THE PERSON OF CHRIST
IN NEW TESTAMENT TEACHING

By the same author

*

THE CROSS OF CHRIST

FORGIVENESS AND RECONCILIATION
A Study in New Testament Theology

THE FORMATION OF THE GOSPEL TRADITION

THE GOSPEL ACCORDING TO ST. MARK
The Greek Text, with Introduction,
Notes and Indexes

JESUS AND HIS SACRIFICE
A Study of the Passion-Sayings in the Gospels

THE LIFE AND MINISTRY OF JESUS

THE NAMES OF JESUS

THE TEXT OF THE NEW TESTAMENT
A Short Introduction

THE
PERSON OF CHRIST

IN NEW TESTAMENT TEACHING

BY

VINCENT TAYLOR

D.D., F.B.A.

MACMILLAN

London · Melbourne · Toronto

ST MARTIN'S PRESS

New York

1966

PREFACE

THE present work consists of Part III of the Speaker's Lectures on 'The Person of Christ in New Testament Teaching' delivered in Oxford during the years 1951–6. Part I was published in 1953 under the title, *The Names of Jesus*. In treating this theme I pointed out that the names and titles, which are far more numerous than is commonly supposed, carry us back to a time when doctrinal motives were only beginning to be operative, and that, in short, they are both the foreshadowing and the precipitate of primitive Christian Christology. In their formation and use, I maintained, liturgical and devotional influences were as strongly operative as the attempt to define the Person of Christ. Part II appeared in 1954 as *The Life and Ministry of Jesus*. In this work I attempted to make a historical survey of this theme in the belief that, before we can apprehend the significance of Christ's Person, we must consider, and endeavour to understand, so far as we can, the records of His earthly life in the earliest sources. This venture was made with the knowledge that any one who attempts to write a life of Christ is vulnerable at a hundred points, but with the conviction that this danger must be incurred if the doctrinal teaching of the New Testament writings is to be apprehended adequately. Part III now undertakes this vital task.

There are two ways in which New Testament teaching concerning the person of Christ can be presented. The older method is to set forth the teaching of individual writings, or groups of writings, in order, beginning with the Gospels and the Acts, and then continuing as far as possible in chronological succession throughout the rest of the New Testament. This method has great advantages. By means of it we can conveniently assemble the New Testament evidence and make a useful exegetical study of the Gospels and the Epistles separately. In particular, we know where to turn to find important passages in these writings, which are treated within the groups in which they appear. This method, however, has corresponding disadvantages. The chronological order is only partially followed, since the Gospels and the Acts, which are late writings containing material both early and late, are treated before the earliest Epistles, especially those of St. Paul. Further, as often happens in the history of exegesis, the method may be followed with implications which cannot be sustained. Many who have adopted this method have assumed the existence of a Christology common to all the writings, to which each book bears witness with varying degrees of clarity, with the result that the omissions or silences of particular writings are not adequately considered or appraised.

The perception of these disabilities has led in recent years to another method, more strictly chronological in its application. In this method one begins with the teaching of Jesus, so far as it can be ascertained, and then examines the thought of the primitive Christian communities, passing on to consider in succession the Christology of the Epistles of St. Paul, the Epistle of the Hebrews, the Johannine writings, and the Pastoral and Catholic Epistles. This is the method adopted in Bultmann's *Theology of the New Testament* and in other studies of the kind. Its merits are manifest. It recognizes the existence of a process of development within the period covered by the New Testament writings. We are introduced to

'Christologies' rather than 'the Christology of the New Testament', so far as either of these expressions is relevant. By this method, it is held, we can see the process in its historical movement. Simpler ideas give place to richer developments. The mind is prepared for those later theological discussions which, beginning in the second century, continue through the third and fourth centuries and culminate in the Christology of Nicaea and Chalcedon. These are great advantages, but there are also drawbacks. The weakness of this method is that inevitably a subjective element enters into the account which is given of the course of the development. The evidence is displayed in accordance with the observer's insight. Passages from the Gospels are cited both at earlier and later stages and evidence for the thought of the primitive period is drawn from the Pauline and Johannine writings and even from the Pastoral and Catholic Epistles. This procedure is necessary and is justifiable, but it is less easy to check since passages of great importance are introduced apart from their contexts at points where they are held to be significant.

I attempted to use this second method in *The Atonement in New Testament Teaching*. In the present investigation I propose to use both methods, the older and predominantly exegetical method and also the more recent and mainly theological method. The value of this double approach does not need to be argued. It secures the advantages of both methods, while the weaknesses of each are controlled by the use of the other. I shall therefore in an exegetical section examine the various New Testament writings singly or in groups, and in a historical and theological study endeavour to trace the movements of thought during the period in relation to the doctrinal issues which are involved.

The inseparable connexion of *The Names of Jesus* with the present subject explains my somewhat frequent references to the book I published in 1953 under that title. For the guidance of the reader I should explain that I have used the prefix 'St.' where the Evangelists as distinct from the Gospels are mentioned. In the main I have quoted the well known English versions, but on occasion I have given a translation of my own.

I regret that Professor Oscar Cullmann's very interesting and valuable work, *Die Christologie des Neuen Testaments* (1957), did not come into my hands until the last stages of the correction of the proofs of this book. I am glad to find that, apart from smaller points, we are independently in close agreement regarding the significance of names and titles of Jesus, and I gladly endorse his judgement that in actual fact primitive Christian theology is almost exclusively Christology.

My best thanks are due to the Rev. W. F. Hewitson, B.A., B.D., and to my wife, for their invaluable help in the laborious task of correcting the typescript and the proofs. I am also grateful to Mr. Hewitson for his kindness in compiling the Index of Proper Names. I am also indebted to many conversations and discussions with students and others at Wesley College, Headingley, Leeds, at Oxford, and at Drew University, New Jersey, U.S.A. Following upon my earlier works on the doctrine of the Atonement, this book embodies many years of thought and research in the problems of Christology, and, despite its imperfections and the manifest impossibility of doing adequate justice to the theme, I trust it may meet difficulties and stimulate reflection upon the greatest of all subjects, the meaning and significance of Christ.

February 2nd, 1957   VINCENT TAYLOR

CONTENTS

PART I: EXEGETICAL

PART II: HISTORICAL AND THEOLOGICAL

x   **CONTENTS**

PART ONE
EXEGETICAL

I
THE GOSPELS: MARK AND LUKE

IN considering New Testament teaching concerning the Person of Christ the Gospels claim attention first, since they contain basic data regarding His sayings and acts which are derived from early sources and the tradition of the primitive Christian communities. While the four Gospels share many features in common, each has interests of its own which call for examination. It is not my purpose at this stage to discuss in detail the many interesting and important historical questions which of necessity arise, but rather to describe as objectively as possible the primitive beliefs the Gospels reflect.

(A) MARK

St. Mark's Gospel claims attention first in view of its early date and its primitive character. The distinctive features of its Christology may be described as follows.

1. The Gospel stands apart by the realism with which it depicts the humanity of Jesus. Jesus is represented as a man subject to the limitations of His human lot. Among the human characteristics attested are His anger (iii. 5), His indignation (x. 14), His surprise (vi. 6), the compassion with which He viewed the multitudes (vi. 34, viii. 2f.), His feelings of disappointment (viii. 17, ix. 19), His requests for information (vi. 38, viii. 27, ix. 21, x. 18), and His want of knowledge about the date of His Parousia (xiii. 32). St. Mark faithfully records the petulant question of the distressed disciples during the storm

3

on the lake, 'Master, do you not care that we are perishing?' (iv. 38), and he does not hesitate to give the
question to the rich suppliant, 'Why do you call me good?
none is good save one, even God?' (x. 18).   In narrating
the fruitless visit of Jesus to Nazareth, he does not shrink
from saying, 'He could there do no mighty work, save that
he laid his hands upon a few sick people, and healed
them', and he adds that He 'marvelled because of their
unbelief' (vi. 5f.).   Along with St. Matthew he records
the cry from the cross, 'My God, my God, why hast thou
forsaken me?' (xv. 34, Mt. xxvii. 46).   There is no doubt
that he portrays a fully human life.

2. It is clear that St. Mark believed Jesus to be the
Messiah.   This belief is illustrated by his narratives of the
Confession of Peter, the Cure of Bartimaeus, the Entry
into Jerusalem, the Trial scenes before Caiaphas and
Pilate, his account of the inscription on the cross, and his
frequent use of the title 'the King of the Jews'.   Nevertheless, nationalistic views of Messiahship are completely
absent, and much is made of the fact that, during the days
of His ministry, Jesus enjoined silence regarding His
Messianic claims.   In St. Mark's Gospel it is only by
implication that Jesus claims to be the Messiah in His
reply to Peter's confession and at His entry into Jerusalem,
and directly only in His reply to the high priest's challenge,
'Are you the Christ, the Son of the Blessed?', 'I am, and
you will see the Son of Man sitting at the right hand of
power, and coming with the clouds of heaven' (xiv. 62).
Even here important manuscripts give His answer in the
form, 'You say that I am', that is, 'The word is
yours', 'That is how you put it', an answer which does
not deny Messiahship, but suggests by its reserve that
His view of its nature is very different from that of
Caiaphas.

3. The Messianic title used in Mark is 'the Son of Man'; it appears in fourteen sayings of Jesus, but is not used of Him by the Evangelist himself. Apparently it is the name which Jesus used in preference to 'the Christ'. Sometimes it bears a present Messianic sense, as in ii. 10 and 28; sometimes it is used eschatologically, to describe the future Messianic dignity of Jesus at His Parousia, as in viii. 38, xiii. 26, and xiv. 62; and frequently it appears in sayings which prophesy His Messianic suffering, rejection, death, and resurrection, in viii. 31, ix. 9, 12, 31, x. 33f., 45, xiv. 21 (*bis*), 41. How far these different ideas were held concurrently by Jesus, and how far they belong to different periods in His ministry, is the problem which these sayings present to us.[1] The eschatological sayings, which reflect the influence of Dan. vii. 13, represent Jesus as a supernatural being; the sayings which speak of suffering and rejection, in terms of the Servant conception of Isa. liii, characterize Him as the Saviour, who 'came not to be served, but to serve, and to give his life a ransom for many' (x. 45). The sayings connected with the forgiveness of sins (ii. 10) and the Sabbath (ii. 28) imply His authority on earth as the Son of Man. In St. Mark's view the Son of Man, who exercises this authority, and yet is to suffer and die, is the same Son of Man who in the future will be seen 'sitting at the right hand of power, and coming with the clouds of heaven' (xiv. 62). He is also the One whose real human life the Evangelist elsewhere depicts. In these representations the whole problem of Christology is present *in nuce*. There is no doubt that, in recording these sayings, St. Mark is reflecting and meeting the needs of the Church of his day. The question, therefore, whether

[1] I have discussed this question in *The Life and Ministry of Jesus*, pp. 142-5.

they are genuine utterances of Jesus is one of first importance.[1]

4. It is important to observe that St. Mark does not apply the title 'the Lord' to Jesus, unless he does so in xi. 3.[2] He contents himself with the names 'Teacher', 'Jesus', and 'Son of Man'. This restraint is remarkable, since the confession 'Jesus is Lord' was widespread in the primitive Christian communities long before he wrote his Gospel. The explanation may be that the Evangelist was aware of the fact that this name was not applied to Jesus until after His resurrection, and this inference is encouraged by the parallel consideration that the title 'Son of Man', which he so freely attests, was no longer in use in the communities, Ac. vii. 56 where it appears being the only example outside the Gospels. The fact, however, that he does not use the title 'the Lord' in no way suggests that he was a stranger to those deep feelings of religious devotion which it expresses. On the contrary, it is probable that for him, as for his readers, the name 'Jesus' often expresses this devotion, although in the nature of the case this suggestion cannot be proved. In any case, the deep significance which he finds in the name 'Son of Man' is sufficient in itself to suggest that attitude of religious veneration unambiguously expressed by the name 'the Lord'.

5. A striking feature of St. Mark's Christology is the close connexion he finds between the Holy Spirit and the life and work of Jesus. At His baptism the Spirit descended upon Him as a dove (i. 10), and subsequently, before His temptation, drove Him into the wilderness (i. 12). It is often maintained that in recording John the

---

[1] Cf. *The Names of Jesus*, 36f.; *The Gospel according to St. Mark*, 199; and *New Testament Studies*, I, No. 3, 159–67.

[2] Cf. *The Gospel according to St. Mark*, 455.

Baptist's prophecy, 'He shall baptize you with the Holy Spirit' (i. 8), St. Mark is thinking of the rite of Christian Baptism. If so, we must assume that he believed baptism into the name of Jesus to be baptism with the Spirit. There is no suggestion in this Gospel that it is in consequence of the descent of the Spirit that Jesus becomes the Messiah, although this view has often been held. The words, 'Thou art my beloved Son, in thee I am well pleased' (i. 11), authenticate a filial consciousness which, so far as we can see, is not created by the gift of the Spirit, but is deepened and enriched by the baptismal experience. The Virgin Birth tradition does not appear to have been known to St. Mark, unless it is implied by the phrase, 'the Son of Mary', in vi. 3.[1] The references to the Spirit are comparatively few in this Gospel (cf. iii. 29, xii. 36, xiii. 11), as indeed in all the Synoptic Gospels. It does not appear to be a part of St. Mark's Christology to explain the supernatural element in Christ's person by the fact that He is 'filled with the Spirit'.

6. St. Mark's highest claim for Jesus is that He is 'the Son of God'. As we have seen, this belief is present in his account of the Baptism in the words of the divine voice, 'Thou art my beloved Son' (i. 11). A divine Sonship is implied in the Parable of the Wicked Husbandmen in the words, 'He had yet one, a beloved son: he sent him last unto them, saying, They will reverence my son' (xii. 6). The belief also appears in the centurion's confession, 'Truly this man was the Son of God' (xv. 39), for whatever the soldier's meaning may have been, the Evangelist appears to have regarded his words as a tribute to the divine sonship of Jesus. The consciousness of sonship is clearly expressed in the saying, 'Of that day or that hour, no one knows, not even the angels in heaven, neither the

[1] For the textual problem cf. *The Gospel according to St. Mark*, 300.

B

Son, but the Father' (xiii. 32). St. Mark interprets the cries of the demoniacs as confessions of the divine origin and dignity of Jesus, probably in i. 24, 'I know thee who thou art, the Holy One of God', and certainly in iii. 11, 'Thou art the Son of God', and in v. 7, 'Thou Son of the Most High God'. If the phrase, 'the Son of God', in the opening words of the Gospel is original, as it probably is, St. Mark's conviction is expressed from the beginning in a passage which is probably to be interpreted as a title to the Gospel. Unquestionably St. Mark believes that Jesus is the Son of God. Whether he goes further and believes in the pre-existence of Christ is doubtful; in any case the idea is not a living element in his theology. He is content to underline a primitive Christian confession and to express it powerfully in the body of his Gospel. This fact is especially important because his theology is not distinctively Pauline. The divine sonship of Jesus is St. Mark's conviction and that of the Church for which he wrote.

In sum, we may say that St. Mark's Christology is a 'high Christology', all the more important because of his fidelity in recording a life lived out upon the human plane. He has no doubt that, as the Messiah and the Son of God, Jesus possessed the most astounding healing powers, and even authority to still storms, to exorcise daemons, to raise the dead, and to multiply loaves and fishes. Whatever explanations we of to-day may give to the 'mighty works' of Jesus, we must not fail to recognize that to the Evangelist they are fitting signs of His divine authority and person. Much is said and written to-day about St. Mark's theology, and with justice, but it cannot be claimed that his theological impulse is great and creative. He gives point and power to existing tradition. It is noteworthy that in his Gospel the application of Old Testament prophecies to Jesus, characteristic as it was of

primitive Christianity as a means of expounding the
meaning of the person of Christ, is not prominent, for
almost all his quotations appear in the recorded sayings
and parables of Jesus, while those that remain are either
literary allusions, as in the Passion narrative (xv. 29), or
are applied to John the Baptist (i. 2f.) and the use of
parables (iv. 11f.). In this matter the situation is very
different in Matthew. Although 'high', St. Mark's
Christology is not a new construction; it reveals his own
beliefs and those of the community for which he wrote,
and there are good reasons for thinking that it stands near
to the ideas of Jesus Himself.

(B) LUKE

I turn next to the Gospel of St. Luke. While pointing
out his distinctive ideas, I desire also to compare his
treatment with the ideas already found in Mark.

1. Like St. Mark, St. Luke also gives a vivid portraiture of the human Jesus. This is especially true of the
material peculiar to the Gospel. As St. Luke represents
Him, Jesus has no love for adulation (xi. 27f.); He knows
the pain of unfulfilled desires (xxii. 15) and the experience
of unanswered prayer (xxii. 32). He is often tempted
(iv. 13, xxii. 28), is divinely strengthened (xxii. 43f.), and
frequently communes with God in prayer (vi. 12, xi. 1,
xxii. 32, 41, 44). On the cross He commends His
spirit into the Father's hands (xxiii. 46). Tender and
compassionate towards outcasts (vii. 36–50, xix. 1–10),
Samaritans (ix. 51–6, xvii. 11–19), and sinners (xviii.
9–14), He makes the strongest demands upon the
loyalty of His disciples (ix. 51–6, xiv. 25–35).

Nevertheless, the human characteristics of Jesus do not
stand out as sharply as they do in Mark. St. Luke modi-
fies some of St. Mark's bolder statements out of motives

of reverence, although not to the same degree as in St.
Matthew's Gospel.   In his account of the cure of the man
with the withered hand he omits the Markan phrase 'with
anger, being grieved at the hardening of their heart'
(Mk. iii. 5), and, instead of reproducing the words,
'Master, do you not care that we are perishing?' (Mk. iv.
38), he has simply 'Master, master, we are perishing'
(Lk. viii. 24).   He has no parallel to the statement that
Jesus could do no mighty work at Nazareth (Mk. vi. 5f.),
does not record the saying in which knowledge of the day
of the Parousia is denied (Mk. xiii. 32), and omits the cry
of desolation on the Cross (Mk. xv. 34).   Some of these
omissions may be partially explained if, as the Proto-Luke
hypothesis affirms, St. Luke uses Mark as a supplemen-
tary source, but even so the absence of these Markan
passages is significant of a desire to soften the boldness of
his source.   On the other hand, we must note that he re-
tains the question of Jesus, 'Why do you call me good?'
(xviii. 19, cf. Mk. x. 18, Mt. xix. 17).   Moreover, in a
manner in striking contrast to the apocryphal Gospels, he
presents a natural picture of the boyhood of Jesus in
ii. 41–52, when he records His question, 'Did you not
know that I must be in my Father's house?' (ii. 49), and
says quite objectively, 'And Jesus advanced in wisdom and
stature, and in favour with God and men' (ii. 52).   We
must conclude that, in a different way from St. Mark, St.
Luke faithfully describes a truly human life of Jesus.

2. Like St. Mark, St. Luke also believes Jesus to be the
Messiah.   In fact, he uses the name 'Christ' more frequently than Mark, but he rarely introduces it into the
sayings of Jesus.   In xxiv. 26 and 46 he connects the title
with suffering and death.   This fact, together with the
note of universalism in his Gospel, shows how decisively the Lukan idea of Messiahship has broken from

its Jewish moorings. For St. Luke Jesus is 'a Saviour,
which is Christ the Lord' (ii. 11), of whom it is written
that He 'should suffer, and rise again from the dead the
third day' (xxiv. 46).

3. Because of his use of Q St. Luke has the title 'Son of
Man' more frequently than St. Mark. In both Gospels it
always appears in sayings of Jesus regarding the Passion
and the Parousia. In agreement with the other Synoptists he makes no attempt to bring out its Christological
importance. As a Gentile he must have found the title
strange. He tends to use it as a personal name for Jesus,
for in xvii. 24f., immediately after the words, 'So shall the
Son of Man be in his day', he adds, clearly with reference to Jesus, 'But first must he suffer many things and
be rejected of this generation'. In xxii. 69 he connects the
title with the exaltation of Christ in the saying, 'But from
henceforth shall the Son of Man be seated at the right hand
of the power of God.' Here nothing is said of His
coming 'with the clouds of heaven' (Mk. xiv. 62).

4. St. Luke's manifest preference is to speak of Jesus
as 'the Lord'. In addition to two examples based on Mk.
xi. 3 he has the title some fifteen times. More than
fidelity to his sources is indicated by his usage since at
least six examples are editorial.[1] The name expresses an
attitude of veneration and religious devotion towards the
Person of Jesus. The Evangelist finds it natural to say
that John the Baptist sent two of his disciples 'to the Lord'
(vii. 19), that 'the Lord' appointed seventy and sent them
two by two before His face (x. 1), and to relate that the
Apostles said 'unto the Lord', 'Increase our faith' (xvii. 5).

5. St. Luke's teaching about the Spirit in relation to
Jesus is an advance upon that of St. Mark. The work of

[1] Cf. Lk. vii. 19, x. 1, xi. 39, xii. 42, xvii. 5f. The examples in xxii. 31
and xxiv. 3 are textually doubtful.

the Spirit is seen in His birth (i. 35) as well as in His
baptism (iii. 22). 'Full of the Spirit', Jesus returns from
the Jordan and is led 'by the Spirit' into the wilderness
(iv. 1). 'In the power of the Spirit', He returns to
Galilee (iv. 14), and in the synagogue at Nazareth He
begins His address to the people with the words of Isa.
lxi. 1f., 'The Spirit of the Lord is upon me' (iv. 18). The
saying concerning the mutual knowledge of the Father
and the Son is introduced by the statement, 'In that hour
he rejoiced in the Holy Spirit' (x. 21), and after the Resurrection Jesus declares, with reference to the Spirit,
'Behold, I send forth the promise of my Father upon you'
(xxiv. 49). In the total presentation the advance upon
St. Mark is notable. Jesus is the Son of God because He
is born of, and possessed by, the Spirit in a manner and to
a degree which surpass anything that is recorded in the
Old Testament concerning the patriarchs and the prophets. Christological interpretation is developing. The
impression we receive, however, is that the development is
not the work of the Evangelist himself, but is rather inherent in the tradition he records.

6. Lastly, St. Luke shares the primitive Christian confession that Jesus is the Son of God. He not only re-
produces sayings in which the titles 'the Son of God' and
'the Son' already appear, but also introduces this terminology into the story of the Annunciation in the words,
'Wherefore also the holy child which is to be born shall be
called the Son of God' (i. 35). Along with St. Matthew,
but in an independent and distinctive form, he records the
Virgin Birth tradition, which presupposes the belief that
in virtue of His divine origin Jesus is the Son of God.
This belief is not inferred from the tradition; on the
contrary the Virgin Birth is felt to be harmonious with
the superhuman dignity of Jesus.

II

THE GOSPELS: MATTHEW AND JOHN

IN these Gospels the primitive tradition is interpreted
to a greater degree than it is in Mark and Luke.

(c) MATTHEW

1. While depicting Jesus as a historical figure with
fidelity to the original tradition, St. Matthew more than
St. Luke softens the bolder realism of St. Mark. Like St.
Luke he omits the references to anger and surprise in
Mk. iii. 5 and vi. 6, and he gives the cry of the storm-
tossed disciples in the prosaic form, 'Save, Lord; we are
perishing' (viii. 25), but he drastically recasts the question
of Jesus to the rich ruler, 'Why do you call me good?'
(Mk. x. 18), so that it becomes, 'Why do you ask me concerning that which is good?' (xix. 17), while retaining the
words, 'One there is who is good'. The miraculous element in the Markan narratives is heightened,[1] and the
narratives peculiar to the Gospel, in i–ii and xxvi–xxviii,
serve the interests of defence against current objections.
The humanity of Christ, although fully displayed, is beginning to be seen through a doctrinal veil. Interpretation of this kind was inevitable and necessary, and its
presence is of great value for the study of the Person of
Jesus. Nevertheless, a comparison with St. Mark's
Gospel shows how great would be our loss if we did not
possess the more objective account contained in that
writing.

2. In agreement with this apologetic tendency the

----

[1] Cf. Mt. viii. 16, xii. 15, xiv. 21, xv. 38, xxi. 19.

13

Messiahship of Jesus is more strongly emphasized. The Matthaean genealogy, ending with the words, 'Jesus, who is called Christ' (i. 16), illustrates this interest. It also appears in the more frequent use of the title 'Son of David',[1] and of the name 'Christ' in the Birth Stories,[2] in sections derived from Mark,[3] and in other editorial passages.[4] There is no trace of nationalistic interpretations of these titles, except in so far as they are used as popular designations. While Messianic, the title 'Christ' is well on its way to becoming a personal name charged with religious meaning, because it describes the One in whom the ancient prophecies are fulfilled. This tendency can be seen when 'Jesus' is explained as 'He that shall save his people from their sins' (i. 21).

3. Characteristic of St. Matthew is the direct application of Old Testament prophecies to Jesus, especially in the twelve passages introduced by the phrase, or its equivalent, 'that it might be fulfilled which was spoken by the prophet'.[5] In two of these passages Servant prophecies are quoted and applied to Jesus (viii. 17 and xii. 17–21) as predictions fulfilled in His ministry. These are of especial interest when compared with that latent use of Isa. liii manifest in the sayings of Jesus in Mk. ix. 12, 31, x. 33f., 45 and in St. Mark's usage in viii. 31. In viii. 17 St. Matthew interprets the healing ministry of Jesus by the words of Isa. liii. 4, 'Himself took our infirmities, and bore our diseases.' In xii. 18–21 he uses the description of the Servant's unostentatious compassion in Isa. xlii. 1–4 to illustrate the charge of Jesus Himself not to make Him known.

[1] Mt. i. 1, 20, ix. 27, xii. 23, xv. 22, xx. 30f., xxi. 9, 15.
[2] Mt. i. 16, 17, 18, ii. 4. [3] Mt. xvi. 16, xxii. 42, xxiv. 23, xxvi. 63.
[4] Mt. xi. 2, xvi. 20f., xxiv. 5, xxvi. 68, xxvii. 17, 22.
[5] Mt. i. 22, ii. 15, 17, 23, iv. 14, viii. 17, xii. 17–21, xiii. 35, xxi. 4f., xxvi. 54, 56, xxvii. 9f.

'Behold, my servant whom I have chosen;
My beloved in whom my soul is well pleased:
I will put my Spirit upon him,
And he shall declare judgement to the Gentiles.
He shall not strive, nor cry aloud;
Neither shall any one hear his voice in the streets.
A bruised reed shall he not break,
And smoking flax shall he not quench,
Till he send forth judgement unto victory.
And in his name shall the Gentiles hope'.

This Christological interest powerfully expresses the primitive Christian conviction that in Jesus the Old Testament prophetic expectations are fulfilled.[1]

4. Like St. Mark, and in contrast with St. Luke, St. Matthew does not use the title 'the Lord' of Jesus except once in xxi. 3 which is based on Mk. xi. 3.

5. As in the other Synoptic Gospels the title 'Son of Man' is found frequently; indeed it appears more often in St. Matthew since, in addition to his sources Mark and Q, the Evangelist also draws examples from M. In the eschatological sayings in xxiv–xxv the name describes a superhuman figure like that depicted in I Enoch. B. T. D. Smith[2] suggests that in using the name St. Matthew thinks of Christ primarily as 'the *Man*' rather than as '*the* Man of apocalyptic prophecy', in a manner not far removed from the usage of Ignatius in *Eph.* xx, 'Jesus Christ ... Son of Man and Son of God'. This suggestion is supported by Mt. xvi. 13 and 16: 'Who do men say that *the Son of Man* is? ... You are the Christ, *the Son of the living God.*' Nevertheless, the eschatological interest is pronounced. The choice of many sayings, especially xxiv. 29–31 with its reference to 'a great sound of a trumpet', shows how closely St. Matthew

[1] See especially C. H. Dodd, *According to the Scriptures.*
[2] *The Gospel according to S. Matthew,* 116.

connects supernatural dignity and power with the Parousia of the Son of Man.

6. St. Matthew shares and deepens the primitive
Christian emphasis on the relationship of the Holy
Spirit to the Person and Work of Jesus. Like St. Luke,
he associates the Spirit with His birth (i. 20), His
baptism (iii. 16), and His temptation (iv. 1). Further, in
quoting the passage Isa. xlii. 1–4, mentioned above, he
includes the words, 'I will put my Spirit upon him', and
where St. Luke has the phrase 'the finger of God' (xi. 20)
he has 'the Spirit of God' in the saying, 'If I by the Spirit
of God cast out devils, then is the kingdom of God come
upon you' (xii. 28). A still greater development is manifest in xxviii. 19, which speaks of baptism into 'the name
of the Father and of the Son and of the Holy Spirit'.
Here we have passed beyond the Christology which sees
in Jesus the Spirit-filled prophet. Although we may not
read into the saying later trinitarian theology, we must
recognize that a step has been taken which was to find its
culmination in the Christology of Nicaea.

7. As compared with the other Synoptists St. Matthew
gives increased prominence to the Sonship of Christ.
He not only takes over from his sources the name 'Son of
God' (iii. 17, iv. 3, 6, xi. 25–7), but also inserts it in his
version of the confession of Peter (xvi. 16) and the walking
on the sea (xiv. 33), and again in his account of the
Crucifixion in describing the taunts of the crowd (xxvii.
40) and of the chief priests (xxvii. 43). Further, at the
climax of his Gospel, in the saying quoted above, the
Eleven are commissioned to make disciples of all the
nations and to baptize 'into the name of the Father and the
Son and the Holy Spirit' (xxviii. 19). In the mind of St.
Matthew Christ is divine both before and after the Resurrection. There is thus a greater Christological de-

velopment in his Gospel than in Mark and Luke corresponding to a fuller experience of the worship of Christ within the Church.   In particular, the Matthaean Birth Stories not only assign the origin of Jesus to the creative act of the Spirit, but reveal this tradition so deeply entrenched in the mind of the Church for which the Gospel was written that objections brought against it are met and refuted (cf. 1. 3–5, 18–25).   We are well on the way to that fuller presentation of the Sonship of Christ which is so pronounced in the Fourth Gospel.

(D) JOHN

The Johannine Christology will be considered later in detail, but even at this point a comparison with the teaching of the Synoptists is needed with special reference to the points already treated.

1. As regards the humanity of Jesus St. John is much more emphatic in insisting that the Son of God came to earth in flesh and lived a truly human life.   Nevertheless, in consequence of his doctrinal interests, the Evangelist is less able to describe the facts of His earthly existence. On the one hand, he insists that the Word 'became flesh' (i. 14), that He shared the conditions of flesh and blood (xix. 34), that He knew weariness (iv. 6) and thirst (iv. 7, xix. 28), that He groaned in spirit and was troubled (xi. 33), and that He wept (xi. 35).   But, on the other hand, the Johannine Christ is never taken by surprise;   He is not limited in knowledge or tempted;   He does not pray for Himself, is not 'greatly amazed and sore troubled' (cf. Mk. xiv. 33),[1] and does not ask that, if it be possible, the cup may be taken from Him (cf. Mk. xiv. 35f. and Jn. xii. 27).[2]   It is this combination of historical tradition

---

[1] But see Jn. xii. 27.
[2] Cf. R. N. Flew, *The Idea of Perfection in Christian Theology*, 117.

and doctrinal interpretation which constitutes the Johannine problem. The determining interest, both when the humanity is affirmed and when the Markan realism is dimmed, is doctrinal; it is the desire to represent the Son of God veiled in flesh. For this purpose it was necessary, on the one hand, to insist that the Son was truly incarnate, and, on the other hand, to avoid elements which might seem to compromise the reality of His Sonship.

2. St. John follows with great fidelity the earliest tradition in his sparing use of the name 'Christ'. He believes that Jesus is the Messiah, but is sure that He is immeasurably more. Only in the high-priestly prayer does Jesus use the name of Himself (xvii. 3), although by implication He accepts it when He says to the woman of Samaria, 'I that speak to you am he' (iv. 26). What is more remarkable, the Evangelist himself uses the name twice only, in i. 17 and xx. 31, and he agrees with the Synoptists in implying that Jesus spoke of His Messiahship with reserve when he represents the Jews as saying, 'How long do you hold us in suspense? If you are the Christ, tell us plainly' (x. 24). Clearly, his usage is both traditional and interpretative. Andrew indeed says, 'We have found the Messiah' (i. 41), but Philip speaks of Him rather as the fulfilment of Old Testament hopes, 'We have found him of whom Moses in the law and the prophets wrote, Jesus of Nazareth, the son of Joseph' (i. 45). We may therefore infer that when he writes, 'These are written that you may believe that Jesus is the Christ, the Son of God' (xx. 31), he is putting a new meaning on the title. He describes a Messiah who is the Son of God.

3. Similarly, the Evangelist's use of the name 'Son of Man' is doctrinal. He has it thirteen times, twelve times in sayings of Jesus.[1] In his usage the eschatological

---

[1] In xii. 34b it is taken up and used by the people of Jerusalem.

meaning of the title has almost disappeared, but, like St.
Mark, he uses it in Passion-sayings.[1] For him the title
describes the humanity of the Son of God in the humiliation, which is at the same time the glory, of His incarnation, from which, by the gate of death, He emerges into
that greater glory which was His before the world was.
Significantly enough, the Evangelist ceases to use the
name after the Crucifixion. His title now is that of 'the
Lord', which, if we allow for the insertions of copyists,[2]
he reserves for the Risen Christ.[3] It may be that i. 51,
'You shall see heaven opened, and the angels of God
ascending and descending upon the Son of Man', represents one of his deepest convictions. The Son of Man
is the link between heaven and earth, whereby the glory
of God is made known to men. Yet another conviction
of the Evangelist is the belief that, through the up-lifting
of the Son of Man in death, believers attain to eternal life
(iii. 14f.) and the knowledge of His Sonship (viii. 28).

4. St. John is fully aware of the Virgin Birth tradition,
but it has no place in his Christology. By wide consent
the Western reading in i. 13 ('who was born') is a later
modification,[4] but probably he has the tradition in mind
when he says that believers 'were born, not of blood nor
of the will of the flesh nor of the will of man, but of God'.[5]
This view, however, is conjectural, and it is equally
possible that the Evangelist is contrasting spiritual birth
with physical generation. E. F. Scott[6] is probably right
when he suggests that St. John preferred the Christology

---

[1] Jn. iii. 14, viii. 28, xii. 23, 34.
[2] In iv. 1, vi. 23, and xi. 2. Cf. J. H. Bernard, *St. John*, 132.
[3] Jn. xx. 2, 18, 20, 25, xxi. 7 (*bis*), 12. Cf. xx. 13, 28.
[4] Cf. Bernard, *St. John*, 17; Hoskyns, *The Fourth Gospel*, 164f.;
Barrett, *St. John*, 137f.
[5] Cf. O. C. Quick, *Doctrines of the Creed*, 16of.: Hoskyns, *op. cit.*, 166–8;
Barrett, *op. cit.*, 137.
[6] *The Fourth Gospel*, 188.

set forth in the prologue to that of the Virgin Birth tradition. 'He does not deny the story, but his own Christology has superior spiritual attractions'.[1]

5. The doctrine of the Spirit in the Fourth Gospel is
so important that it must be reserved for discussion in the
chapter on the Johannine Christology.[2] Meantime, in
order to compare the teaching of the four Gospels, we note
that, like the Synoptists, St. John speaks of the Holy
Spirit descending as a dove and abiding upon Jesus (i. 32)
and of His baptism 'with the Holy Spirit', and he explains
the fact that He speaks God's words by the grace of Him
who 'does not give the Spirit by measure' (iii. 34). Dr.
Temple interprets this statement to mean that Jesus
'received the Spirit in all the fulness of the divine gift',[3]
but this idea is not distinctive in the Evangelist's teaching.
His distinctive teaching is the doctrine of 'the Paraclete'
in xiv–xvi. By his description of the Paraclete as Christ's
gift (xv, 26, xvi. 7, cf. xx. 22), as well as the gift of the
Father (iii. 34, xiv. 16, xv. 26), and by the phrase 'another
Paraclete' (xiv. 16), he raises questions which were to
prove of vital importance to the doctrine of the Trinity.

6. The most outstanding feature in St. John's Christology is the doctrine of the Logos. This question also will
be considered later,[4] but it must be mentioned now because it reveals a degree of reflection which we do not find
in the Synoptic Gospels. Many scholars maintain that
the Logos conception dominates the thought of the
Fourth Gospel, and others that it focuses the Evangelist's
Christology. The latter, I think, is the better view, because the word *logos* is used differently in the rest of the
Gospel, a feature which is strange if the Evangelist of set
purpose wrote to embody in his narratives and sayings the

[1] V. Taylor, *The Historical Evidence for the Virgin Birth*, 19.
[2] Pp. 111–20. [3] *Readings in St. John's Gospel*, 55. [4] Pp. 107–11.

ideas first set forth in i. 1–18. If we infer that the Prologue was written last, as a summary of St. John's apprehension of the significance of the incarnation of the Son of God, we account better for the traditional element combined with interpretation present in the Gospel. The same inference is warranted if, as some have thought, he took over and adapted in i. 1–18 a pre-Johannine hymn. As he contemplates the Gospel Story the Evangelist's deepest conviction is that in Jesus Christ 'the word became flesh and tabernacled among us' (i. 14).

7. The high point in St. John's Christology is the Sonship of Christ and His incomparable relation to the Father. In this matter the contrast with the Synoptists is one of range rather than of quality, and in the extent to which its different aspects are presented. With them he shares the abiding sense of the Sonship of Jesus and of the mutual knowledge existing between the Father and the Son; but he takes up, and presents to a remarkable degree, that exclusive Sonship which in the earlier Gospels flames out in episodes, as at the Baptism and the Transfiguration, and in the ecstatic Shout of Joy recorded in Lk. x. 21f. and Mt. xi. 25–7. In the Fourth Gospel Sonship is displayed on an even plane; in the Synoptics it is visible on the highest contours. In the factual sense of the term the more historical account is that of the Synoptics, but it is of the greatest possible importance to us that we also possess the interpretation of the Fourth Evangelist.

SUMMARY

The outstanding feature of the Christology of the Gospels is the combination of traditional teaching with doctrinal ideas which in a dynamic manner foreshadow later developments.

1. A fully human life is described in all the Gospels,

but from the beginning, and notably in Matthew and John its doctrinal significance is increasingly seen and expressed.

2. All the Gospels affirm the Messiahship of Jesus. They see His Messiahship as the fulfilment of prophecy, but they are not content with this representation as an adequate account of His person.

3. Contrary to Christian usage at the time when the Gospels were compiled, all four Evangelists use the name 'Son of Man' freely. They do so in terms of suffering and rejection, but with an eschatological emphasis which is most pronounced in Matthew and Mark. In John the name describes the divine Son in the circumstances of His earthly lot and as prophetic of His predestined glory.

4. The four Gospels support the view that the name 'the Lord' describes Jesus as risen and glorified and as the object of religious devotion. Its virtual absence from the accounts of the earthly ministry of Jesus, except the L source used in Luke, confirms this view.

5. From the beginning a close connexion between the Holy Spirit and Jesus is recognized, which becomes more prominent in the later Gospels, in the Virgin Birth tradition in Luke and Matthew and in the Paraclete teaching in John. Nowhere is there a disposition to be satisfied with the idea of Jesus as a Spirit-filled prophet.

6. All the Gospels affirm the divine Sonship of Jesus. In the Synoptics it is connected with His Baptism and Transfiguration and in sayings derived from Mark and Q. In these early Palestinian sources the name 'the Son' is attested as one used by Jesus of Himself. In Mt. xxviii. 19 and in the Johannine sayings the use of the name illustrates growing doctrinal interests which stand in close and lineal connexion with earlier and later tradition. The development which can be seen is not a mark

of corruption, but a process of interpretation made necessary as the tradition is understood better and is expounded in the light of the missionary expansion of the primitive Church.

c

III

THE ACTS OF THE APOSTLES

I

IN spite of its late date the Acts of the Apostles is a very valuable authority for the study of the Person of Christ in New Testament teaching, since, in view of the use of early sources, it supplies important evidence concerning the preaching and beliefs of the earliest Christian communities. Harnack declares that not a trace of the so-called higher Christology is to be found in the Acts and in Luke. Their Christology he describes as 'absolutely primitive'.[1] J. Weiss[2] speaks in the same strain of one of the main sources used in the early chapters of the Acts, and B. H. Streeter writes, 'What Acts really represents—modified a little by later experience and touched only here and there with a phrase caught up from Paul—is *pre-Pauline Gentile Christianity*'.[3] With equal truth the same can be said of Palestinian Christianity. We can see what was believed and taught in the earliest days.

It would be mistaken to suppose that the Acts of the Apostles is our only source of information about primitive Christianity. Already from the Gospels themselves we have seen evidence pointing to this period, especially as regards the Lordship of Christ and the interest taken in the fulfilment of prophecy. But much fuller information is available to us. One of the main insights of modern New Testament study is the degree to which almost all the

---

[1] *The Date of the Acts and the Synoptic Gospels,* 108f.
[2] *The History of Primitive Christianity,* 10.
[3] *The Four Gospels,* 556.

Epistles, Pauline, Pastoral, and Catholic, as well as the Epistle to the Hebrews and the Apocalypse of John, depend upon primitive Christian tradition. This indebtedness is manifest, not only in the great writers, but also, as we shall see, in the latest New Testament writings composed at a time when the distinctive contributions of St. Paul, the author of Hebrews, and St. John had not yet been assimilated. We cannot, therefore, assume that the Acts gives us a complete account of primitive Christian Christology. This point is important. The history of New Testament theology illustrates the perils of this assumption, which is revealed in the bare account often given of the beliefs of the earliest communities derived from the Acts alone and in the exaggerated estimates of 'Paulinism' and of its influence upon later writers. The real importance of the Acts lies in its positive testimony; its silences and 'omissions' need to be assessed in the light of other evidence.

II. THE ACTS AND THE FOUR GOSPELS

Before proceeding further it will be useful to compare in a summary manner the Christological teaching of the Acts with that already found in the Gospels. Its teaching concerning the humanity of Christ, His Messiahship, and His Lordship will be found to be full, but other elements conspicuous in the Gospels receive much less attention. For example, although it is highly characteristic of the Acts to dwell upon the work of the Holy Spirit in connexion with Christian baptism and the life of the early communities, there is no marked emphasis upon the relation of the Spirit to Jesus Himself. It is emphasized, and the fact is important, that through baptism into the name of Jesus believers receive the gift of the Spirit (ii. 38, cf. ix. 17), and the belief is expressed that Jesus was anointed with the Spirit. In his address before Cornelius and his friends Peter speaks of Jesus of Nazareth and declares that 'God anointed him with the Holy Spirit and with power' (x. 38). This is clearly a belief of the Jerusalem community, but it is not otherwise emphasized in the primitive tradition, and for a further development of the relation of the Spirit to Jesus we have to turn to the great New Testament writers. Of the Virgin Birth tradition there is no trace in the Acts. Again, the title 'the Son of Man', so frequently found in the Gospels, appears once only in the words of Stephen, 'Behold, I see the heavens opened, and the Son of Man standing on the right hand of God' (vii. 56). This silence manifestly calls for notice. Further, and more surprising, the name 'the Son of God' is applied to Jesus only once in St. Luke's editorial reference to the preaching of St. Paul at Damascus, 'And straightway in the synagogues he proclaimed Jesus, that he is the Son of God' (ix. 20).[1] Why, we are compelled to ask, does not this name appear more often in the admittedly brief records of the first sermons in the Acts?

The almost complete absence of the title 'the Son of Man' can only mean that it conveyed little or nothing to the people of Jerusalem. Known perhaps in the Galilean country, where apocalyptic hopes burned high, it was incomprehensible to the crowds addressed by Peter. This situation is illustrated in the Fourth Gospel, when the multitudes say to Jesus, 'We have heard out of the law that the Christ abides for ever: and how do you say, The Son of Man must be lifted up? who is this Son of Man?' (Jn. xii. 34). There can be no clearer indication of the fact that, when Jesus used this title in preference to 'the Christ', He still preserved His reserve in public con-

---

[1] The phrase 'my Son' also appears in the quotation from Psa. ii. 7 in Ac. xiii. 33.

cerning His Messiahship. It was a name He used in teaching His disciples, and the Synoptic Gospels show that it was the cause of much perplexity (cf. Mk. viii. 32, ix. 32, Lk. ix. 45). Its presence is not to be expected in the early preaching, and still less when Gentile audiences were addressed.

The absence of the title 'the Son of God' from the primitive preaching is also to be explained by the fact that it was not a popular Messianic designation. It is significant that in the one place in which it appears in the Acts it is used in synagogue teaching (ix. 20). It was not a term suitable for use in the open air. This fact does not bring into disrepute the Synoptic tradition, since it is attested by both Mark and Q. It was a name into which Jesus poured new meaning, and, as we shall see, naturally emerges in the teaching of the great New Testament writers without any necessity to trace its origin to Hellenistic usage. This question will need further discussion. Meantime, we must examine carefully the Christological beliefs actually attested in the Acts.

III. THE CHRISTOLOGY OF THE ACTS

1. Acts reveals that in the primitive preaching the reality of Christ's manhood was clearly assumed. This fact is illustrated in ii. 22, in the sermon on the Day of Pentecost, when Peter speaks of 'Jesus of Nazareth' as 'a man approved of God unto you by mighty works and wonders and signs, which God did by him in the midst of you, even as you yourselves know', and again, in the passage x. 38, in the address to Cornelius mentioned above when Peter describes Jesus as one 'who went about doing good, and healing all that were oppressed of the devil'. To this second passage the explanatory clause is added, 'for God was with him', almost as if no more than a

remarkable healer and prophet was in mind. It is significant that the name 'Jesus' is used in the Acts three times as often as 'Christ' and that six times we read of 'Jesus' or 'Jesus Christ of Nazareth'.[1] Twice, moreover, in iii. 22 and vii. 37, He is identified with 'the prophet' mentioned in Deut. xviii. 18 in the words, 'Moses indeed said, A prophet shall the Lord God raise up unto you from among your brethren, like unto me; to him shall you hearken in all things whatsoever he shall speak unto you'.[2] This passage reflects the conviction that Jesus is the Second Moses; but the express claim is not made in the sermons in which the emphasis lies upon the crucifixion and resurrection of Jesus as recent and well known historical events. 'Him', declared Peter, 'being delivered up by the determinate counsel and foreknowledge of God, you by the hand of lawless men did crucify and slay: whom God raised up, having loosed the pangs of death: because it was not possible that he should be holden of it' (ii. 23f.). So objectively is Jesus described in these primitive sermons that, if other teaching in the Acts is disregarded, it would be possible to infer that He is no more than a Spirit-filled prophet rejected and slain by His fellow-countrymen. Only the significant claim that God raised Him up from the dead and that it was impossible for Him to be held captive by death forbids this inference to be drawn from the manner in which the human life of Jesus is mentioned.

2. Acts reveals a deep interest in the Messiahship of Jesus. The title 'the Christ', in the sense of 'the Messiah', appears at least twelve times, and in many cases the name

---

[1] See *The Names of Jesus*, 7.

[2] In the Hebrew text the latter part of Deut. xviii. 18 reads, 'And I will put my words in his mouth, and he shall speak unto them all that I shall command him'.

'Jesus Christ' seems to be more than a merely personal designation.[1] David is said to have spoken of 'the Christ' (ii. 31) and, with reference to God, Jesus is described as 'his Christ' (iii. 18). St. Luke speaks of preaching Jesus as 'the Christ' (v. 42), of proclaiming 'the Christ' (viii. 5), of proving or testifying that He is such (ix. 22, xvii. 3, xviii. 5, 28), and of showing that 'the Christ must suffer' (xvii. 3, xxvi. 23). There is no trace in the preaching of the idea that Jesus is a political Messiah. On the contrary, it is explained that heaven must receive Him 'until the times of restoration of all things' (iii. 21). Further, other Messianic designations are ascribed to Him. He is described as 'the Righteous One' (iii. 14, vii. 52, xxii. 14), and as 'the Stone', set at nought by the builders 'which was made the head of the corner' (iv. 11, cf. Rom. ix. 32f., I Pet. ii. 5–8). This increased interest is due to the influence of the Resurrection upon the minds of the first preachers, and to the fact that the reserve practised by Jesus in speaking of His Messiahship was now a distant memory. 'Let all the house of Israel therefore know assuredly', says Peter, 'that God made him both Lord and Christ, this Jesus whom you crucified' (ii. 36).

3. Acts is characterized by its teaching that Jesus is the Servant of the Lord. We have seen that, like the Gospels, it teaches that the Christ 'must suffer' (xvii. 3, xxvi. 23, *v. supra*), but, unlike the Gospels, it definitely uses the name 'Servant' of Jesus (iii. 13, 26, iv. 27, 30). Delivered up and denied before the face of Pilate, 'his Servant Jesus' is 'glorified' and 'raised' by God (iii. 13, 26). He is addressed in prayer as 'thy holy Servant Jesus, whom thou didst anoint' (iv. 27), and boldness in

---

[1] Harnack, *Date of the Acts and the Synoptic Gospels*, 104–6; cf. H. J. Cadbury, *The Beginnings of Christianity*, v. 357; V. Taylor, *The Names of Jesus*, 21.

speaking the word is sought 'that signs and wonders may be done through the name of thy holy Servant Jesus' (iv. 30). The phrases used suggest that the Suffering Servant is in mind, and this interpretation is confirmed by the narrative of viii. 26–40, in which the Ethiopian eunuch's question, 'Of whom speaks the prophet this? of himself, or of some other?', is followed by the statement that Philip 'beginning from this scripture, preached unto him Jesus' (viii. 35). Already beginning to be in eclipse by the time of St. Paul, this teaching is plainly an element in the earliest Christology.[1]

4. But the most notable characteristic of the Christology of the Acts is the conviction that Jesus is Lord (cf. Rom. x. 9, 1 Cor. xii. 3, Phil. ii. 11). I have pointed out in *The Names of Jesus*[2] that Hawkins estimates that the Acts has the name 'the Lord' twenty times, in addition to the names 'the Lord Jesus', 'the Lord Jesus Christ', and 'Our Lord Jesus Christ'. The first Christians believed that the Resurrection had shown Jesus to be both Lord and Christ (ii. 36). This name carries with it the attitude of religious devotion. Prayer is addressed to Jesus by Stephen in the words, 'Lord Jesus, receive my spirit' (vii. 59). This fact is attested also by the phrase, 'all that call upon thy name' in ix. 14 (cf. ix. 21, xxii. 16). 'Such passages', writes Kirsopp Lake,[3] 'show that the name of Jesus was invoked by his followers, and that he was regarded as able to help them'. 'It is doubtful', he adds, 'whether they prove that he was prayed to in the same way as God', and he finds a parallel in the later Christian invocation of the saints. This alleged parallel is not adequate, for the practice of 'calling upon the name of the Lord' does not stand alone. Into the name of Jesus be-

---

[1] Cf. V. Taylor, *New Testament Studies*, I, No. 3, 159–67.
[2] *Op. cit.*, 44.　　[3] *The Beginnings of Christianity*, iv. 15.

lievers are baptized (ii. 38, viii. 16). He is the object of faith (iii. 16). Indeed, it is expressly affirmed that 'in none other is there salvation', that 'neither is there any other name under heaven, that is given among men, wherein we must be saved' (iv. 12). Further, He is described as 'the Prince' or 'Pioneer of life' (iii. 15, v. 31), and as 'a Saviour' exalted 'to give repentance to Israel and remission of sins' (v. 31, cf. xiii. 23f.). In the light of all the facts it is impossible to describe the Christology of the Acts as 'Adoptionist'. Although the designation 'the Son of God' does not belong to the vocabulary of the Acts, its religious values appear in the manner in which He is described. One must agree with Dom Gregory Dix when he writes, 'The real difficulties of harmonizing Acts with the Pauline Epistles are almost entirely those of harmonizing silences. But the difficulties of harmonizing those Epistles with the theory of a permanent separation between S. Paul and the Jewish Christians are those of harmonizing contradictions'.[1]

[1] *Jew and Greek: A Study in the Primitive Church*, 50.

IV

THE EPISTLES OF ST. PAUL

We turn next to St. Paul's teaching concerning the Person of Christ.

The Apostle is the first Christian teacher who meditates upon and develops the Christological teaching which he had received from the Christian communities at Jerusalem and Antioch. He does not write in the air, for he is dependent upon tradition, but he does not merely hand on the tradition. Under the influence of Old Testament teaching and in response to the stimulus of Greek religious thought he reflects upon it and interprets it in the light of his Christian experience and his missionary labours. His influence upon later New Testament writers, and in particular the author of the Epistle to the Hebrews and the Fourth Evangelist, is less than has been commonly supposed, but his teaching has left a deep impress upon Christian thought throughout the centuries and especially since the Reformation. It is an exaggeration to say that he completely transformed the Christian message under the influence of Hellenistic ideas, so that it became something quite different from the beliefs of the first Christian communities and the teaching of Jesus, but there can be no doubt that his eager and penetrating mind was responsive to prevailing currents of thought, with the result that he was able to give to the Gospel a new and a rich setting. The effects of his teaching can be seen in all subsequent Christological teaching down to the present day and are of abiding importance for the Church.

It is significant that St. Paul's teaching is conveyed in

letters and not in formal treatises. This form gives to them an intimacy and a facility of expression which have greatly contributed to their influence. The Epistles are letters to Churches at important centres of the Roman Empire and on this account have a communal as well as a personal interest. In a sense they are occasional writings, since they are addressed to existing circumstances and conditions in particular Churches. It would be a mistake, however, to think of them in terms of a passing correspondence between the Apostle and his friends. Many sections in them bear signs of prolonged thought and are probably transcripts of earlier teaching formulated as St. Paul travelled and taught during his missionary journeys or while he was in bonds in prisons.

The Epistles have a unique value because, with the possible exception of Ephesians, there is no doubt of their genuineness. Half a century ago it was often said that we could be sure of the authenticity of at least four of the Epistles, those accepted by the Tübingen school, Galatians, Romans, and 1 and 2 Corinthians, although even then it was being increasingly recognized that other letters were genuine also. In addition to the four already mentioned we have to-day no good reason to question Philippians, Philemon, and 1 Thessalonians. If there is some hesitation about Colossians, especially the Christological passage i. 15–17, I believe the decisive word was spoken by E. F. Scott when he said that this passage is 'integral to the whole argument and indeed supplies its philosophical groundwork'.[1] The doubts which have been expressed from time to time about 2 Thessalonians do not seem to be of serious moment in view of the evi-

---

[1] *The Epistles to the Colossians, to Philemon, and to the Ephesians* (*The Moffatt New Testament Commentary*), 12 ; C. F. D. Moule, *The Epistles of Paul the Apostle to the Colossians and to Philemon* (1957).

dence supplied by the vocabulary, diction, and ideas, especially if, with J. Weiss,[1] we think that this Epistle was written before 1 Thessalonians. Ephesians is another matter. The case for the non-Pauline authorship of the Epistle has recently been restated and ably supported by C. L. Mitton,[2] who commends the hypothesis of E. J. Goodspeed,[3] that it was written in dependence on St. Paul's letters to form the preface to the corpus of Pauline writings about the period A.D. 87–92. The argument is carefully based on linguistic and stylistic considerations, the use of words, theological differences, and above all the striking similarities between Ephesians and Colossians. The question is still under debate, but whatever conclusion is reached, it remains true by agreement on both sides that Ephesians is the crown and climax of Pauline teaching although as a later development if the Epistle is non-Pauline. I feel therefore at liberty to use all the ten Epistles in studying the Apostle's Christology.[4]

I. ST. PAUL'S USE OF PRIMITIVE CHRISTIAN TRADITION

I have said that St. Paul is dependent upon the early tradition of Jerusalem and Antioch, and it is important at the outset to estimate his debt to that tradition as fully as we can.

A useful pointer is his use of names and titles. Some of the names found in the Gospels and the Acts he does not use at all. These include 'Rabbi', 'Rabboni', 'Teacher', 'Master', 'Prophet', 'Son of David', 'Son of Mary', 'Son

---

[1] *The History of Primitive Christianity*, 289. But see L. Morris, *The Epistles of Paul to the Thessalonians* (1956), 27–30.

[2] *The Epistle to the Ephesians*, (1951).

[3] *The Meaning of Ephesians* (1933).

[4] The teaching of the Pastoral Epistles is discussed separately. See pp. 129–33.

of Joseph', 'Son of Man', 'King of Israel', 'He that cometh', 'the Pioneer', 'the Holy One', and 'the Righteous One'. Manifestly, he does not feel these names to be adequate to express his veneration for Jesus. The traditional names he uses are 'Jesus', which appears in his letters with relative frequency, 'Christ', which is repeatedly found by itself and in combination with other names, 'Lord', of which the same is true, 'Son of God', which surprisingly is found four times only, 'the Son' which he has twice, and 'His Son' which is used eleven times. To these we must add 'the Head of the Corner', 'the Stone', 'the Rock', and perhaps 'the Power of God'.

Among the new names which St. Paul uses are 'the Image of God', 'the Firstborn', 'the Beloved', 'the Wisdom of God', and 'the Last Adam'. The list is surprisingly small, and so reveals the extent to which the Apostle is dependent on names current in the Christian communities. His conservatism in this respect is also illustrated by the fact that he does not use important names which subsequently became current, including 'Shepherd', 'Mediator', 'Lamb', 'High Priest', 'Advocate', 'the Expiation', 'the Radiance of (God's) Glory', 'the Logos', and the names used in the Fourth Gospel connected with bread, life, light, door, way, truth. Even the name 'Saviour', present with some frequency in the latest New Testament writings, appears twice only in his letters, in Phil. iii. 20 in an eschatological sense, and in Eph. v. 23 in the phrase 'the Saviour of the body'. Apart from the new expressions listed above his usage is that of the Churches.

The Apostle's dependence on primitive Christianity, however, goes far beyond names and titles. Many of his ideas are not new, but borrowed and adapted. His undoubted originality must not blind us to this fact. Fre-

quently his testimony is based on earlier usage. Bultmann
has illustrated this indebtedness in his *Theology of the New
Testament*, and it will be of advantage to recall some of the
examples he cites. He points out that the death of Jesus
had already been conceived as an expiatory sacrifice in the
earliest Church, and says that St. Paul is visibly leaning
upon traditional formulations in such passages as Rom.
iii. 24f. and iv. 25.[1] The latter, he says, 'makes the impression of a quotation'.[2] Rom. i. 3, he suggests, 'is
evidently due to a traditional formula', and it attests the
use of the title 'Son of God' to describe the messianic king
as already current before St. Paul.[3] Again, the eschatological prayer '*Marana tha*', 'Our Lord, come' (1 Cor.
xvi. 22), 'certainly comes out of the earliest Church',
although not, Bultmann maintains, as an invocation of
Jesus.[4] 'Without doubt', he writes, 'Paul is alluding to a
creedal formula in Rom. x. 9, 'If you confess with your
mouth that Jesus is Lord and believe in your heart that
God raised him from the dead, you will be saved.'[5] 'The
idea of the "new covenant", of which the death of Christ is
held to be the instituting sacrifice, was evidently alive before Paul, as the liturgy of the Lord's Supper which had
come down to him indicates (1 Cor. xi. 25).'[6] Bultmann
several times refers to 'the Christ-hymn in Phil. ii. 6–11',
maintaining in agreement with E. Lohmeyer that it has
been taken over by the Apostle, not composed by him.[7]
He is even ready to say that the matter-of-fact way in
which St. Paul speaks of Christ as the mediator in creation
inclines one to conclude that he was not alone in doing so,
and that the same impression is made by his description of
Christ as 'the image of God' (2 Cor. iv. 4).[8] 'Besides

[1] *Op. cit.*, I. 46f. [2] *Op. cit.*, I. 47. [3] *Op. cit.*, I. 50.
[4] *Op. cit.*, I. 51f. [5] *Op. cit.*, I. 81. [6] *Op. cit.*, I. 98.
[7] *Op. cit.*, I. 27, 125, 129, 131, etc. [8] *Op. cit.*, I. 132.

Jn. i. 1ff.', he declares, 'Hebrews attests that Christ as the Son of God was regarded as a cosmic figure by others than Paul and his school'.[1] Similar opinions are expressed regarding the sacraments. St. Paul, it is said, was not the first to give to baptism the 'mystery interpretation' found in Rom. vi. 2ff., and he is 'the earliest witness to the sacrament of the Lord's Supper'. 'He created it no more than he did baptism; rather *he found it already present in Hellenistic Christianity*'.[2]

I have quoted these opinions because they have a certain force as coming from one who cannot be suspected of writing with an apologetic tendency. They show how mistaken it is to suppose that the Apostle is 'the great innovator'. His thought is steeped in traditional Christianity. However far he may rise on the wings of speculation, and no matter how ecstatic his utterances may sometimes be, as, for example, in 2 Cor. xii. 1–10, he is always in the closest touch with the brown earth of common Christian belief.

II. ST. PAUL AND THE JESUS OF HISTORY

From what has already been said the question arises, 'In what relation does St. Paul stand to the Jesus of History?' Part of the answer is given by affirming his knowledge of the tradition into which he entered, but special and more detailed issues are involved.

It has been held that St. Paul had actually seen Jesus in Jerusalem and had witnessed His crucifixion.[3] This may be true, but the evidence is far from being conclusive. It is clear, however, from many incidental references in his Epistles that he was well acquainted with

[1] *Ibid.*

[2] *Op. cit.*, I. 141, 150. The italics are his.

[3] Cf. J. H. Moulton, *Expositor* (1911), ii. 18ff.; J. Weiss, *Paul and Jesus*, 42ff.; C. A. Anderson Scott, *Christianity according to St. Paul*, 11f.

many facts in His life and ministry. He knows, for
example, of His Davidic descent (Rom. i. 3), His human
birth (Gal. iv. 4), His self-humiliation (Phil. ii. 6–11, 2
Cor. viii. 9, Rom. viii. 3), His meekness and gentleness
(2 Cor. x. 1), His refusal to please Himself (Rom. xv. 3),
His betrayal and Last Supper (1 Cor. xi. 23–5), His death
and resurrection, which are frequently mentioned, and
His ascension (Eph. iv. 8). Further, St. Paul's ethical
teaching in Rom. xii. 19–21 implies a knowledge of the
teaching of Jesus concerning love to enemies (Mt. v.
43–8). He is acquainted with sayings of Jesus concerning
divorce (1 Cor. vii. 10) and the support of missionaries
(1 Cor. ix. 14, cf. Lk. x. 7). In Ac. xx. 35 he quotes a
saying not otherwise attested.

It is necessary to recall these things, since his knowledge of the life and ministry of Jesus has often been
underestimated. Nevertheless, when all the evidence has
been collected, it is very small in extent, especially when
we recall very many incidents and sayings about which he
is completely silent; and this limitation is not adequately
explained when it is pointed out that his letters deal with
practical situations which do not always lend themselves
to biographical allusions. St. Paul refers to no event in
the life of Christ between His birth and betrayal and to
none of the major aspects of His teaching with the exception of love. When speaking of the Law he does not
quote the sayings, although he knows what Jesus had said
about the greatest commandment (Rom. xiii. 9f.). The
want of a biographical interest is, of course, true of the
earliest community, but it has special prominence in St.
Paul's letters because he is concerned above all with the
significance of Christ's person and work. 'From now
on', he writes, 'we regard no one from a human point of
view; even though we once regarded Christ from a human

point of view, we regard him thus no longer' (2 Cor. v.
16).[1] The meaning of this passage has often been debated. It does not necessarily imply that he had seen
Jesus, nor is it merely an admission for argument's sake,
nor again an allusion to his vision of Christ on the
Damascus road; it seems to refer to a knowledge of
Christ as a teacher and prophet in the days of His flesh,
as He appeared outwardly to human eyes. St. Paul's
interest, on the contrary, lies in the supernatural aspects of
Christ's person and in His creative power. This interest
appears to be implied in the words that follow: 'Therefore
if any one is in Christ, he is a new creation; the old has
passed away, behold, the new has come' (2 Cor. v. 17).

The question arises, 'In what way does St. Paul think
of the humanity of Jesus?' He certainly thinks and
speaks of Christ as a man (cf. Rom. v. 15, Phil. ii. 8), but
it is a challenging fact that he does not say that He
'became man' or 'became flesh'. We do not find in his
writings any express statement comparable to Jn. i. 14,
'The Word became flesh'. Always when speaking of the
humanity of Christ he has a qualifying phrase: 'in the
likeness of men' (Phil. ii. 7), 'in fashion as a man' (Phil.
ii. 8), 'in the likeness of sinful flesh' (Rom. viii. 3). One
cannot be surprised that a suspicion of Docetism in his
teaching has sometimes arisen. J. Weiss observes that,
in thinking of the Incarnation, he permitted himself to
waver more or less in the balance between an actual
humanity and a merely external assumption of a human
body, and claims that he 'grazes the later heresy of
"Docetism" '.[2] 'He does not wish to state', says Weiss,
'that Christ had borne flesh which, like our own, was ruled

[1] Cf. A. Plummer, *The Second Epistle of St. Paul to the Corinthians*,
175–9.
[2] *The History of Primitive Christianity*, 490.

D

by sin. It would have seemed to him like blasphemy.
Therefore he uses—we cannot put it differently—an
expression of double meaning'.[1] Bousset gives a better
account of St. Paul's words when he says that in them
there are all the beginnings which could issue in Docetism,
that the Apostle glides over conceptions of this kind, but
that he has never seriously applied himself to the question,
how the divine pre-existent being in Jesus was connected
with an actual humanity.[2] The truth would appear to be
that St. Paul has no doubt of the true humanity of Jesus,
and indeed asserts it in 2 Cor. viii. 9, Gal. iv. 4, and Phil.
ii. 6–11, and that there is a reason for his qualifying
phrases in his conviction that 'the flesh', as we know it, is
the sphere in which sin is entrenched (Rom. vii. 14–25).
Believing Christ to be sinless (2 Cor. v. 21), he is driven
to introduce the phrases, 'in the likeness of' and 'in
fashion as', which safeguard his belief. Thus, there is
only an appearance of Docetism in these expressions.
Docetism itself he would roundly have rejected. He
wishes to say that the humanity of Christ was like our
own, except that in His flesh sin had no place. Sanday
and Headlam put the truth well when they write: 'The
flesh of Christ is "like" ours inasmuch as it is flesh;
"like", and only "like", because it is not sinful'.[3] P. C.
Boylan expresses a similar view in his commentary on
Romans.[4] To this explanation we must add that, while
St. Paul himself did not graze the edge of Docetism, his
words furnished its exponents with weapons. Thus, the
Johannine teaching, with its concentration upon the
reality of the Incarnation, was a necessary supplement to
Pauline teaching.

---

[1] *Op. cit.*, 489.   [2] *Kyrios Christos*, 152f.
[3] *The Epistle to the Romans*, 193.
[4] *St. Paul's Epistle to the Romans*, 132.

III. JESUS AS THE MESSIAH

St. Paul's attitude to the Messiahship of Jesus is an interesting illustration of his preoccupation with higher theological interests.

There can be no doubt that for him Jesus is the Messiah. Thus, he speaks of 'His Son, who was born of the seed of David according to the flesh' (Rom. i. 3), and of the Jews as those 'of whom is the Messiah according to the flesh' (Rom. ix. 5), if we are justified in so rendering 'the Christ' in that passage. His words in 2 Thess. ii. 8 about the Lord Jesus, who shall consume the wicked with the breath of His mouth, and shall destroy him with the brightness of His coming, show that he assigned Messianic functions of judgement to Christ at His Parousia. So too his emphasis elsewhere that Christ is the Judge (Rom. ii. 16, 2 Cor. v. 10), especially his solemn assertion that we must all appear before the judgement seat of Christ. His interest in Messiahship is eschatological.

Nevertheless, it cannot be said that the idea of Christ as the Messiah is a central and dominating thought in his theology. It is part of the primitive tradition which he takes over, but it does not represent the main direction of his Christological interests. This view is illustrated by the fact that, while he echoes the soteriological aspects of Messiahship, as in Rom. iv. 25 and other passages, he does not dwell upon and develop this teaching preserved in the Passion-sayings of Mark. Christ, moreover, is Judge, not only because He is the promised Messiah, but because He is the 'Lord Christ', the object of devotion and obedience. Had it been otherwise, His Messiahship would have received greater emphasis in St. Paul's teaching, and not have remained in the background; whereas, as we can see from his letters, 'Christ Jesus',

'Jesus Christ', 'Christ', and 'the Lord Jesus Christ' are predominantly proper names. Jesus Himself is the centre of his teaching.

IV. JESUS AS LORD

Although taken over from primitive usage, the conception of Christ as 'Lord' is the dominating idea in the Pauline theology. 'For Paul', says Bultmann, ' "Lord" and not "Christ" is Jesus's title'.[1] As used by him the name, to an overwhelming degree, is redolent of religious veneration. 'It gave to Him', writes Anderson Scott, 'a religious significance hardly to be distinguished from that which men assigned to God'.[2]

Four passages, in particular, convey this impression. First must be mentioned the exultant and scornful words of 1 Cor. viii. 5f.: 'For though there be that are called gods, whether in heaven or on earth; as there are gods many, and lords many; yet to us there is one God, the Father, of whom are all things, and we unto him; and one Lord, Jesus Christ, through whom are all things, and we through him'. Then, there is the emphatic statement in 1 Cor. xii. 3: 'I give you to understand, that no man speaking in the Spirit of God says, Jesus is anathema; and no man can say, Jesus is Lord, but in the Holy Spirit'. Again, the Christian confession in Rom. x. 9 points in this direction: 'If you shall confess with your mouth that Jesus is Lord, and shall believe in your heart that God raised him from the dead, you will be saved'. Lastly, there is the magnificent climax in Phil. ii. 6–11: 'That at the name of Jesus every knee should bow, in heaven and on earth and under the earth, and every tongue confess that Jesus Christ is Lord, to the glory of God the Father'. These statements and others of like character

---

[1] *Op. cit.*, I. 80.   [2] *Op. cit.*, 254.

leave us in no doubt that in St. Paul's religion, and in that of the Hellenistic communities, the confession 'Jesus is Lord' expresses an attitude of religious devotion.

This is the opinion of Bousset. In the endeavour to refute his explanation of the origin of the Christian use of the Kyrios-title, many of his penetrating observations are often forgotten. Thus, he observes that the living experience of the Lord Christ, present in the worship and life of the community, stands behind the Pauline mysticism of 'being in Christ', and that the passion of St. Paul's Christ-piety took fire, not in the historic Jesus, nor even in the first case in the Christ who appeared to him at Damascus, but rather in the powerful reality (*machtvollen Wirklichkeit*) of the Kyrios, as St. Paul came to know it in the first Hellenistic communities.[1] In many of St. Paul's statements there is an unmistakable atmosphere of awe, while the relationship between himself and the living Lord is that of slave and Master. 'We preach not ourselves', he writes, 'but Christ Jesus as Lord, and ourselves as your servants for Jesus's sake' (2 Cor. iv. 5). 'Christ', he declares, 'died and lived again, that he might be Lord both of the dead and the living' (Rom. xiv. 9). When he thinks of the living Christ, he thinks of Him as the Lord who reigns, exercises His power, and issues His commands, and while the believer's attitude is one of faith in Him, it is no less one of obedience to Him. All this must be taken seriously into account in considering the Apostle's Christology. It is especially relevant in estimating what he has to say of Christ's Sonship.

v. JESUS AS THE SON OF GOD

Besides repeatedly referring to the Lordship of Christ St. Paul speaks also, but much less frequently, of His

[1] *Op. cit.*, 106. Cf. also J. Weiss, *op. cit.*, 465ff.

Sonship. He uses the name 'Son of God' four times only, in Rom. i. 4, 2 Cor. i. 19, Gal. ii. 20, and Eph. iv. 13, 'the Son' twice, in 1 Cor, xv. 28 and Col. i. 13,[1] and the phrase 'His Son' eleven times, in Rom. i. 3, 9, v. 10, viii. 3, 29, 32, 1 Cor. i. 9, Gal. i. 16, iv. 4, 6, and 1 Thess. i. 10.[2] The disparity between this terminology and the use of the name 'the Lord' is startling, for the latter is found at least 138 times, apart from the expressions 'Our Lord', 'Our Lord Jesus Christ', 'The Lord Jesus Christ', and kindred names. If we add these names the number is not less than 222. It is true that he also speaks of God as 'the Father' of Jesus Christ, as in 2 Cor. i. 3, xi. 31, Col. i. 3, and Eph. i. 3. Even so a problem remains.

In *The Names of Jesus* I attempted to account for the disparity by claiming that the names 'the Son' and 'His Son' were associated with teaching rather than with worship, and I observed that, while the first Christians fervently believed in 'the Son', they invoked in worship 'the Lord'. In using the name 'the Lord' they confessed their personal relation to Christ; in speaking of 'the Son' they described His divine status.[3]

This explanation, I think, is sound, but manifestly more needs to be said when we are speaking of St. Paul. The disparity suggests that pre-eminently he is the man of religion rather than the theologian and that he is deeply influenced by the liturgical tradition of the primitive communities. It is also due to the fact that his letters are addressed to believers. As belonging to the language of devotion, the name 'the Lord' means everything to the worshipper of Christ, but when he reflects upon His significance, and wishes to convey it to others, a fuller

---

[1] Here the phrase 'the Son of his love' is used.
[2] Rom. viii. 3 and 32 speak of 'His own Son'.
[3] *Op. cit.*, 52, 57.

terminology is necessary. In meditation he can say 'My Lord', but if he wishes to bear testimony, like Thomas he must say, 'My Lord and my God' (Jn. xx. 28). He can speak of Christ as 'the Lord' to other believers, but to un-believers or to catechumens, and even to believers in need of further instruction, he must add other names. Now the Pauline letters are written to believing communities by one whose faith is as fire. That is why St. Paul uses the language of Lordship so freely; but when he is con-cerned to say what this language means, he must use the terminology of Sonship, and all the more because ac-cording to the tradition the name 'the Son' had been used by Jesus of Himself. It is less adequate to say that the Kyrios-title was embarrassed by its pagan associations, even though the fact is undoubted, because the same can be said of the name 'the Son of God' in Greek religion. It cannot be too often remembered that all the names of Christ which struck a responsive chord in the ears of Gentile audiences were capable of being misunderstood. It is along such lines that we must account for the fact, so far as we can explain it at all, that St. Paul speaks of Christ so much more often as 'the Lord' than he does of Him as 'the Son' or 'the Son of God'. One cannot but notice his marked preference for the more intimate name 'His Son'.

What, then, is the content of the language of Sonship as applied to Christ in Pauline teaching, and how far is it in line with the explanation advanced above?

Let us turn, first, to the passages listed above. The association of teaching with this terminology is especially manifest in each of the four passages in which 'the Son of God' is mentioned. Rom. i. 4, 'designated Son of God with power, according to the spirit of holiness, by the re-surrection of the dead', is by wide consent the language of a primitive creed. In Gal. ii. 20 the name is used by the

Apostle to define the faith by which he lives; it is that grounded in 'the Son of God' who, he says, 'loved me and gave himself up for me'. 2 Cor. i. 19, 'the Son of God, Jesus Christ, whom we preached among you', also has a formal ring, and expressly mentions preaching. In the fourth passage. Eph. iv. 13, the Sonship of Christ is associated with 'knowledge' in the words, 'till we attain unto the unity of the faith, and of the knowledge of the Son of God, unto a fullgrown man'. In all these passages teaching or exhortation is in question.

The same may be said of other passages, especially Rom. i. 3 and 8, which connect 'His Son' with 'the gospel' in the phrases 'the gospel concerning his Son' and 'the gospel of his Son'. Again the title is connected with teaching.

In the passages which speak of 'the Son' and 'His Son' a new point emerges; the terminology is used because Jesus Christ is mentioned over against God. In 1 Cor. xv. 28 the time is contemplated when 'the Son' will be subjected to God, 'that God may be all in all'. In Col. i. 13 Christ is described with reference to God as 'the Son of his love'. In Rom. v. 10 reconciliation with God is 'through the death of his Son'. In Rom. viii. 3 God sends 'his own Son', and in Rom. viii. 29 He predestines men 'to be conformed to the image of his Son'. In Rom. viii. 32 it is said that He 'did not spare his own Son, but delivered him up for us all'. 1 Cor. i. 9 speaks of 'the fellowship of his Son', Gal. i. 16 of the good pleasure of God 'to reveal his Son', Gal. iv. 4 of God's act in sending forth 'his Son', Gal. iv. 6 of His sending forth 'the Spirit of his Son into our hearts', and, finally, 1 Thess. i. 10 of waiting for 'his Son from heaven, whom he raised from the dead, even Jesus'. These are all the passages in question, and it is significant that the Godward relationship which is implicit in the names is expressly brought out by the Apostle. It is manifestly his intention to use these names in defining Christ's relation to God.

What, then, is the relationship? We may say at once that it is far more than that of Messiahship. It is not that of the Messianic king. To use the luminous phrase of C. A. Anderson Scott, it is 'personal, ethical, and inherent';[1] it involves 'a community of nature between the Father and the Son'.[2] Bousset is justified when he says that, whether St. Paul has gone back to an older Messianic title or not, the name 'Son of God' receives from him a new impress, with which Jewish teaching has nothing more to do. 'The Son of God in Paul', he writes, 'appears as a supra-mundane being standing in the closest metaphysical relationship to God'.[3]

This statement of Bousset uses the language of a later time, and if we press it, it is tempting to ask whether St. Paul's teaching ultimately implies the truth of the *homoousios* and the hypostatic union between the Persons of the Trinity. But we have only to state the question to see that it is inappropriate while considering Pauline teaching, since St. Paul does not use philosophic terms and does not contemplate such questions. We must continue the inquiry as far as we can in Pauline terms. If, from this standpoint, we ask what is the content of the Sonship he describes, there can be no doubt that it is appreciated best by considering his teaching concerning the relationship of Christ to man, to the universe, to the Spirit, and to God. The Sonship is estimated best in terms of its functions.

VI. ST. PAUL'S VIEW OF CHRIST'S RELATIONSHIP TO MAN

In this matter three aspects of the Apostle's teaching claim attention: (*a*) Christ as the Second Adam; (*b*) the

[1] *Op. cit.*, 255.   [2] *Op. cit.*, 256.   [3] *Op. cit.*, 151.

work of God in Christ; (c) the faith-relationship between the believer and Christ.

(a) St. Paul's teaching concerning Christ as the Second Adam[1] is found in Rom. v. 12–21 and 1 Cor. xv. 21f., 45–7. It certainly has an old-world ring, since it is based on the historical character of the Genesis creation story, a postulate we no longer accept. It would be wrong, however, to neglect his teaching on this account. Quite apart from the historical character of the narrative the teaching is of the greatest importance, since the story is only the medium by which it is conveyed.

In contrasting the disobedience and trespass of Adam with the obedience and righteous act of Christ St. Paul assigns to both Adam and Christ a representative relationship to man. The same idea recurs in 1 Cor. xv. 45, where it is said that Adam became 'a living soul', but Christ 'a life-giving spirit'. The teaching is Rabbinic in character. It has been held that the Apostle is using the widespread myth of the Heavenly Man who descends from the upper world of light to free men from the bonds of matter.[2] It seems more probable that the 'Man from heaven' (1 Cor. xv. 47) is St. Paul's equivalent for 'the Son of Man',[3] a name which he does not use. It may be that he knew of the pagan myth, but there is no reason to think that he is deeply influenced by it, since in his teaching Christ comes to deliver men from sin, not from the entanglements of matter. These questions are of great interest, but for our purpose the significant thing is the representative function he attributes to Christ. This idea is implicit in the Pauline theology as a whole, especially in the doctrine of the work of God in Christ. Its bearings

[1] Cf. V. Taylor, *The Names of Jesus*, 153–5.
[2] Cf. Bousset, *op. cit.*, 140–3; Bultmann, *op. cit.*, I. 166f., 174
[3] Cf. J. Weiss, *op. cit.*, 484f.

upon Christology are manifest. Later theologians spoke of Christ as 'Man', as in the well known sentence of R. C. Moberly, 'He was not generically, but inclusively, man'.[1] St. Paul does not say anything like this, but we must undoubtedly conclude that, in giving Christ a representative significance in relation to man, he imparts a supernatural character to his doctrine of Christ's Sonship, with consequent implications, which are not worked out, concerning the nature and being of God.

(b) St. Paul's teaching concerning the work of God in Christ leads to the same conclusion, for while the saving work is God's (Rom. v. 8, viii. 3), Christ is presented as an active agent, not a passive medium. 'Christ died for us', he writes (Rom. v. 8); and 'Christ died for our sins' (1 Cor. xv. 3). In describing His vicarious act he brings out its representative character unmistakably in such expressions as 'one died for all' (2 Cor. v. 14) and 'made to be sin on our behalf' (2 Cor. v. 21, cf. Gal. iii. 13). I have maintained elsewhere[2] that this teaching approaches the verge of substitution, from which it is distinguished negatively by the absence of definitely substitutionary language, 'instead of', 'ransom', 'to ransom', and positively by the strong emphasis laid upon the experience of union with Christ by faith. This teaching would not be self-consistent if it did not carry with it the doctrine of a supernatural Sonship. In St. Paul Soteriology and Christology are inseparable.

(c) Precisely the same conclusion follows from the Apostle's teaching about faith-union with Christ in the many passages in which he speaks of 'being in Christ' or 'in the Lord', and of 'dying', 'suffering', 'being crucified', 'being buried', 'being raised', 'quickened', and 'glorified'

[1] *Atonement and Personality*, 86.
[2] *The Atonement in New Testament Teaching*, 85–7.

with Him.[1] We rightly prize the devotional value of such teaching, but it is Christological as well. Language of this kind is gross exaggeration if it used of a prophet or teacher, or even of a deified man. We can have fellowship with men, but the kind of fellowship with Christ which St. Paul describes, union or communion with Him, without the loss of personal identity, in faith, worship, and the sacraments, is possible only if the object of fellowship is a supernatural person. 'The Jesus Paul knows', Bousset writes, 'is the pre-existent supra-mundane Christ, who was rich and became poor for our sakes, who was in the divine form and assumed the form of a servant, the Son of God whom the Father gave as an offering, the One who fulfils the prophecies and completes the promises'.[2] It is this supernatural Christ with whom the believer has fellowship.

VII. ST. PAUL'S VIEW OF CHRIST'S RELATIONSHIP TO THE UNIVERSE

The relationship of Christ to the universe is manifestly bound up with His Sonship. This conception is more directly expressed in Jn. i. 3 and Heb. i. 2f. and is found in St. Paul in its earlier stages. Its Christological importance stands out when the strong Jewish emphasis upon God as the sole Creator is remembered (cf. Isa. xliv. 24).

The first passage to consider is 1 Cor. viii. 6: 'Yet to us there is one God, the Father, of whom are all things, and we unto him; and one Lord Jesus Christ, through whom are all things, and we through him'. We are often rightly warned against stressing the grammatical niceties on which the earlier commentators loved to dwell; but this is not a case in which we can afford to neglect the fact

---

[1] *Forgiveness and Reconciliation*, 113–19.   [2] *Op. cit.*, 105.

that, in speaking of the Father, St. Paul uses the pre-
position ἐκ, whereas with reference to Christ he uses διά.
The two statements in the passage are not parallel. The
more direct statement is made concerning the Father.
He is the ultimate ground of the existence of the universe.
He is the Creator '*of* whom' or '*from* whom are all things'.
A great claim, but not the same claim, is made concerning Christ. He is the mediate cause of the universe
and of man; '*through* whom are all things, and we
through him'. We note the difference indicated by the
prepositions, and it is manifest that we are introduced to
that idea of subordination we shall have to consider later
when we consider how St. Paul speaks of Christ's relationship to God. Meantime the sublimity of the statement must be noted. The words 'and we through him'
relate to the new spiritual creation of man, and suggest
that in the earlier phrase 'through whom are all things' the
Apostle is thinking of Christ as the ordering and ener-
gizing power in the universe. The idea has strong
affinities with the doctrine of the Logos. The affirmation
is staggering when it is read alongside the words 'born of
the seed of David' (Rom. i. 3) and 'born of a woman, born
under the law' (Gal. iv. 4). That the Apostle implies the
pre-existent dignity of the divine Christ does not need to
be argued.

The second passage, Rom. xi. 36, 'For of him, and
through him, and unto him, are all things', is less immediately relevant, since it refers to God and not directly
to Christ. It is not possible to agree with Aquinas that
the three clauses refer to the Persons of the Trinity.[1] It
states that God is the source and inspirer and goal of all
things;[2] it is an impressive statement of St. Paul's mono-

---

[1] Cf. Boylan, *St. Paul's Epistle to the Romans*, 190.
[2] Cf. Sanday and Headlam, *The Epistle to the Romans*, 340.

theism, with parallels in Stoicism[1] as well as in the Old
Testament. It is quoted here because it is the same
writer who finds a cosmic significance in Christ.

The third passage is the great Christological statement
of Col. i. 16f.: 'For in him (ἐν αὐτῷ) were all things
created, in the heavens and upon the earth, things visible
and invisible, whether thrones or dominions or principalities or powers; all things have been created through
him (δι' αὐτοῦ), and unto him (εἰς αὐτόν); and he is
before all things (πρὸ πάντων), and in him (ἐν αὐτῷ)
all things consist (συνέστηκεν)'.[2] Here undoubtedly we
have an advance upon 1 Cor. viii. 6, but there is a
fundamental affinity between the two passages. St.
Paul may be using an earlier hymn, but in my view the
agreement and the development are sufficiently explained
by the fact that he is meeting the claims of the false
teachers at Colossae. How much is to be read into the
phrase 'in him' it is difficult to say, but it is not pedantic
to observe that he still witholds the explicit phrase 'by
him' (ὑπ' αὐτοῦ). 'In him' appears to anticipate the verb
'consist' (συνέστηκεν), by which he intends to say that
in Christ all things 'find their place', as the keystone holds
an arch together. Alternatively ἐν is instrumental, but
in either case it seems to be deliberately chosen as being
less explicit than either ἐκ or ὑπό. As in 1 Cor. viii. 6
'through him' suggests the idea of mediate creation, but
'unto him', with its suggestion of a goal, makes the same
statement concerning Christ which in Rom. xi. 36 is made
about God.

The teaching of the passage resembles that of the Stoics
with reference to the Logos. It may reflect the influence

---

[1] Cf. Bultmann, *Theology of the New Testament*, I. 70f.
[2] For the view that this passage may be part of a pre-Pauline hymn see
p. 62f.

of Stoic teaching upon the Apostle's mind. If so, he does not borrow it in a mechanical way and straightway apply it to Christ; he finds the teaching luminous when he reflects upon Christ's cosmic functions. He believes, and again the idea is of the most far-reaching importance, that all the powers which bring the universe into being and sustain it are resident in Him. The bearing upon his Christology of 1 Cor. viii. 6 and Col. i. 16f. cannot be mistaken. These passages cannot be applied to a man, or even to a deified man. The Christ to whom they refer is a Christ who belongs, in a manner which is not defined, to Deity itself. Here, as elsewhere, we see that, high as St. Paul's Christology is in statement, its ultimate implications are higher still.

VIII. ST. PAUL'S VIEW OF CHRIST'S RELATIONSHIP TO THE HOLY SPIRIT

The relationship between Christ and the Holy Spirit is undeniably close. In the opinion of some scholars it amounts to one of identity, but in the light of the evidence as a whole it is best described in C. A. Anderson Scott's phrase as 'an equivalence of function'.[1]

First may be noted, in Pauline teaching, aspects of the Christian experience associated with Christ which are also connected with the Spirit. For example, just as the believer is said to be 'in Christ', so also he is said to be 'in the Spirit' (Rom. xiv. 17). Christ 'dwells' in believers, but so does the Spirit (Rom. viii. 9, 1 Cor. iii. 16). Love (Col. i. 8), Justification (1 Cor. vi. 11), and Life (Rom. viii. 2, 11), are all associated with the Spirit as with Christ.

Among the passages which appear to identify Christ with the Spirit are Rom. viii. 9, in which 'the Spirit of God' and 'the Spirit of Christ' are mentioned in the same

---

[1] *Op. cit.*, 260.

verse, and, in particular, 2 Cor. iii. 17, where it is explicitly said, 'Now the Lord is the Spirit: and where the Spirit of the Lord is, there is liberty'. As regards the second clause conjectures made by commentators are of much interest, but are hardly adequate. Thus, Baljon and others suggest the reading, 'Now where the Lord is, there is the Spirit', and Hort suggests the reading of the adjective κύριον, and so translates, 'Where the Spirit is sovereign, is freedom'.[1] The better explanation is that in the passage κύριος refers to Ex. xxxiv. 34 which speaks of Moses and the veil, and which St. Paul has in mind in the immediate context (2 Cor. iii. 13–16) so that the meaning is, 'Now κύριος in the passage I have just quoted denotes the Spirit: and where the Spirit of the Lord is, there is liberty'.[2]

This explanation is supported by two considerations. First, it is impossible to suppose that it is a matter of indifference whether we think of Christ or of the Spirit in the many passages in which either of them is mentioned alone. Secondly, there are many important passages in which the Apostle expressly distinguishes Christ and the Spirit. A conspicuous example is Rom. viii. 16f.: 'The Spirit bears witness with our spirit, that we are children of God, . . . and joint heirs with Christ'. The same is true of 1 Cor. vi. 11, xii. 3, 2 Cor. xiii. 14, and Eph. ii. 18. In the last-named passage we read: 'For through him (that is, Christ) we both have our access in one Spirit unto the Father'.

Our conclusion must be that in St. Paul's teaching the relationship between Christ and the Spirit is not one of identity, but is singularly close in range and function. But if so, we must go further. The intimate relationship

[1] Cf. A. E. J. Rawlinson, *The New Testament Doctrine of the Christ*, 155.
[2] Cf. C. Gore, *The Reconstruction of Belief*, 550.

between the two implies that Christ is divine and suggests the existence of distinctions of personal relationships within the Godhead. The doctrine of the Trinity is not taught, but its presuppositions in Pauline teaching are laid bare.

IX. ST. PAUL'S VIEW OF CHRIST'S RELATIONSHIP TO GOD

Bultmann observes that 'in describing Christ as "God" the New Testament still exercises great restraint', and he contrasts its usage in this respect with that of Ignatius at the beginning of the second century.[1] Except for Jn. i. 1 and xx. 28, he says, this assertion is made 'at least by any probable exegesis' only in 2 Thess. i. 12, Tit. ii. 13, and 2 Pet. i. 1. In a footnote he adds, 'The doxology in Rom. ix. 5 is scarcely to be referred to Christ; in Jn. i. 18 and 1 Tim. iii. 16 "God" is a secondary variant'.

Of the Pauline passages named the most important is the doxology in Rom. ix. 5, which according to the Revised Version says of Christ, 'who is over all, God blessed for ever'. On this passage critical opinion is more sharply divided than Bultmann's note suggests. Sanday and Headlam, G. G. Findlay, P. C. Boylan, and many others agree with the Revised Version in relating the doxology to Christ; but H. A. W. Meyer, J. Denney, C. A. Anderson Scott, C. H. Dodd, and other commentators,[2] think that it is addressed to God and should be rendered, 'God who is over all be blessed for ever'. The American Revised Standard Version adopts this rendering and the margin of the English Revised Version gives a similar translation.[3]

---

[1] *Op. cit.*, I. 129.
[2] See the commentaries of the writers named on Romans *in loc*.
[3] Moffatt has, 'Blessed for evermore be the God who is over all!'

E

The decisive argument is the fact that nowhere else does St. Paul call Christ 'God'. He does not do so in 2 Thess. i. 12, where the absence of the definite article before κυρίου ᾿Ιησοῦ Χριστοῦ by no means excludes the rendering 'the grace of our God and the Lord Jesus Christ' (RV and RSV). Moreover, the passages which suggest the idea of subordination, 1 Cor. iii. 23, xi. 3, xv. 28, and Gal. iv. 4, to which reference will be made later, suggest that to speak of Christ as 'God' is inconsistent with Pauline usage. We have only to read the many passages in which Ignatius speaks of Jesus Christ as 'our God'[1] to be conscious of the fact that this mode of speech is not Pauline.

If this interpretation of Rom. ix. 5 is accepted, we are at once introduced to the real problem of St. Paul's Christology, for, while he does not call Christ 'God', we have seen that he brings Him within the orbit of Deity when he thinks of His relationships with man, with the universe, and with the Holy Spirit. Again, he uses words of Christ which in the Old Testament are used of God, as, for example, when he adapts Joel ii. 32 in 1 Cor. i. 2 in the phrase 'all who call upon the name of our Lord Jesus Christ'. Moreover, he applies great names[2] to Christ which give to Him an incomparable divine status. Thus, he speaks of Him as 'the image of God' (2 Cor. iv. 4, Col. i. 15), 'the Firstborn' (Rom. viii. 29, Col. i. 15), 'the Lord of Glory' (1 Cor. ii. 8), 'the Power and the Wisdom of God' (1 Cor. i. 24). Most significant of all, he thinks of Christ as pre-existent. Pre-existence is implied when he says, 'You know the grace of our Lord Jesus Christ, that though he was rich, yet for your sake he became poor, that you through his poverty might become rich' (2 Cor.

---

[1] *Eph.* pr., xv. 3, xviii. 2; *Rom.* pr., iii. 3; *Pol.* viii. 3.
[2] I have discussed these titles in *The Names of Jesus*.

viii. 9), when he speaks of Him as 'being in the form of God' (Phil. ii. 6), and again of God sending forth His Son when the fulness of the time came (Gal. iv. 4). Pre-existence, it may also be held, is implicit in such phrases as 'The rock was Christ' (1 Cor. x. 4) and 'The second man is of heaven' (1 Cor. xv. 47).

In the light of such teaching it seems incomprehensible to many Christians that the Apostle does not speak of Christ as 'God', and in discussing such questions we may appear to be splitting hairs. The well known correspondence between Sir William Robertson Nicoll and Dr. James Denney illustrates this situation.[1] Nicoll went so far as to say that, for all his apparent orthodoxy, there was a singular vein of scepticism in Denney, and Denney admitted that the aversion he had to such expressions as Jesus is God was linguistic as much as theological. 'Jesus', wrote Denney, 'is man as well as God, in some way therefore both less and more than God; and consequently a form of proposition which in our idiom suggests inevitably the precise equivalence of Jesus and God does some kind of injustice to the truth'.

In discussing this question we are in danger of entangling the exegetical problem with Christological theories. Our immediate concern is with St. Paul's teaching. We return, then, to the question how it is that he can make the highest of claims for Christ's divinity without using the language of Ignatius. The whole problem, however, is not before us until attention is given to the several passages in his Epistles already mentioned which assign to Christ a status of subordination in relation to God.

The first of these passages is 1 Cor. iii. 23, 'All are

---

[1] *Letters of Principal James Denney to W. Robertson Nicoll, 1883–1917*, 120–6.

yours; and you are Christ's; and Christ is God's'. Here, in an ascending scale, believers, Christ, and God are mentioned. A similar scale appears in 1 Cor. xi. 3, 'But I would have you know, that the head of every man is Christ; and the head of the woman is the man: and the head of Christ is God'. Man is mentioned first, but the order implied is the ascending series, woman, man, Christ, God. If these passages stood alone, we might not regard them as being of much importance. But a third passage shows that they are in fact theologically significant. This passage is 1 Cor. xv. 28, 'And when all things have been subjected to him, then shall the Son also himself be subjected to him that did subject all things to him, that God may be all in all'. Whether πάντα ἐν πᾶσιν is rendered 'absolutely everything' or 'everything in all things',[1] a climax is reached in which the intermediate link between things and the pre-eminence of God is the Son. He stands between them and God.

The language about 'subjection' is suggested by the Apostle's use of Psa. viii. 6, 'Thou hast put all things in subjection under his feet'. All things, says St. Paul, are put in subjection to the Son, and finally He Himself will be subjected to God. Too much must not be made of the word 'subjected', as if it implied the idea of a demi-god greater indeed than man, but less than God, an idea entirely alien to the Pauline Christology, with its emphasis upon Christ as 'the image of God'. A relative degree of subordination is implied, but it is far removed from the 'Subordinationism' of Arian and later controversy.[2] The distinction in order must be understood in terms of love, since in the mind of St. Paul Christ is the Son of God's

---

[1] Cf. C. F. D. Moule, *An Idiom-Book of New Testament Greek*, 75, 160.
[2] Cf. J. Bethune-Baker, *An Introduction to the Early History of Christian Doctrine*, 151f., 161–3, 177.

love (Col. i. 13) and 'the Beloved' (Eph. i. 6).[1] No doubt
this love is more fully emphasized in Johannine teaching,
but it is present also in St. Paul's theology, and it must be
remembered that in the Fourth Gospel Christ says, 'My
Father is greater than I' (xiv. 28). Basil observed that
comparisons may properly be made between things which
are of the same nature, and wrote, 'If, then, comparisons
are made between things of the same species, and the
Father by comparison is said to be greater than the Son,
then the Son is of the same essence as the Father'.[2]

The quotation reveals the theological distance which
intervenes between New Testament teaching and Patristic speculation. Neither St. Paul nor St. John makes observations of this kind, but, at the same time, each takes
steps which inevitably lead thought in this direction, St.
Paul by the virtual adoption, and St. John by the express
use, of a Logos or Wisdom Christology. In St. Paul's
Epistles the teaching is unsystematized. He speaks of
Christ as divine, applies to Him names and titles which
give Him no less a status, assigns to Him soteriological
functions such as no man or demi-god can exercise, gives
Him a place in the creation of the universe, and all but
identifies Him with the Spirit of God. Above all, he
represents Him as the object of worship, and as One with
whom the closest faith relationships can be known. And
yet, he does not call Him God, but distinguishes Him
from God, and presents Him in a relation of subordination to God! We must not attempt to simplify his
teaching by imposing upon it a harmony unattained by
him, for we can make no greater mistake than to short-
circuit primitive Christology. It will not serve, for
example to affirm that when St. Paul says that the Son

---

[1] Cf. *The Names of Jesus*, 159f.
[2] *Ep.* 8. The Epistle is assigned to a later hand by patristic scholars.

will be subjected to God he is thinking only of the historical Christ or Christ as incarnate, or to suppose that,
when in Rom. ix. 5 he says 'God blessed for ever', he
must be thinking of Christ. The instructive paradox of
Pauline theology is that he does not identify the Pre-
existent Christ with Deity. There is nothing but gain for
the modern theologian when he faces this fact.

The situation is like that which obtains in the history
of the physical sciences at the point before inclusive
hypotheses are framed. We see facts recognized and un-
co-ordinated, and apparently contradictory, but all the
more instructive just because they have not been con-
taminated by premature hypotheses. The wise procedure
is to recognize the situation for what it is and to account
for it as best we can. If we follow this course two important considerations stand out. First, we note the
dominating place of monotheism in St. Paul's Christology.
He will not compromise his belief that God is One God,
not even for Christ's sake. Always in his Christological
statements the emphasis is upon God, and upon God as
acting. He appears to avoid an immanental Christology.
His nearest approach to this is in Col. i. 19, in the words
'For it was the good pleasure of the Father that in him
should all the fulness dwell', or as the Revised Standard
Version translates the passage, 'For in him all the fulness
of God was pleased to dwell' (cf. RVmg). This statement however stands alone, for in 2 Cor. v. 19 the verb is
periphrastic, and the passage should be rendered, not
'God was in Christ . . .', but 'In Christ God was recon-
ciling the world to himself'. Central to his teaching is
the declaration that, when the time had fully come, 'God
sent forth his Son' (Gal. iv. 4).

Secondly, and equally clearly, we see that St. Paul's
monotheism is not Islamic. It is destined to become an

enriched version of Old Testament monotheism, one in which personal distinctions are implicit within the unity of the Godhead. The ultimate implications of his theology are trinitarian. We cannot quote a passage in which the doctrine of the Trinity is explicit, but we are well on the way to it in the Apostolic benediction of 2 Cor. xiii. 14, 'The grace of the Lord Jesus Christ and the love of God and the fellowship of the Holy Spirit be with you all', and in Eph. ii. 18, 'For through him we both have our access in one Spirit unto the Father'. It is not a thing to be lamented that we see these preliminary stages in Pauline teaching, except for those whose doctrine of inspiration compels them to find the same theology in every part of Scripture. Looking back from the standpoint of Nicene theology we have reason to be thankful that foreshadowings of later teaching are found in St. Paul's Christology, and not premature attempts at definition which might have compromised the course of later discussion, and further that the Apostle's emphasis is religious rather than philosophical, and devotional rather than dogmatic. What he says compelled Christian thinkers to move forward under the guidance, as we may well believe, of the Holy Spirit, without fetters and with lights for walking. If he does not say that Christ is 'God', he stimulated the teachers and doctors of the Church in the endeavour to find a place for Him within a richer conception of the Godhead.

St. Paul's teaching, however, points the way to this development in a passage more explicit than any we have yet noticed. This passage is the great Christological statement in Phil. ii. 6–11. It is of such importance that it calls for separate and detailed treatment, and to it we now turn.

V

THE CHRISTOLOGICAL 'HYMN'
IN PHIL. ii. 6–11

I

IN view of recent discussions it will be of interest first to consider the form of the passage.

The present tendency is to explain the passage as a pre-Pauline 'Hymn to Christ'. E. Lohmeyer[1] so describes it on grounds of vocabulary and style, and a similar view is taken by M. Dibelius,[2] R. Bultmann,[3] P. Bonnard,[4] and other scholars. *Hapax legomena*, it is pointed out, appear in the words μορφή, ἁρπαγμός, ἴσος, ὑπερυψόω, and καταχθόνιος. The balanced clauses, it is suggested, have a poetic form such as might belong to an early hymn, and the exhortations in ii. 1–5 appear to be adapted in content to it. Bonnard says that if the verses are read slowly and aloud, they are seen to possess a rhythm which is obedient to the best known law of religious Hebrew poetry, namely parallelism such as we find in the Psalms of the Old Testament and the Odes of Solomon.[5] He himself is inclined to accept the view that the pericope is 'a parenetic adapation by Paul of a hymn which sang, in Judaeo-Gnostic terms, of the appearance of the Heavenly Man on earth'.[6] Lohmeyer thinks that the motif is that of Servant of Isa. liii. Some scholars trace it

---

[1] *Kyrios Jesus, Eine Untersuchung über Phil.* ii. 5–11 (1928).
[2] *An die Thessalonicher I, II. An die Philipper*, 72–82.
[3] *Theology of the New Testament*, I. 125, 131, 175, II. 153, 155.
[4] *L'Épître de saint Paul aux Philippiens*, 41–9.
[5] *Op. cit.*, 47.   [6] *Op. cit.*, 49.

to the early communities at Damascus and Antioch, and others think that it may be of Marcionite origin.

It may well be that the 'hymn' is pre-Pauline. The argument from *hapax legomena* does not carry us far, for there are other passages in the Pauline Epistles of equal length in which as many words of the kind can be found. The argument from the rhythmical style is stronger, but here again other passages, for example, 1 Cor. i. 26–31 and 2 Cor. xi. 21–9, have similar characteristics. The strongest argument is the contention of Lohmeyer and Bonnard that the Servant theology of Phil. ii. 6–11 is pre-Pauline,[1] for in Rom. iv. 25, Gal. ii. 20, and Eph. v. 2 the use of Isa. liii is traditional.[2] But in any case, whether St. Paul is using a 'hymn' composed by himself or by a predecessor, he uses it to express his beliefs concerning the person of Christ.

There is less to be said for the parallel suggestion that Col. i. 15–20 is also a pre-Pauline hymn.[3] Here again the case is based on *hapax legomena* and the liturgical style of the passage. C. Masson suggests that the poem has five strophes, each with four lines containing a more or less regular number of syllables and marked by assonance and alliteration. He further suggests that an unsuitable preliminary strophe has been omitted, and that the words, 'And he is the head of the body, the Church', in 18a, were

---

[1] Bonnard says: On comprend les christologies de Paul and du quatrième évangile comme des développements de ces versets, mais non point comme des formulations préparant celles de l'hymne. Après les épîtres pauliniennes et les écrits johanniques, nos versets trouveraient difficilement leur place dans le développement de la christologie primitive, *op. cit.*, 48.

[2] I have discussed St. Paul's comparative neglect of the Servant-conception in *The Atonement in New Testament Teaching*, 65f.

[3] Cf. R. Bultmann, *Theology of the New Testament*, I. 132, 176n., 178, II. 134; E. Käsemann, in his essay 'Eine christliche Taufliturgie', *Festschrift für Rudolf Bultmann*, 1949, pp. 133–48; C. Masson, *L'Épître de saint Paul aux Colossiens* (1950), pp. 97–107.

added to the poem by the author of Ephesians who has inserted the whole into its present context. This uneasy combination of the critical views of H. J. Holtzmann with the new liturgical suggestions is far from being convincing. The opinion endorsed earlier,[1] that in Col. i. 15–20 St. Paul is meeting the claims of the false teachers at Colossae and is perhaps using some of their terms, is much more probable.

I have already referred to Col. i. 15–20 in discussing St. Paul's view of the relation of Christ to the universe, and shall need to consider it again in Part II.[2] Phil., ii. 6–8 has a larger Christological range. I propose, therefore, to examine it in some detail in this chapter in the light of some of the most important critical discussions.

II. EXPOSITION

'Who being (ὑπάρχων) in the form of God (ἐν μορφῇ θεοῦ) counted it not a prize (οὐχ ἁρπαγμὸν ἡγήσατο) to be on an equality with God (τὸ εἶναι ἴσα θεῷ), but emptied himself (ἀλλὰ ἑαυτὸν ἐκένωσεν), taking the form of a servant (μορφὴν δούλου λαβών), being made in the likeness of men; And being found in fashion as a man, he humbled himself, becoming obedient even unto death, yea, the death of the cross. Wherefore also God highly exalted him, and gave to him the name that is above every name, that in the name of Jesus every knee should bow, of things in heaven and things on earth and things under the earth, that every tongue should confess that Jesus Christ is Lord, to the glory of God the Father'.

1. The classical exposition of this passage is that of J. B. Lightfoot in his commentary, *The Epistle to the Philippians* (3rd. ed. 1873, pp. 110–15, 127–37). It will be of advantage to compare his discussion with those of later commentators.

The 'form' (μορφή) he says, is not the 'nature' or the 'essence' or 'substance' of God, but its possession in-

[1] See p. 33.　　　　　[2] See p. 235f.

volves participation in the 'essence'. It implies, not the external accidents, but 'the essential attributes' of God. With it he compares 'the image of God' (2 Cor. iv. 4, Col. i. 15), 'the express image of his essence' (Heb. i. 3), and 'the Logos' (Jn. i. 1–18). 'Being', he says, denotes 'prior existence', but not necessarily 'eternal existence'. Ἁρπαγμόν is 'a prize', 'a treasure to be clutched and retained at all hazards'; for, while nouns ending in -μος primarily denote a process, they frequently describe a concrete thing, and the context shows that it is used as the equivalent of ἅρπαγμα 'a piece of plunder'. Therefore the meaning is: '*Though* He pre-existed in the form of God, *yet* He did not look upon equality with God as a prize which must not slip from His grasp, *but* He emptied Himself, divested Himself, taking upon Him the form of a slave'.[1] It will be seen that Lightfoot emphasizes the idea of something renounced. The AV rendering 'robbery', he maintains, disconnects the clause from its context.

The word ἴσα in τὸ εἶναι ἴσα θεῷ is adverbial, 'on an equality'. The distinction between ἴσος εἶναι and ἴσα εἶναι is that the former refers to the *person*, the latter to the *attributes*. He interprets ἀλλὰ ἑαυτὸν ἐκένωσεν as meaning that He divested Himself 'of the glories, the prerogatives, of Deity'. He stripped Himself of 'the insignia of majesty'. With this action the phrase 'by taking the form of a servant' is coincident in time; it does not describe the external semblance only (cf. σχῆμα in ii. 7), but the characteristic attributes as in verse 6. In 'being found in fashion as a man' the opposition is expressed 'between what He *is* in Himself, and what He *appeared* in the eyes of men'. The 'name' given to Him in His exaltation is best explained in the Hebrew sense

[1] The italics are Lightfoot's.

of the 'Name of God' used in the Old Testament 'to denote the Divine Presence or the Divine Majesty, more especially as the object of adoration and praise'. At the same time Lightfoot recognizes that, if St. Paul were referring to any one term, Κύριος 'would best explain the reference', for it appears in the context in verse 11.

The main points in Lightfoot's discussion indicate the issues upon which subsequent discussion has turned. It has been objected that his interpretation is too theological, since the Apostle's aim is practical, as indicated in the counsel, 'Have this mind in you which was also in Christ Jesus' (ii. 5). This objection is urged by many who hold that the passage is liturgical. I doubt if this criticism can be sustained, since a practical interest does not exclude a doctrinal emphasis. Moreover, as the hymns of Luther and the Wesleys show, a liturgical composition often contains doctrine in solution. The questions for discussion are (1) whether 'being in the form of God' implies a pre-existent state, (2) whether οὐχ ἁρπαγμὸν ἡγήσατο is passive ('prize') or active ('robbery') in meaning, indicating renunciation rather than attainment, (3) how 'to be on an equality with God' is related to 'being in the form of God', (4) how ἐκένωσεν is to be interpreted, and (5) what is the name above every name. We may shorten the discussion by saying that by wide consent the 'name' is that of 'Lord'.

2. It will be useful first to recall Moulton and Milligan's comments on ἁρπαγμός in *The Vocabulary of the Greek Testament*, p. 78. They show that in the papyri and in Hellenistic writers many nouns ending in -μος support the practical identity of ἁρπαγμός with ἅρπαγμα, 'spoil' or 'prize', that is, its passive use. But they also say that by far the larger number of such nouns (forty or more) denote the action of the verb and so are active. This

means that the rendering 'robbery' is also possible, and that, therefore, in the end the decision must turn on the context. This fact is recognized by Lightfoot.[1] Moulton and Milligan agree with Kennedy that μορφή in later Greek had come to have a vague, general meaning, far removed from its philosophical use in Plato and Aristotle, but, they say, it 'always signifies a form which truly and fully expresses the being which underlies it'.[2] In this respect it differs from 'the more outward σχῆμα', as Lightfoot contends.

With this preface I turn to the views of other commentators.

3. I begin with the commentary of J. Eadie,[3] now almost forgotten, but still of real value. It was first published in 1859 and a second edition followed in 1884. Eadie interprets μορφή as Lightfoot does; it is 'that by which we know or distinguish anything', and in Phil. ii. 6 it refers to the pre-incarnate life of Christ. The participle ὑπάρχων, he says, has a fuller meaning than ὤν; not in itself quite 'pre-existing', it indicates something on which stress is laid. Τὸ εἶναι ἴσα θεῷ, the object of ἡγήσατο, is 'a parity with God', and this parity consists in the possession of the μορφή. Anticipating Moulton and Milligan, Eadie says that philology gives no firm ground of explanation for ἁρπαγμόν, but he believes that it means, not 'robbery', which is not in harmony with the passage, but 'a thing to be caught at', 'a catch'. The reference to self-emptying, he holds, forms a contrast to what is previously said; it is a veiling of the μορφή and a

---

[1] The meaning to be assigned to the word, he says, is 'the one which best suits the context'. His submission is that the passive sense, 'a prize', as almost universally recognized by the Greek Fathers, does this. *Op. cit.*, III, 135.

[2] The quotation is from Kennedy's commentary. *V. infra.*

[3] *The Epistle to the Philippians.*

foregoing of the equality for a season. Christ 'descended with His splendour eclipsed'. In μορφὴν δούλου λαβών the aorist is coincident and a pointed contrast is made with ἐν μορφῇ θεοῦ ὑπάρχων. 'Being made in the likeness of men' implies that 'He was identical in all respects with other men', and 'He humbled himself' describes a further act. The exaltation is a recompense. Here Eadie differs from most commentators in holding that 'the name which is above every name' is 'Jesus'. A theological point is made in the statement: 'The economical subordination of the Son to the Father is implied, both in the obedience and in the reception of the reward'.[1]

It will be seen that, in the main, Eadie's views are in close agreement with those of Lightfoot.

4. The next commentator to be considered, H. A. W. Meyer,[2] reveals greater differences of opinion. Meyer agrees with Lightfoot in holding that the initial statement 'being in the form of God' refers to Christ 'in the pre-human state'. In this matter he differs from Lutheran commentators, who maintain that the reference is to the incarnate Christ. The μορφή is the divine δόξα; it 'denotes the form of being corresponding to the essence and *exhibiting* the condition'. Ὑπάρχων describes 'the subsisting state', not the divine majesty of Jesus in word and deed in His human existence. In substance, the same thing is denoted by τὸ εἶναι ἴσα θεῷ and ἐν μορφῇ θεοῦ ὑπάρχων. But at this point a different opinion is registered. Ἁρπαγμόν, Meyer holds, does not mean *praeda*, 'booty', or that which is seized upon; it is active and means 'robbing', 'making booty'. So the meaning is, 'Not as a robbing did He consider the being equal with

[1] *Op. cit.*, 126.
[2] *Meyer's Commentary on the New Testament, The Epistle to the Philippians* (1876), 77–88.

God'.[1]   There is, however, no question of seizing what did not belong to Him.   His self-renunciation was His refusal to grasp at earthly honours by means of His equality with God.   Throughout the New Testament, it is claimed, the Son appears as subordinate to the Father. In the light of later opinions it is interesting to see that the idea that the passage alludes to Gen. iif. is rejected.

5.   Meyer's commentary is of outstanding merit and has naturally influenced the views of later writers. Similar views, for example, are put forward by J. A. Beet.[2] Agreeing with Lightfoot as regards the reference to a pre-existent state in the opening clauses, he decisively rejects his explanation of ἁρπαγμόν.   He argues that the verb underlying the substantive 'always denotes taking hold of, or snatching, something not yet in our hands'.   Hence his translation, 'No high-handed self-enrichment did He deem the being equal with God'.[3]   He holds that the suggestion of refusing to let go that which one already securely holds is a sense which the verb never has.   The emphasis, therefore, must lie upon attainment rather than renunciation.   In this matter Beet agrees with Meyer and Hofman.   At the same time he maintains that, even when Christ emptied Himself, He was in truth essentially God. The Son, he suggests, deliberately laid aside the full exercise of His divine powers, thus permitting them to become for a time latent.   In this opinion one sees an anticipation of the position adopted later by Forsyth.[4]

6.   Marvin R. Vincent, in the *International Critical Commentary*,[5] agrees closely with Lightfoot.   It is true

---

[1] *Op. cit.*, 82.

[2] *Ephesians, Philippians, Colossians, Philemon* (1890), 63–73.

[3] *Op. cit.*, 64.   [4] See later p. 263.

[5] *The Epistles to the Philippians and to Philemon* (1897), 78–90.

that he explains μορφὴ θεοῦ as 'chiefly a rhetorical anti-thesis to μορφὴ δούλου', but agrees that μορφή is pur-posely selected instead of σχῆμα 'with a recognition of a peculiar relation of the word to the essential and permanent nature of that which is expressed or embodied'. It ex-presses 'the essential nature of the being to whom it be-longs'. With the Greek Fathers, Augustine, and most Reformed expositors, he identifies the parity with God with the divine μορφή. He explains ἁρπαγμόν as Light-foot does, and rejects the views of Meyer and Beet, saying that the endeavour to preserve the active force, 'a means of grasping', 'seems desperate'. 'If this had been Paul's meaning', he writes, 'I can conceive of no mode of ex-pression which he would have been less likely to choose'.[1] St. Paul's aim is to show the magnitude of the renunciation from the pre-incarnate and heavenly point of view, and the renunciation consisted in Christ's relinquishment of heavenly glory and majesty.

7. I turn next to the suggestive commentary of H. A. A. Kennedy.[2] Kennedy agrees with Lightfoot as regards μορφή and the passive sense of ἁρπαγμόν, but he takes a different line in holding that τὸ εἶναι ἴσα θεῷ is 'some-thing still future', res rapienda. The equality is lordship (κυριότης), the high dignity attained by the path of hu-miliation, suffering, and death in contrast with the first Adam who was tempted to be as God (Gen. iii. 5). A real likeness to man, he says, is connoted by ὁμοιώματι, 'yet Paul feels that it did not express the whole of Christ's nature'.[3] The position to which He was highly exalted (ὑπερύψωσε) was, in a certain sense, higher than that which He occupied when 'in the form of God'. 'The Divine glory which He always possessed', he explains,

[1] Op. cit., 89.
[2] The Expositor's Greek Testament (1903), iii. 435–9.   [3] Op. cit., 438.

'can never be enhanced. But now, in the eyes of men and claiming their homage, He is on an equality with God'.[1] The name is Kyrios, the equivalent of the Old Testament Jehovah.

8. Kennedy's views, as well as those of Lightfoot, are endorsed in J. H. Michael's valuable commentary on Philippians.[2] Michael agrees with Lightfoot and others in thinking that Phil. ii. 6–11 probably embraces the pre-incarnate as well as the incarnate life of Christ, and with Lightfoot, Moulton and Milligan, and Kennedy as regards the meaning of μορφή. He accepts Moffatt's translation, 'Though he was divine by nature', and agrees with G. G. Findlay[3] in the rendering, 'He was in nature essentially Divine'. But he follows Kennedy in rejecting the identity of μορφή with 'equality with God'. This parity, he holds, was achieved at the exaltation. Ἁρπαγμόν, he agrees, is passive, but means 'booty to be snatched', not 'booty to be retained'. C. A. Anderson Scott takes the same view in his *Christianity according to St. Paul*: 'He could have grasped it by the assertion of Himself, by insistence on His own interests. But He refused . . .'.[4]

9. The commentary of M. Dibelius[5] is of interest because it draws attention to the liturgical character of Phil. ii. 6–11. He mentions three considerations which, in his opinion, tell against the doctrinal interpretation of the passage. (*a*) St. Paul, he affirms, says nothing which decides between the idea of a dignity as possessed, though not in use (*res rapta*) and one to be acquired (*res rapienda*);

---

[1] *Ibid.*
[2] *The Epistle to the Philippians* (*Moffatt New Testament Commentary*) (1928), 82–97.
[3] *The Epistles of St. Paul*, 199.   [4] *Op. cit.*, 272.
[5] *An die Thessalonicher I. II. An die Philipper* (1911. 3rd ed, 1937), 72–82.

F

(*b*) he does not show how equality with God is related to the form of God and to the Kyrios-title; (*c*) he does not say what was renounced. These points, he claims, favour a liturgical interpretation of the passage. How far this submission rules out a doctrinal exposition is, of course, a point to be considered, and this question will be taken up later.[1]

10. In commenting on Phil. ii. 6–11 Karl Barth[2] stresses the idea that the self-emptying of Christ was willed by Him, and with great effect he quotes the words of Calvin, that, like a curtain the *humilitas carnis* covers the *divina majestas*. Nevertheless, he strongly affirms that the divinity of Christ is not lost in the circumstances of the incarnation. '*Er ist Gott fortan*', he says, '*gleich in der Verborgenheit der Knechtsgestalt*' ('He is God continuously equally in the obscurity of the form of a servant').[3] This conviction explains why Barth is unwilling to think of the exaltation of Christ, as described in Phil. ii. 9–11, as merely or only His reward, but insists that it is the revelation of what is true of Him throughout the course of His humiliation. This combination of a strong emphasis upon the reality of the veiling of the divine glory with the insistence that, although covered, it is still present in Christ's person, is the presupposition of a virile doctrine of the incarnation.

11. Finally, it will be of interest to note the views of C. Masson[4] mentioned above since he is one of the most recent commentators on the Epistle. Masson renders μορφή by 'condition'.[5] He believes that the first Adam (Gen. iii. 5) is in mind. He thinks that there is no radical opposition between the view that equality with God is a

---

[1] See p. 74.
[2] *Erklärung des Philipperbriefes* (1928), 53–62.   [3] *Op. cit.*, 56.
[4] *L'Épître de saint Paul aux Philippiens* (1950), 41–9.   [5] *Op. cit.*, 43.

prize to be retained and the claim that it is one to be sought, but that the text combines both ideas. Christ did not consider the divine condition, which He possessed, as 'a springing-board' (*tremplin*)[1] in order to prevail against God and thus to attain equality with Him. On the contrary He assumed voluntarily the humble and despicable lot of a slave. No loss of personal identity is implied by 'emptied'. Christ remains what He was in His divine condition, but now assumes all the historical risks of a human existence. Masson stresses the reality of Christ's humanity and maintains that a continual obedience is described by 'He humbled himself', a phrase suggested by Isa. liii. 7f. The reference to death is qualitative and not merely temporal. Throughout God is the principal actor. There is no logical or psychological link in 'Wherefore' (verse 9). The link between the Cross and the Exaltation exists only in the authority and grace of God. Christ, it is held, receives a condition and an authority greater than that which He possessed before His humiliation.[2] The name *Kyrios*, 'Lord', is used in the Old Testament sense in which it is applied to God Himself, but in the reference to 'the glory of God' monotheism is safeguarded.[3]

No apology, I think, is needed for giving at length the opinions of leading commentators, and of course the above is only a selection. It seems to me that the only way to enter into the meaning of a sublime, but difficult, passage is to summarize the views of many commentators and then to leave the summaries in storage for ten years.[4] By that time the vital phrases stand out in the mind, and we grow familiar with conflicting views, so that out of the welter of opinions we can form conclusions of our own.

---

[1] *Ibid.*   [2] *Op. cit.*, 46.   [3] *Op. cit.*, 47.
[4] Masson's commentary falls, of course, within this period.

In those I shall state below I have no thought of making *ex cathedra* utterances, but only opinions formed by the use of such a method, and with these the reader can compare his own thoughts. I suggest that some conclusions emerge with relative clarity, and that, while differences of interpretation must persist, the main points are reasonably clear.

III. SUGGESTED CONCLUSIONS

The following conclusions seem to be suggested.

1. While liturgical in form, the passage is also doctrinal in content. It is true, as Dibelius has claimed, that St. Paul says nothing which expressly decides between the idea of a dignity possessed, though not in use, and one to be acquired, that he does not show how equality with God is related to the divine form and to the title 'Lord', and that he does not indicate what Christ renounced. These omissions are not strange in a hymn. Nevertheless, conclusions upon all these points can be drawn even though differences of opinion are inevitable. The key to the interpretation of the passage is the exhortation, 'Have this mind in you which was also in Christ Jesus', and the counsels which precede it in verses 2–4. St. Paul earnestly desires the Philippians to do nothing through faction or vainglory, to count others better than themselves, not to look to their own things, but to the things of others. These exhortations suggest that, when he goes on to speak of 'the mind of Christ', he intends to describe a supreme act of renunciation on His part, a refusal to look to His own things, but to the needs of men.

2. This emphasis upon renunciation is a governing consideration in deciding between ambiguous alternatives in the phrases used. The participle ὑπάρχων does not necessarily mean 'being originally', but in this context

it can hardly mean less. St. Paul means to describe the renunciation of the glory of Christ's pre-incarnate life, just as he does in 2 Cor. viii. 9, where he speaks of the grace of Him who for our sakes became poor. As many commentators have seen, it is too philosophical an explanation to say that by μορφή he means 'nature' or 'substance'. He must mean to refer to a visible form which was characteristic of Christ's being, just as 'the form of a slave' is that by which the slave is recognized and known. Of this 'form of God' the best thing we can say is that it is His 'glory', the shining light in which, according to Old Testament thought, God was pictured. This view of Meyer and other commentators is powerfully expressed by J. Weiss when he writes: 'The "divine form" which he possessed before becoming man (Phil. ii. 6) was nothing less than the divine *Doxa*, and may we not understand this statement to mean, in the Pauline sense: Christ was from the beginning no other than the *Kabōd*, the *Doxa*, of God himself, the glory and radiation of his being, which appears almost as an independent hypostasis of God and yet is connected intimately with God?'[1] Further, it would appear that when he uses the phrase 'on an equality with God', there is a backward reference to 'the form of God'. In other words, as Eadie and others have maintained, parity with God consists in the possession of the divine 'form'. This view seems superior to the alternative explanation, that the phrase describes something achieved in the exaltation, true though it is that, as exalted, Christ has 'the name that is above every name', the name 'Lord'. St. Paul's thought

---

[1] *The History of Primitive Christianity*, 478; cf. J. Behm, *Theologisches Wörterbuch*, iv. 759. M. R. Vincent, *op. cit.*, 81f., maintains that δόξα is not the equivalent of μορφή, to which εἰκών approximates more closely, but says that δόξα 'is and must be included in μορφὴ θεοῦ'.

appears to be that 'the mind that was in Christ Jesus' was the mind of One who possessed, and renounced, heavenly majesty.

3. This interpretation harmonizes best with Lightfoot's view, that ἁρπαγμὸν ἡγήσατο is 'to clutch greedily 'or 'prize highly' 'a prize' or 'booty' (*praeda*) rather than 'to account it as robbing' or 'robbery' (*rapina*) to be on an equality with God. Moulton and Milligan have shown that the point cannot be decided linguistically, since both 'prize' and 'robbery' are possible renderings, but the context seems to me to support the former. It should be noted, however, that even the rendering 'robbery' would not convey a meaning alien to St. Paul's thought, provided that the parity with God is something possessed; but it seems less apposite to the passage. It is somewhat pedantic to insist that the underlying verb (ἁρπάζω) must always mean to seize something not yet possessed; it can mean to grab at booty, and so to hold on to it, or, as Barth puts it, 'to hold something convulsively', as a bandit clutches his prize. This Christ refused to do. It is quite possible that in the thought there is an implicit contrast with Adam who was tempted to 'be as God, knowing good and evil', and in this case it is natural to think of the Temptation experience recorded in Mt. iv. 1–11; but the nature of the temptation in the two instances is so different as to render the contrast doubtful. It has not perhaps been sufficiently considered that, if St. Paul is using a hymn composed in the first case by some one else, the ambiguous language in ἁρπαγμὸν ἡγήσατο is one upon which he has to impose his own meaning. This meaning, there can be little doubt, is the refusal to put personal interests first, signalized in renunciation.

4. The idea of renunciation is strongly attested by

ἀλλὰ ἑαυτὸν ἐκένωσεν, 'but emptied himself' or, if the rendering be preferred, 'but despoiled himself'. The words underline the exhortation, not to mind one's own things, and are weakened if τὸ εἶναι ἴσα θεῷ describes a future parity with God. How much is to be read into ἐκένωσεν is the theologian's problem. If we decline to think that the Apostle has the attributes of omniscience, omnipotence, and omnipresence in mind, we must conclude that he is thinking of the divine glory which was His in the beginning. And it is most in accord with the whole passage if the reference is to a pre-incarnate renunciation coincident with the act of 'taking the form of a servant'. Here indeed the Philippians are reminded of the mind of Christ. Christ let the light of His glory die down, so that its flame, hidden by the dark lantern of His humanity, was no longer visible save to the eyes of faith.

5. Further, the same emphasis on renunciation is seen in Christ's acceptance of a full humanity. He was 'made in the likeness of men'. He knew weariness, hunger, thirst, trial, temptation, disappointment, fear, the hampering conditions of space, want of knowledge, restricted power. The Apostle does not say this, but in the light of history, we see that all these experiences are involved in the words, 'He humbled himself, becoming obedient even unto death'. He accepted an incognito. He became the Unknown whom men might deride, the Stranger on whom they might spit. Such, St. Paul is saying, was the mind of Christ. In particular, that mind was revealed in His obedience 'even unto death'. 'Yes', St. Paul adds, 'the death of the cross'. Those commentators are amply justified who suggest that these words must have made a deep impression on the minds of the Philippians, since, as we know from Ac. xvi. 19–40, they prided themselves on their Roman citizenship. St. Paul reminds

them that the acceptance of a cross, so horrible to a Roman, was the mind of Christ.

6. Lastly, the seal set on renunciation was the exaltation. The choirs of heaven and earth confess that Jesus Christ is Lord, to the glory of God the Father. The exaltation is His reward, but it may be that this is but half St. Paul's thought, and that Karl Barth is right in contending that the exaltation recognizes that Christ is Lord already, even in His humiliation. *Er ist Gott fortan gleich in der Verborgenheit der Knechtsgestalt.* The exaltation tears away the veil. What is true all the time is confessed by heaven and earth. If so, the idea of renunciation persists to the end, and Christ's word is illustrated in Himself, 'If any man would be first, he shall be last of all, and minister of all' (Mk. ix. 35).

I can only refer in passing to the doctrine of the Kenosis, of which so much has been made, but which appears to be out of favour to-day. In this matter we cannot press upon St. Paul the ideas of Giessen or those of Tübingen. St. Paul says nothing about the abandonment of the attributes of God. We must distinguish between the kenosis he describes and kenosis as a Christological hypothesis. It seems to me that the time is ripe for new thoughts upon this question, for the popular theology which would have us be content with the view that God is like Jesus is altogether too facile. We cannot afford to jettison the biblical doctrine of God or to ignore the teaching of the centuries that He is love and is all-knowing, all-powerful, and unconfined by time and place. If this is so, it is a legitimate inquiry how far the self-emptying of Christ, God's Son, involves these divine qualities, even when we allow that St. Paul is not thinking of such questions in Phil. ii. 6–11. These inquiries are not our immediate concern, but we cannot doubt that this

great hymn is bound up with them.   The hymn speaks of
the majesty of the glory of Christ's pre-incarnate life, His
renunciation of this glory and His full acceptance of a
human lot culminating in obedience unto death, and the
exaltation which reveals all that is true of Him.   Who can
doubt that in this matchless hymn is the creative material
of a living Christology?

VI

THE FIRST EPISTLE OF ST. PETER

THE Christology of this Epistle is important because it combines primitive Christian data with elements which foreshadow later developments. Such a combination is the mark of a living tradition. The date and authorship of the Epistle are disputed questions.[1] The case for the Petrine authorship and a date in A.D. 63 or the first half of A.D. 64 is ably and, I think, convincingly argued by E. G. Selwyn in his commentary, *The First Epistle of St. Peter* (1946). This is the traditional view maintained in modern times by a succession of scholars including C. Bigg,[2] F. J. A. Hort,[3] A. S. Peake,[4] J. Moffatt,[5] A. H. M'Neile,[6] and J. C. W. Wand.[7] Non-Petrine authorship and a late date for the Epistle are advocated by many other scholars, notably by H. Windisch[8] and F. W. Beare.[9] Fortunately the date of the Epistle does not seriously affect its importance for our immediate purpose, for by wide consent it contains many traditional elements, and Primitive Christianity extends beyond the period covered by the Pauline Epistles. In particular, several scholars have recently maintained that

[1] I have previously discussed these questions in *The Atonement in New Testament Teaching*, 25–7.

[2] *The Epistles of St. Peter and St. Jude.*

[3] *The First Epistle of St. Peter* (i. 1–ii. 17).

[4] *A Critical Introduction to the New Testament*, 94f.

[5] *Introduction to the Literature of the New Testament*, 339.

[6] *Introduction to the New Testament*, 2nd ed., 223.

[7] *The General Epistles of St. Peter and St. Jude*, 16f.

[8] *Die katholischen Briefe*, 50f.

[9] *The First Epistle of Peter* (1947).

fragments of early Christian hymns and confessions are embedded in 1 Peter, and, as we shall see, primitive features appear in its Christology.

1. Among the primitive features in the Petrine Christology the following may be noted. The hope of the Parousia of Christ is strong (i. 5, 7, 13, v. 4) and as in the earliest preaching the importance of the Resurrection is stressed. In these matters there are many striking parallels between the Epistle and St. Peter's speeches in the Acts.[1] In the Epistle the writer declares that it was according to His great mercy that God 'begat us again unto a living hope by the resurrection of Jesus Christ from the dead', and the goal of the Christian hope is described as 'an inheritance incorruptible, and undefiled, and that does not fade away' (i. 3f.). This teaching is expanded by further allusions to the Resurrection in iii. 18 and 21.

2. Again, as in Ac. iv. 11 and Rom. ix. 33, Christ is spoken of as 'the Stone' in 1 Pet. ii. 4–8. With Acts the saying of Jesus about 'the stone which the builders rejected' is quoted in 1 Pet. ii. 7 and, in common with Rom. ix. 33, the two stone-passages in Isa. viii. 14 and xxviii. 16 are combined in 1 Pet. ii. 6 and 8.[2] It has long been held that 1 Peter is dependent on Rom. ix. 33, and sometimes the opposite view has been maintained; but the opinion is growing that both writers used a common written source, a collection of Messianic proof-texts or, as both Windisch[3] and Selwyn[4] suggest, an early Christian hymn. Selwyn persuasively argues that the first strophe of the hymn is to be found in 1 Pet. ii. 6–8 and the second in 1 Pet. ii. 9f. The use and combination of these stone-passages shows how closely 1 Peter is in touch with pri-

[1] Cf. Selwyn, *op. cit.*, 33–6   [2] Cf. *The Names of Jesus*, 93–6.
[3] *Op. cit.*, 58.   [4] *Op. cit.*, 274–7, 281.

mitive Christian ideas, and the same view is suggested by
the use of the imagery of the Shepherd in ii. 25, where
Christ is designated as 'the Shepherd and Bishop of your
souls' and in v. 4 as 'the chief Shepherd'. Hort maintained
that in i. 11 τὰ εἰς Χριστὸν παθήματα means 'the
sufferings destined for the Messiah'.[1]

3. A further sign of primitive Christian teaching is the
use of the Servant-conception in 1 Pet. ii. 22–4. The
name 'the Servant' is not used, but Christ's sinlessness,
patience, and submission are described in close agreement
with the teaching of Isa. liii. 5 and 12. Here again
Windisch[2] speaks of a '*Christuslied*' lying behind the
passage, and Bultmann[3] takes the same view. The
presence of this teaching in 1 Peter is a very primitive
feature if we are right in tracing a diminishing emphasis
upon the Servant idea in the New Testament.[4] Whether
the hypothesis of a 'hymn' is accepted or not, an early
Christology is reflected in the words, 'For hereunto were
you called: because Christ also suffered for you, leaving
you an example, that you should follow his steps' (ii. 21),
and in the description of Him as One 'who did no sin,
neither was guile found in his mouth: who, when he
was reviled, reviled not again; when he suffered,
threatened not; but committed himself to him that judges
righteously: who his own self bore our sins in his body
up to the tree, that we, having died unto sins, might live
unto righteousness; by whose stripes you were healed'
(ii. 22–4). Along with a doctrinal interpretation a true
human life is pictured. Elsewhere in the Epistle it is

---

[1] *Op. cit.*, 54f. Selwyn, 156, 263, prefers 'the sufferings of the Christ-ward road'.

[2] *Op. cit.*, 65. Cf. also Wand, *op. cit.*, 81.

[3] See his article 'Bekenntnis- und Liedfragmente im ersten Petrus-brief', *Coniectanea Neotestamentica*, xi. 12–14.

[4] See earlier p. 30.

emphasized that He suffered, 'being put to death in the flesh' (iii. 18. cf. iv. 1) and frequent references are made to His sufferings (i. 11, iv. 1, 13, v. 1), which are the ground for the exhortation, 'Arm yourselves also with the same mind' (iv. 1). The names 'Jesus Christ' (9 times) and 'Christ' (13 times) have become personal designations.

4. The distribution of the names and titles assigned to Christ in the Epistle is so remarkable as to call for comment. The names 'the Son', 'His Son' and 'the Son of God' do not appear at all. This fact is perhaps not as surprising as it appears if, as we have claimed, these names were associated in Primitive Christianity with teaching rather than with worship. What is surprising is the fact that, in an Epistle with a distinctly liturgical atmosphere, the personal names, 'Jesus Christ' and 'Christ', are found about six times as often as the title 'Lord'. 'Lord' is used four times only, in i. 3, ii. 3, 13, and iii. 15.[1] Is this usage confirmatory, so far as it goes, of Petrine authorship? Who more than he is likely to have preferred the more personal names? What, however, the use of the name 'Lord' lacks in extent is more than compensated for by the quality of the passages in question. In the formal opening of the Epistle God is described as 'the God and Father of our Lord Jesus Christ' (i. 3). In ii. 3 the words of Psa. xxxiv. 8, 'Taste and see that the Lord is gracious' (LXX), are applied to Christ in the form, 'If you have tasted that the Lord is gracious', as the context in ii. 4 clearly shows. In ii. 13 the readers are exhorted to be subject to every ordinance of man 'for the Lord's sake'. Finally, in iii. 15 Christ is to be sanctified in the heart 'as Lord', that is, He is to be declared holy, a passage which recalls Isa. viii. 13 in which 'him' is replaced by 'Christ'.

[1] In i. 25 and iii. 12 (*bis*) 'Lord' is used of God.

We must infer that in all these passages the use of the name 'Lord' reflects an attitude of deep veneration.

5. Other passages in the Epistle show that a divine status is assigned to Christ. In i. 8 He is mentioned as the object of love and of faith, and in iii. 22 He is described as 'on the right hand of God, having gone into heaven; angels and authorities and powers being made subject to him'. Further, in iv. 11 charity and humility are enjoined 'that in all things God may be glorified through Jesus Christ', and a doxology is added, which is probably addressed to Christ, in the words, 'whose is the glory and the dominion for ever and ever. Amen'.[1] This divine status is also implied by the sacrificial ministry which the Epistle assigns to Christ. His 'precious blood' is described as that of 'a lamb without blemish and without spot' (i. 19). Christ is said to have suffered 'for you' (ii. 21). In words already quoted it is declared that He 'bore our sins in his body up to the tree, that we, having died unto sins, might live unto righteousness; by whose stripes you were healed' (ii. 24). Again, the assurance is given that He suffered for sins once, 'the righteous for the unrighteous', with the purpose that He might bring us to God (iii. 18). In all this teaching appears the paradox of the Gospel, that these things are said of One who lived and died in the flesh. Without doubt the Christ depicted in the Epistle is divine.

Both Selwyn and Bultmann independently see a credal formula embedded in iii. 18–22. Selwyn[2] suggests that, though the passage is not itself quoted from a hymn, it rests on the credal hymn which is quoted in 1 Tim. iii. 16. Bultmann[3] thinks that the passage is drawn from a primitive confession rather than a hymn. He re-

[1] Cf. Selwyn, *op. cit.*, 220.   [2] *Op. cit.*, 277, 325.
[3] *Coniectanea Neotestamentica*, xi. 14.

constructs this confession from i. 20+, iii. 18f., and 22 and conjectures that it may have been introduced by some such phrase as 'I believe in the Lord Jesus Christ'. Admittedly these suggestions are somewhat speculative, as all attempts at reconstruction must necessarily be. What is not speculative is the Christological importance of the passage in its allusions to Christ's Sacrifice, His death, resurrection, ascension, and victorious session at the right hand of God.

6. The emphasis laid upon Baptism in the Epistle has also Christological importance. The view of F. L. Cross,[1] that 1 Peter is a Paschal Liturgy descriptive of the Celebrant's part in the baptismal rite, is one of much interest. Even if the suggestion cannot be pressed to the point of demonstration, the fact that it can be so persuasively argued is a testimony to the marked baptismal setting of the Epistle, seen in the reference to baptism in iii. 20f. and the allusions to regeneration in i. 3, 23, and ii. 2. Whether the Eucharist is meant in the enigmatic phrase 'spiritual sacrifices' in ii. 5 is hard to decide. The negative views of Hort and of Bigg stand on one side and the positive opinion of Lohmeyer,[2] favourably commended by Selwyn,[3] stands on the other. One would expect a clearer reference to the rite if it is actually meant, unless this is a case in which the view that the Eucharist is an *arcanum*, a secret to be guarded from profane eyes, is present. In the circumstances it is not possible to build a Christological argument on the phrase. On the other hand the importance of the baptismal allusions is unmistakable. The connexion of baptism with the re-

[1] *I Peter: A Paschal Liturgy* (1954).
[2] *Theologische Rundschau* (1937), 296.
[3] *Op. cit.*, 294–8. Hort prefers the view that 'acts of self-oblation to God for the service of the community' are meant, *op. cit.*, 112.

surrection of Christ and His session on high in iii. 21f.
gives added weight to this passage, since in the primitive
Church men are baptized 'in' or 'into' the name of Christ.

7. Some of the most interesting elements in the writer's
Christology are those which appear to be anticipations—
we cannot say more—of later developments. Windisch[1]
thinks that pre-existence is implied in the phrase 'the
Spirit of Christ' (i. 11) and he points to i. 20 in which
Christ is spoken of as 'foreknown indeed before the
foundation of the world'. This interpretation is far from
being assured, since Christians are also the objects of
God's foreknowledge (cf. Rom. viii. 29), but there is
force in Selwyn's suggestion that the position assigned to
Christ 'needs the doctrine of the Incarnation to set it
forth'.[2] It may be that we are entitled to say that a conception of pre-existence, rudimentary as compared with
that implied in Phil. ii. 6 and 2 Cor. viii. 9, is implicit in
the Petrine passages. Two different aspects of Christ's
person are mentioned in iii. 18, 'being put to death in the
flesh, but quickened in the spirit'. Here Christ is seen
from different points of view, the natural physical order
($\sigma\alpha\rho\kappa\iota$) on the one hand, and the supernatural ($\pi\nu\epsilon\acute{\upsilon}\mu\alpha\tau\iota$)
on the other hand. In this distinction it would be wrong
to see the later doctrine of two natures in one Person,
but it is out of such simple beginnings that the doctrine of
the Creeds arose. Finally, the same may be said of the
'trinitarian' language used in i. 2, 'God the Father ...
the Spirit ... Jesus Christ'. This is not the doctrine of
the Trinity, but here are some of the data which that
doctrine was formulated to include. The order of the
names, the Father, the Spirit, Jesus Christ, and the
absence of the title 'the Son', show the primitive character
of the passage. A distinction of 'Persons' does not appear

[1] *Op. cit.*, 55.   [2] *Op. cit.*, 249.

to be intended, but Christian thought has begun to tread the road which was to lead to Chalcedon. Of the Christology of the Epistle, Selwyn writes that it 'contains the roots of later Catholic doctrine, but not yet its flower, so far as conscious formulation is concerned: in particular, its metaphysical implications are not yet considered'.[1]

8. Finally, reference must be made to the passages which speak of Christ's descent into Hades; in iii. 19f. 'He went and preached to the spirits in prison, which aforetime were disobedient, when the longsuffering of God waited in the days of Noah', and in iv. 6, 'For to this end was the gospel preached even to the dead, that they might be judged according to men in the flesh, but live according to God in the spirit'.[2] This teaching in iii. 19, of which there are echoes in Rom. x. 6–8, Eph. iv. 8–10, Phil. ii. 10, and Apoc. v. 13, is not the later doctrine of 'the Harrowing of Hell', nor is it necessary to trace its origin to legendary sources which tell of the descent of Greek heroes and gods to the underworld. It has a two-fold source in the desire to express the universal scope of the Gospel and reflection upon the meaning of the three days' interval between the Crucifixion and the Resurrection. The 'spirits in prison' are defined as the 'disobedient' in the days of Noah, and the preaching mentioned in iii. 19 is the proclamation of Christ's victory over death. In iv. 6 the reference seems to be to dead Christians (cf. 1 Thess. iv. 13f.) who by human standards ('according to men') might seem to be already judged, but who now have the gospel preached to them that, in accordance with the will of God, they might live 'in the spirit'. There is no need to assign this teaching to a late

---

[1] Op. cit., 249.

[2] For a full treatment of these passages see Essay I in Selwyn's commentary, pp. 314–62.

G

date; it is the kind of reflection which might arise at any time in the first generation of Christianity when questions connected with Christ's resurrection and ascension were considered and when baptism, which is expressly mentioned in iii. 21 in connexion with the deluge and the story of Noah, was in mind. The Christological significance of this teaching is the point of primary importance for us, and in this respect it is clear that the references to Christ's ministry in the underworld after His crucifixion are an added reason for believing that in the Epistle He is presented as divine.

VII

THE EPISTLE TO THE HEBREWS

THE importance of the Epistle to the Hebrews is beyond question, for while its Christology has strong affinities with that of St. Paul and St. John, it has also markedly distinctive features. Written about A.D. 80[1] by a writer whose identity remains a matter of speculation, the Epistle stands midway between the Pauline and the Johannine writings, reminding us of the teaching of St. Paul in Colossians and anticipating the theology of St. John. Its dominant ideas reflect the influence of Alexandrian thought mediated by the teaching of Philo and illustrated in the Book of Wisdom. These ideas, therefore, have both a Jewish and a Greek heritage; they are derived from the Old Testament and reveal the impress of the Platonic philosophy.

The main interest of the Epistle for theology lies in its soteriology, but its concentration upon the work of Christ has clear Christological implications which appear in its opening verses.

The absence from the writing of the usual epistolary beginning, when there is a real epistolary ending in chapter xiii, has led to the conjecture that its original introduction is lost and even to the suggestion that i. 1–3 was added later. These interesting opinions lack adequate foundation. It was manifestly necessary that the writer, who wished to dwell almost exclusively upon the

---

[1] For a strong and persuasive argument in favour of a date about A.D. 60 see W. Manson, *The Epistle to the Hebrews* (1951), 162–7.

highpriestly work of Christ, should preface his letter by a statement concerning His Person.

The background of the Christology of the Epistle is the belief that, while Judaism belongs to the transient order of the present age, Christianity belongs to the eternal world of reality. Plato[1] had taught that the world was a 'copy' ($\epsilon\dot{\iota}\kappa\dot{\omega}\nu$) of the eternal 'pattern' ($\pi\alpha\rho\dot{\alpha}\delta\epsilon\iota\gamma\mu\alpha$), and Philo[2] had used this teaching in his distinction between the 'copy' and the 'pattern' or 'archetype'. The book of Wisdom (ix. 8) speaks of the Temple and the altar as 'a copy of the holy tabernacle' prepared by God from the beginning, and similar ideas appear in the Epistle to the Hebrews in viii. 2, 'the true tabernacle, which the Lord pitched, not man', in viii. 5, 'a copy and shadow of the heavenly things', and in ix. 23f. and x. 1. In many ways the writer's presentation of the person of Christ recalls Philo's teaching concerning the Logos, or Word of God, but he does not actually use this name, and he differs radically from Philo in affirming the humanity and the personal Sonship of Christ. Characteristic of the Epistle is the conception of Christ as the 'high priest' and the 'mediator' of the New Covenant made possible by the sacrifice of Himself. Philo also speaks of the Logos as 'the Son of God', 'the high priest', 'the firstborn' ($\pi\rho\omega\tau\dot{o}\gamma\rho\nu\rho\varsigma$), 'the mediator' between God and man, the $\ddot{o}\rho\gamma\alpha\nu\rho\nu$ or instrument in the creation of the world, 'the impress' ($\chi\alpha\rho\alpha\kappa\tau\dot{\eta}\rho$) of God's seal.[3] In Wisd. vii. 25f. Wisdom is described as 'the radiance' ($\dot{\alpha}\pi\alpha\dot{\upsilon}\gamma\alpha\sigma\mu\alpha$) or effulgence of everlasting light. Both the indebtedness of the writer and the vital differences in his Christology are manifest in the Epistle.

---

[1] *Timaeus*, 28C, 29B, *Respublica*, 500E.
[2] *De Opificio Mundi*, 15f. See C. K. Barrett, *The New Testament Background*, 174f.
[3] Cf. J. Moffatt, *The Epistle to the Hebrews*, 11, 38.

It will be useful to study the writer's Christology by examining his treatment of (1) the humanity of Christ, (2) His Messiahship, (3) His Sonship, (4) His representative ministry, (5) His relationship to the universe, and (6) His relationship to God.

I. THE HUMANITY OF CHRIST

'Nowhere in the New Testament', writes H. R. Mackintosh,[1] 'is the humanity of Christ set forth so movingly'. The writer uses the name 'Jesus' ten times generally holding it back as a kind of climax.[2] He knows that He belonged to the tribe of Judah (vii. 14), that He endured the contradiction of sinners (xii. 3), and suffered outside Jerusalem (xiii. 12). He speaks of Him as 'faithful to him that appointed him' (iii. 2), as touched with the feeling of our infirmities, 'in all points tempted like as we are, yet without sin' (iv. 15). Most significantly of all, he pictures Him as having offered up prayers and supplications in the days of His flesh 'with strong crying and tears unto him that was able to save him from death', thus clearly referring to the Agony in Gethsemane. The author declares that 'though he was a Son, yet learned he obedience by the things which he suffered', and that 'having been made perfect, he became unto all them that obey him the author of eternal salvation' (v. 7–9). Much more than St. Paul he assigns the greatest importance to the Gospel Story. He does so because he believes that Christ's sinlessness and His perfect humanity were essential to His mission. 'Since then the children are sharers in flesh and blood', he writes, 'he also himself in like manner partook of the same' (ii. 14, cf. v. 9, *supra*).

[1] *The Doctrine of the Person of Jesus Christ*, 79.
[2] Cf. V. Taylor, *The Names of Jesus*, 7.

A. E. J. Rawlinson[1] observes that 'in combining a "Wisdom" Christology with so strong an insistence upon the importance of the human story of our Lord's life the writer of Hebrews may be regarded as having anticipated, and perhaps actually influenced, the theology of the Fourth Gospel'. In declaring that He was tempted in all points like as we are, 'yet without sin' (iv. 15), the writer means that He did not yield to sin; He resisted, beyond the point where others fail, to the climax of victory.[2]

II. THE MESSIAHSHIP OF JESUS

This primitive Christian belief recedes into the background in the Epistle, but it is still alive in the writer's expectation of the Parousia. 'Christ' (iii. 6, ix. 11, 24), 'the Christ' (iii. 14, v. 5, vi. 1, ix. 14, 28, xi. 26), and 'Jesus Christ' (x. 10, xiii. 8. 21) have become personal names, and surprisingly in an Epistle in which the note of worship is prominent the name 'Lord' appears but rarely (ii. 3, vii. 14, xiii. 20, xii. 14 (?)).[3] Further, as we shall see, the term 'Son of God' has far more than Messianic significance. Christ, as Bousset[4] has said, is *der überweltliche Sohn Gottes*. The hope of the Parousia is voiced in the words, 'So Christ, having been once offered to bear the sins of many, shall appear a second time, apart from sin, to them that wait for him, unto salvation' (ix. 28). Here, however, the hope is theologically conceived. 'Salvation', Westcott[5] maintains, indicates 'the attainment of the ideal of humanity', and 'without sin' implies that His atoning work is final and complete.

---

[1] *The New Testament Doctrine of the Christ*, 189.

[2] For the reading 'without God' in ii. 9 cf. Moffatt, *op. cit.*, 26f.

[3] Contrast the six columns in Moulton and Geden's *Concordance to the Greek Testament* which record the instances of κύριος in the Pauline Epistles.

[4] *Kyrios Christos*, 284.   [5] *The Epistle to the Hebrews*, 278.

III. THE SONSHIP OF CHRIST

Distinctive of the writer is the emphasis he lays upon the Sonship of Christ. In various ways he applies the name 'Son' to Him no less than twelve times.[1] 'Sonship and Salvation', declares J. S. Lidgett, is 'the master-theme, the unifying conception, of the Epistle'.[2] It is 'in a Son', the writer insists, that God has made His final revelation to us (i. 2). Twice Psa. ii. 7, with its declaration, 'Thou art my Son', is applied by him to Christ (i. 5, v. 5). He is 'the Son' in contrast with angels (i. 8), and as 'the Son of God' He is our high priest (iv. 14). Although the Logos conception is used in the Epistle, like St. John the writer clearly preferred to think of Christ as 'the Son of God' (iv. 14, vi. 6, vii. 3, x. 29). The implications of this name are seen in the unique functions he assigns to Him in relation to man, to the universe, and to God.

IV. THE REPRESENTATIVE MINISTRY OF CHRIST

Every reader of the Epistle knows that again and again Christ is described by the writer as man's representative before God. He does this when he speaks of Him as our High Priest, of His Sacrifice, and of His session at the right hand of God.[3] 'Christ', he writes, 'entered not into a holy place made with hands, like in pattern to the true; but into heaven itself, now to appear before the face of God for us' (ix. 24). He is 'the surety of a better covenant' (vii. 22) of which He is 'the mediator' (viii. 6, ix. 15, xii. 24). The Christological implications of this teaching are our present concern, and they are fully in harmony with, if they do not actually transcend, all that

---

[1] Cf. *The Names of Jesus*, 57.　　[2] *Sonship and Salvation*, 13.
[3] Cf. *The Atonement in New Testament Teaching*, 57.

the writer directly says of Christ. If Moffatt[1] is right in maintaining that 'all hope for the Christian rests in what Jesus has done in the eternal order by his sacrifice', He cannot be less than the divine Son of God and the high priest of our salvation.

V. THE RELATIONSHIP OF CHRIST TO THE UNIVERSE

The same inference must be drawn from all that the writer says of Christ's relationship to the universe. The Son of God, he claims, was appointed by God 'heir of all things, through whom also he made the worlds ... upholding all things by the word of his power' (i. 2f.). The interest which prompts this claim is not primarily cosmological, but religious, and it is of the most far-reaching character. By 'appointed' a pre-temporal act is meant, 'a relationship which belongs to the eternal order',[2] and by the words 'bearing all things' may be implied, not only the act of sustaining the world, but also that of bringing it into being, as Gregory of Nyssa taught, in fulfilment of its divine end. The commentators[3] remind us that Philo speaks in the same way of the creative activity of the Logos.

In this teaching there is a marked similarity with that of St. Paul in Col. i. 15–17. God is the Creator (Heb. xi. 3); the Son is the Agent of creation (δι' οὖ, Heb. i. 2). Similarly the Fourth Evangelist says of the Logos that 'all things were made through him (δι' αὐτοῦ), and without him was not anything made' (i. 3). Complete loyalty to the Jewish insistence that God alone is the creator of the world is preserved, but a vital function, which is not that of a passive instrument, is assigned to the Son in the making and sustaining of all things. The author feels that no less

---

[1] *Op. cit.*, 89.　　　[2] Moffatt, *op. cit.*, 5, Westcott, *op. cit.*, 7.
[3] Cf. Moffatt, *op. cit.*, 6, Westcott, *op. cit.*, 14.

dignity must belong to Him who sat down at the right hand of the Majesty on high, when He had made purification for sins (i. 3). Unquestionably a richer form of the doctrine of God is demanded by this Christology than anything we find elsewhere in the New Testament. It is not an example of grammatical pedantry to insist that neither in Hebrews nor in the Pauline and Johannine Epistles is ὑπό used to describe the creative activity of the Son, but only ἐν and διά. We must infer that these prepositions are consciously chosen, and then accept the consequence that later theological discussions in the early centuries, however barren they may sometimes appear, were inevitable and necessary.

VI. THE RELATIONSHIP OF CHRIST TO GOD

We have already seen that the relationship of Christ to the created universe implies the writer's belief in His pre-existent activity (cf. i. 2f.). The same belief is implied in all that he says of the Son's superiority to angels (i. 4–14, ii. 5–9). It was not unto angels, he says, that God subjected the world to come, but to Jesus, 'because of the suffering of death crowned with glory and honour' (ii. 9). Pre-existence is also suggested by the high epithets he ascribes to Jesus, ἀπαύγασμα, 'the effulgence' or 'radiance' of God's glory, χαρακτὴρ τῆς ὑποστάσεως αὐτοῦ, 'the impress of His essence', and πρωτότοκος, 'the Firstborn' (i. 3, 6).[1] These names had already been applied by Philo to the Logos, except that he uses πρωτόγονος instead of πρωτότοκος. Names used of the Logos are claimed by the writer for Christ. In i. 8, where Psa. xlv. 6f. is quoted with reference to the Son, He is virtually called 'God': 'But of the Son he says, Thy

[1] These terms are discussed in detail in *The Names of Jesus*, 127f., 129f., 147–9.

throne, *O God*, is for ever and ever'. Nothing can be
built upon this reference, for the author shares the re-
luctance of the New Testament writers to speak explicitly of Christ as 'God', and later in the same quotation
he says, 'Therefore God, *thy God*, hath anointed thee with
the oil of gladness above thy fellows' (i. 9).

Nevertheless, in fidelity to Jewish monotheism, the
writer ascribes a subordinate position to the Son in His
relationship to God, in this respect agreeing with St.
Paul[1] and, as we shall see, with St. John.[2]   The Son is
'appointed' heir of all things (i. 2), He is *'made'* high
priest (v. 5), He is *'brought again'* from the dead by the
God of peace (xiii. 20), and in His exalted life He sits,
not upon the throne, but *'at the right hand'* of the Majesty
on high (i. 3, etc.).

A reconciliation of these positions, supreme dignity and
subordinate rank, is not attempted in the Epistle.   There
is no doctrine of renunciation corresponding to Phil.
ii. 6–11.   Nor does the writer, like St. John, use the term
'Logos'.   He is willing to apply to Christ the highest
Alexandrian epithets, other than 'Logos', but prefers to
speak of Him as the Son, in a sense transcending the
believer's sonship (xii), but which he does not attempt to
define.   His nearest approach to an explanation is in ix.
14, when he says that it was 'through eternal spirit', or
'through His eternal spirit', that Christ offered Himself
without blemish to God.   Here the reference is not to the
Holy Spirit, but to the spirit of Christ which is 'eternal',
that is, as belonging to the divine order.[3]   With this
passage we may compare vii. 16, where Christ is said to be
a priest 'after the power of an endless life' ($\kappa\alpha\tau\grave{\alpha}$ $\delta\acute{\upsilon}\nu\alpha\mu\iota\nu$

---

[1] See earlier, p. 57–60.　　　[2] See later, p. 104–7.
[3] Cf. Moffatt's translation, 'who in the spirit of the eternal'.   See also
Westcott, *op. cit.*, 261f., Moffatt, *op. cit.*, 124, Peake, *op. cit.*, 185.

ζωῆς ἀκαταλύτου). But beyond this reference to quality he does not go.

The want of a closer definition is only partially explained by the fact that we have only a single letter from the author's pen, for there is a parallel feature in his failure to define how the One Sacrifice of Christ annuls sin, in spite of the fact that his main interest centres in this doctrine in his endeavour to present Christianity as the absolute religion. Elsewhere[1] I have attempted to explain this omission by his meagre presentation of the love of God, his want of emphasis upon the self-identification of Christ with sinners, and his silence about faith-union with Christ, sacramental communion, and dying with Him. It may well be that his lack of emphasis upon the love of God explains his unresolved teaching concerning the subordination of the Son, for, as we shall see when considering the Johannine writings, subordination is robbed of all the sting of inferiority in the manifold relationships of love which exist between the Father and the Son. Although the striking phrase 'the Father of spirits' is used of the readers in xii. 9, it is a significant fact that only in a quotation in i. 5 from 2 Sam. vii. 14, 'I will be to him a Father, and he shall be to me a Son', is there any allusion to the relationships of Father and Son in the Christology of Hebrews, although these, of course, are implied when Christ is called 'the Son'. And not even here is love mentioned. ἀγάπη, indeed, appears but twice in the Epistle, in vi. 10 and x. 24, in neither case with reference to Christ, and ἀγαπάω only in two Old Testament quotations (i. 9 and xii. 6). It is abundantly clear that, without a full use of the idea of divine love, all attempts to present the doctrine of the Person of Christ must fail. The Christology of Hebrews is profound, but it suffers from

[1] In *The Atonement in New Testament Teaching*, 126-30.

this defect. On this matter, however, reflection is chastened by the consideration that it may not have been the writer's desire to expound more fully the secrets of Christ's Person, and that we are not warranted in looking for Christological speculation in the New Testament period. We must be grateful for the precious heritage that is given, recognizing that in the Epistle to the Hebrews, as in the Pauline letters, we receive Christological teaching which cries out for a still higher Christology.

VIII

THE FOURTH GOSPEL

THE Fourth Gospel claims attention next, for more than any other New Testament writing it has contributed richly to the doctrine of the Person of Christ. The Johannine Epistles will be treated separately. The case for assigning 1 John to a different author has been ably and persuasively argued,[1] but not, I think, established.[2] Nevertheless, since in some respects the teaching of the Gospel and the Epistle presents distinctive aspects, it will prove useful to examine the two writings in turn. I have previously compared the Christology of the Gospel with that of the Synoptics and have drawn attention to its traditional features. It is now necessary to consider its distinctive teaching.

It will be of advantage to recall the points previously noted. In considering the Christology of the Four Gospels attention was given to the Fourth Evangelist's emphasis upon the reality of the humanity of Jesus, the infrequency with which he uses the name 'Christ', his repeated use of the name 'Son of Man' before the Resurrection, his restriction of the use of the name 'the Lord' to the period after the Resurrection, his strong insistence that Christ is 'the Son of God', his Logos teaching, and his treatment of the doctrine of the Holy

---

[1] Cf. C. H. Dodd, *Bulletin of the John Rylands Library*, vol. 21, no. 1 (April 1937), 129–56, *The Johannine Epistles* (1946), xlvii–lvi; C. K. Barrett, *The Gospel according to St. John* (1955), 49–51.

[2] Cf. A. E. Brooke, *The Johannine Epistles* (1912), i–xix; W. F. Howard, *The Journal of Theological Studies*, xlviii (1947), 12–25.

Spirit. This earlier comparison reveals the central ideas of the Johannine Christology. Some of those mentioned are traditional ideas which he has taken over for polemical or historical purposes, but even if they do not illustrate the main elements in his teaching, it is important to observe the distinctive form which he gives to them. Thus, against the Jews of his day, he insists that Jesus is the Messiah, giving prominence to the name 'the King of the Jews', and rescuing it from the obloquy with which it is associated in the Synoptic Gospels.[1] The name 'the Son of Man', used thirteen times, takes on the wider connotation of 'the ideal Man',[2] and the post-Resurrection use of the title 'the Lord' expresses a deep sense of wonder and awe. Most of all, the new names given to Christ, in addition to the traditional names, 'Jesus', 'Rabbi'. 'Prophet', 'Bridegroom', 'He that cometh', and 'the Holy One of God', namely, 'the Bread of Life', 'the Light of the World', 'the Door of the Sheep', 'the Good Shepherd', 'the Resurrection and the Life', 'the True Vine', and 'the Way, and the Truth and the Life',[3] disclose an attitude of veneration indistinguishable from worship.

The central and basic ideas reflected in the Evangelist's portraiture of Jesus are (1) that He truly appeared in flesh; (2) that He is the divine Son of God; (3) that He is the eternal Logos; (4) that the Holy Spirit is His *alter ego*, while distinct from Himself; (5) that He is 'the Lamb of God', the Saviour; and (6) that, as the Risen and Living Christ, He is the subject and the object of a communion which exists between Himself and the believer. All these truths have Christological implications, and these we must now consider.

[1] Cf. V. Taylor, *The Names of Jesus*, 75–7; C. H. Dodd, *The Interpretation of the Fourth Gospel*, 229f.

[2] Cf. Dodd, *op. cit.*, 241–9.   [3] Cf. Taylor, *op. cit.*, 89f., 104–6, 131–46.

I. THE HUMANITY OF CHRIST

That the Word became flesh and tabernacled amongst men, and that His glory was seen, is the dominating theme of the Fourth Gospel (i. 14). It is this interest which leads the Evangelist to say that Jesus 'needed no one to bear witness of man; for he himself knew what was in man' (ii. 25), to describe Him as bearing His own cross (xix. 17), to declare that, when he was pierced by the lance, there came from His side both water and blood (xix. 34), and to record the word to Thomas, 'Have you believed because you have seen me? Blessed are those who have not seen, and yet believe' (xx. 29). These and other examples were noted earlier, when the Person of Christ in the Four Gospels was considered, and the opinion was expressed that the determining interest is doctrinal. This question now requires further consideration.

That the writer's interest is doctrinal more than historical is shown by his omission of the examples of bold historical realism in Mark, of the narratives of the Baptism, Temptation, Transfiguration, and the Agony, of stories of exorcism, and of sayings like Mk. vi. 6 and xiii. 32 which imply limitations in power and in knowledge. The doctrinal interest may also be seen in the heightened miraculous element in the narratives of the turning of water into wine (ii. 1–11), the impotent man at Bethesda (v. 2–9), and the raising of Lazarus (xi. 1–44), for the emphasis upon the idea of Jesus as the giver of life dominates these stories. The position of the story of the cleansing of the Temple (ii. 13–22) and the consequent importance assigned to it presuppose the Evangelist's desire to present Jesus as establishing a new order in the Church which is His Body, in contrast with that of the Temple system (ii. 19).

But, although the historical interest is subordinate to an over-riding doctrinal purpose, it would be wrong to suppose that it is wanting. On the contrary it is essential to the Evangelist's aim. The frequent references to places, times, feasts, and customs, and the account given of the Passion scenes, show that he had access to good historical tradition. Moreover his polemical reaction to docetic teaching, later so strongly assailed by Ignatius and Polycarp,[1] and illustrated in xix. 17 and 34f., reveal his concern to insist that Jesus did not appear in semblance, but in actual fact upon the plane of history. Without this insistence his polemic loses point. Essential to all that he writes is the fact that the Word was made flesh (i. 14). That Jesus 'came' and was 'sent' into this world is the pivot on which all his doctrinal purposes turn. It cannot be too strongly emphasized that for him the incarnation of the Son of God was veridical.[2]

II. THE RELATION OF THE SON TO THE FATHER

In *The Names of Jesus*[3] it is pointed out how frequently the Evangelist uses the terminology of Sonship. The title 'the Son of God' appears eight times in the Gospel, in the words of the Baptist (i. 34), of Nathanael (i. 49), of Martha (xi. 27), of the Jews (xix. 7), of the Evangelist himself (xx. 31), and in three of the sayings of Jesus (v. 25, x. 36, xi. 4). He has the phrase 'the only begotten Son (of God)' in i. 18, iii. 16, and 18. He prefers, however, the name 'the Son', which appears no less than sixteen times (iii. 17, 35, 36 (*bis*), v. 19 (*bis*), 20, 21, 22, 23 (*bis*), 26, vi. 40, viii. 36, xiv. 13, xvii. 1). 'Thy Son' is

---

[1] Bousset, *Kyrios Christos*, 162, maintains that the Gospel was written to meet this situation, not as a supplement to, but as a substitute for the Synoptic Gospels. Cf. H. Windisch, *Johannes und die Synoptiker* (1926).
[2] Cf. E. Hoskyns, *The Fourth Gospel*, 66, 91, 120.   [3] P. 56.

also found in xvii. 1 and the correlative phrase 'My Father'
about thirty times. This greatly enhanced use of the
terminology of Sonship raises historical problems when
compared with the examples in the Synoptic Gospels,[1]
but at the moment the point to consider is its distinctive
place in the Fourth Gospel.

More important than the number of these expressions
is the character of the Sonship described in the Gospel.

Like the Father, the Son has life in Himself (v. 26).
Like the Father, He has quickening power (v. 21),
authority to judge (v. 22), and is worthy to receive
honour (v. 23). He is in the bosom of the Father (i. 18)
and was loved by Him 'before the foundation of the
world' (xvii. 24). To see the Son is to see the Father
(xiv. 9). He is 'in the Father' and the Father is 'in him'
(x. 38, xiv. 10), and in the giving of 'eternal life' He and
the Father 'are one' (x. 30), a saying which is interpreted
by the Jews as blasphemy 'because', as they say, 'you,
being a man, make yourself God' (x. 33). These sayings
need not only to be read, but pondered. They leave no
doubt that, in the mind of the Evangelist, Christ is the
divine Son of God in a relationship which is fully ethical
and spiritual, but also one of being and nature.

This interpretation is confirmed by sayings which
imply the pre-existence of Christ: viii. 58, 'Before
Abraham was, I am';[2] xvii. 5, 'And now, O Father,
glorify thou me with thine own self with the glory which
I had with thee before the world was'; xvii. 24, 'Thou
lovedst me before the foundation of the world'.[3] 'This

---

[1] See later pp. 143–51, 180–6, 197.

[2] For ἐγώ εἰμι, 'I am', see the commentaries of J. H. Bernard, cxvi–
cxxi, C. K. Barrett, 242f., 282f., and R. H. Lightfoot, 134f. Lightfoot
says that at viii. 24, 28, 58 and xiii. 19 we should probably see a reference
to the Lord's divinity, and that the reader is meant to perceive the same
meaning in xviii. 5, 6, 8.   [3] Cf. also viii. 56, xii. 41.

H

pre-temporal (or more properly, non-temporal) existence of the Son is affirmed with emphasis, and assumed all through the Gospel'.[1]   In harmony with these great claims the Gospel reaches its climax in the words of Thomas, 'My Lord and my God' (xx. 28).

Nevertheless, along with this exalted teaching, the same intractable element of subordination which we have already encountered in the Pauline Epistles and the Epistle to the Hebrews appears also in the Fourth Gospel. Indeed, it is present in a more emphatic form.   Jesus is 'sanctified' and 'sent'[2] into the world by the Father (x. 36, cf. xvii. 18).   His divine life, His authority to execute judgement, and His glory are all the Father's gifts (v. 21f., 26f., xvii. 22).   The charge to lay down His life He has received from the Father (x. 18).   'I can of myself do nothing', He says (v. 30), and explicitly He declares, 'The Father is greater than I' (xiv. 28).   It is not possible to explain these sayings convincingly as reflecting the conditions of the incarnate life of Christ, for unlike St. Paul the Evangelist does not think of that life as one of humiliation, except in so far as he speaks of the departure of the Son from the world as His glorifying (xvii. 1, 5, xiii. 32).   In the sayings quoted above, the context shows that in each case Christ is thinking of His glory as maintained during the conditions of His life on earth.   In the same moment that He speaks of being consecrated and sent by the Father He asks if His claim to be the Son of God is regarded as blasphemy (x. 36).   His life-giving power, His authority to execute judgement, and His glory, although they are the Father's gifts, are divine aspects of the Son's incarnate life (cf. v. 21–7, xvii. 2).   With

[1] C. H. Dodd, *The Interpretation of the Fourth Gospel*, 260.

[2] Lightfoot, 150, points out that the emphasis on 'sending' (present in one form or another 42 times) is a fundamental trait of the Gospel.

reference to the Father's charge to lay down His life He says, 'I have power to lay it down, and I have power to take it again' (x. 18). His statement that He can do nothing of Himself relates to His divine authority to execute judgement (v. 30), and when He declares that the Father is greater than Himself, He is speaking of His going to Him (xiv. 28). The subordination, then, is not merely a temporary condition which obtains while He lives on earth, but an eternal relationship which is mani-fested amid the conditions of His human existence.

The eternal character of this relationship accentuates the subordination, but it also gives a clue to its true nature. It belongs to relationships of love which are interior to the life of the Godhead. It is as far as possible from the 'subordinationism' of the Arian controversies and the 'adoptionism' current in Spain and France towards the close of the eighth century.[1] It is not a servant and master relationship, or that of an inferior and a superior, but that of two in perfect unity in an eternal fellowship of love. It is a state of being in which direction is the function of the one and obedience is that of the other in a relationship of love which robs direction of superiority and obedience of inferiority. It is our limited experience of such a unity which leads us to think of obedience as servility and of direction as lordship. And yet we are not without some knowledge of this unity. Even in military relationships in moments of extreme danger, and sometimes in industrial associations of long standing, it can be reflected; most of all in the highest expressions of human love in which service is perfect freedom.

The Fourth Evangelist does not explain the relation-

---

[1] Cf. J. F. Bethune-Baker, *An Introduction to the Early History of Christian Doctrine*, 151, 161–3, 180 *n*. 1; R. L. Ottley, *The Doctrine of the Incarnation*, ii. 151–61.

ship between the Father and the Son beyond giving the vital clue in his emphasis upon love (xvii. 24); and it may not be within our power to envisage it because our ideas of unity are conditioned by imperfect human relationships. He himself suggests that the opposite approach is better, to begin in thought not with man but with God, when he bases the idea of the unity of the Church upon the communion which exists between the Father and the Son. 'I pray . . . for them also that believe on me through their word; that they may all be one; even as thou, Father, art in me, and I in thee, that they also may be in us: that the world may believe that thou didst send me' (xvii. 20f.). Only when we allow the vision of divine unity to shine upon us shall we attain our own unity, and when this is consummated, it will seem to us the natural language of love when the Son says, 'I can do nothing of myself', and 'The Father is greater than I'. In this matter it is to be remembered that the Evangelist gives us only the words of the Son. His deep reverence and his inherited monotheism allow him only on occasion to give the words of the Father, as, for example, when in response to the prayer of the Son, 'Father, glorify thy name', the Father replies, 'I have both glorified it, and will glorify it again' (xii. 28). We may surmise that, had he ventured further, and matched the highpriestly prayer of the Son with the reply of the Father, he would not have confined his rhapsody to the majestic words of a Creator and Lord, but would have startled us by words of love apparently at variance with His known attributes of knowledge and of power; for it is the language of love to affirm, not dignity and power but complete dependence upon the one who is loved. We may be glad that the Evangelist did not enter on this forbidden path, but the remembrance that it exists may be enough to remove many difficulties from the idea of the subordination of the Son. He would not be the Son if He spoke otherwise. He so speaks because His fellowship with the Father is the fellowship of love.

III. THE LOGOS CONCEPTION

In discussing the Christology of the four Gospels attention was drawn to the question whether the idea of the Logos dominates the Fourth Gospel or whether it is used to focus its teaching.[1] Preference was given to the latter view. The question is important because it is bound up with the further question of the extent to which philosophical ideas determine the subject-matter of the Gospel. E. F. Scott[2] traces the influence of the Logos conception throughout, in the peculiar stress laid upon the miracles of the Gospel, in the omniscience and majesty of the Johannine Christ, His aloofness, His absolute freedom and self-determination, and the character of His sayings. 'It is never said in definite terms', he writes, ' "I am the eternal Word", but this is the implied meaning of the discourses when we read them in connection with the prologue'.[3] This argument does not seem conclusive, for it can just as easily be contended that the features mentioned, so far as they are present, suggested to the Evangelist the propriety of using the Logos conception in order to commend his teaching concerning Christ to his Greek readers; and this view is supported by the fact that the Logos is not mentioned apart from the Prologue and that, from first to last, the dominating theme of the Gospel is the Sonship of Christ. Although Philo speaks of the Logos as 'the Son of God',[4] it is not his teaching which

[1] Cf. W. F. Howard, *Christianity according to St. John*, 44.

[2] *The Fourth Gospel: its Purpose and Theology* (1906), 163–75.

[3] *Op. cit.*, 172. R. H. Lightfoot says that the implications of the Logos conception are never far from the Evangelist's mind, *op. cit.*, 52.

[4] Cf. Dodd, *op. cit.*, 67, 252.

determines the Evangelist's use of this title; on the contrary, it is the fact that he believes Jesus to be 'the Christ, the Son of God' (xx. 31) which reminds him of the Logos.

It should, however, be recognized that the Prologue itself is theological and that, in spite of vital differences, it reflects a knowledge of Greek religious ideas. The tendency of many modern scholars to insist that the Prologue is religious in spirit, and not philosophical, does not exclude this dependence. The origins of the Logos conception and its use in the Fourth Gospel are discussed in *The Names of Jesus*,[1] and the opinion is there expressed that Old Testament teaching concerning the Word of God is not a complete explanation of the Evangelist's teaching, and that we are compelled to look also for contributory factors in the Logos of Philo, in the Wisdom theology, and in the Jewish idea of the Torah. In this matter I am glad to be able to quote the opinion of C. H. Dodd[2] who writes: 'While therefore the statements of the Prologue *might* be understood all through on the assumption that λόγος is the Word of the Lord in the Old Testament sense, yet it seems certain that any reader influenced by the thought of Hellenistic Judaism, directly or at a remove, would inevitably find suggested here a conception of the creative and revealing λόγος in many respects similar to that of Philo; and it is difficult not to think that the author intended this'. If, as Dodd says,[3] 'the substance of a Logos-doctrine similar to that of Philo is present all through the gospel', it is because the Evangelist has seized upon, and used, contemporary ideas as a vehicle for expressing convictions independently reached and which at crucial points, especially in i. 14,[4] are without

[1] Pp. 161–6.   [2] *Op. cit.*, 277.
[3] *Op. cit.*, 279.   [4] *Op. cit.*, 284.

parallel in Philo's teaching or in Jewish speculation concerning Wisdom.[1]

As illustrating both the dependence and the independence of the Evangelist's teaching it is useful to recall what he affirms in i. 1–18. The Word, he says, was 'in the beginning', distinguished from God ('with God') and divine (θεός, but not ὁ θεός) (i. 1f.), the medium of creation and the seat of life (i. 3f.), immanent in the world and constituting the life of men (i. 5, 9). From i. 11 onwards it is difficult to decide how far the Evangelist is speaking of the Logos and how far he is thinking of Christ, but undoubtedly from that point, and perhaps from the beginning, he has Christ as the Word principally in mind. Unrecognized by the world, Christ came to His own people and gave the right to those who received Him to become the children of God, born not of the flesh but of the will of God (i. 11–13). He became flesh and tabernacled among us and out of His fulness we have received grace upon grace (i. 14, 16). No one has seen God at any time, but the only begotten Son has made Him known (i. 18).

In this teaching it is clear that the Evangelist is putting his own stamp upon the idea of the Logos by describing Him as personal, and still more by insisting that He became flesh and was seen in the Person of Christ. It may be too much to say, with H. R. Mackintosh,[2] that 'the Word is interpreted by Jesus, not Jesus by the Word'. The two processes go hand in hand. The Word is interpreted by Jesus, and Jesus by the Word. But the epigram is forceful as giving point to Mackintosh's claim, that 'so far from being captured for speculation, the Logos

[1] See the instructive tables given by Dodd, *op. cit.*, 274–7. See also C. K. Barrett, *The Gospel according to St. John*, 129.
[2] *The Doctrine of the Person of Jesus Christ*, 118.

receives a connotation which is fundamentally ethical, personal, soteriological'.[1]

The immediate success of the identification of the Logos with the Person of Christ was undoubted, as the use of this conception in the writings of Ignatius, Justin Martyr, and Origen shows, and as its importance during the Arian and Apollinarian controversies testifies. It suggested, and made room for, the idea of distinctions within the Godhead, and so enabled Christian thinkers to adjust their experience and knowledge of Christ with montheism in the discussions which issued in the Creed of Nicaea. Its ultimate advantages are more open to question. E. F. Scott[2] declares that, when all is said, the idea of the Logos 'was an artificial hypothesis, and was utterly inadequate to set forth the true significance of the revelation in Christ'. L. Hodgson[3] says that its association with the doctrine of the Trinity has 'outlived its usefulness'. The question is one about which differences of opinion are inevitable. Certainly the idea of Sonship is a far richer conception that that of the Logos, as the emphasis the Fourth Evangelist lays upon the love between the Father and the Son reveals, and it was only by transforming the Logos conception that he was able to use it at all. Whether the subsequent course of Christological speculation might have been pursued more happily, without the excessive intellectualism which the Logos idea fostered, is a very pertinent question. Mackintosh points out that when Athanasius came to the discussion of the Person of Christ, 'he was forced to put the Logos Christology aside'.[4] 'Experience', he says, 'had proved that the term Logos too easily lent itself to cosmological

---

[1] *Ibid.*   [2] *The Fourth Gospel; its Purpose and Theology*, 162.
[3] *The Doctrine of the Trinity*, 113. See also G. L. Prestige, *God in Patristic Thought*, 129.   [4] *Op. cit.*, 144.

theories with no bearing on salvation, and tended to denote a mediating Being, essentially distinct from God'.[1]

The Logos conception, we may conclude, served a providential purpose in the development of Christology, but,
except in its Hebraic counterpart of the Word of God
going forth with an existence and activity of its own, it is
not an idea with which Christian thought of to-day can set
out with confidence on its Christological quest.

The ideas of Sonship and the Logos are used directly
by the Evangelist in his portraiture of Christ, but indirectly light is thrown upon his Christology by his
doctrine of the Holy Spirit, especially by the idea of the
Paraclete; and to this theme we now turn.

IV. THE HOLY SPIRIT IN RELATION
TO THE FATHER AND THE SON

Thus far we have seen that in the Fourth Gospel
Christ, as the Logos-Son, has an eternal relationship to
the Father within the unity of a mutual love. Sublime as
this teaching is, it is not the whole of the Evangelist's
thought. A still richer character is given to his Christology by his teaching concerning the Holy Spirit, the
Paraclete.

The teaching about the Paraclete is a distinctive element in the Gospel; in some respects it matches the idea
of the Logos. Its true character is seen only when it is
distinguished from the basically traditional teaching concerning the Holy Spirit in the rest of the Gospel. This
background may with advantage be considered first.

If we set aside iv. 24, 'God is Spirit', which does not
refer to the Holy Spirit, but to the essential nature of

---

[1] *Op. cit.*, 187. See also L. S. Thornton, *The Incarnate Lord*, 311:
'Before Nicaea he (Athanasius) wrote to the Logos. After Nicaea he,
like everyone else, was occupied with the Divine Sonship'.

God, and vi. 63, 'It is the spirit that quickeneth; the flesh profiteth nothing',[1] which illustrates the antithesis between 'spirit' and 'flesh' (cf. iii. 6), only five passages in the Gospel refer to the Holy Spirit apart from the Paraclete-sayings in xiv–xvi.   The first, i. 32f., belongs to the Baptist's account of the descent of the Spirit upon Jesus at His Baptism, and describes Him as 'He that baptizeth with the Holy Spirit' (cf. Mk. i. 8).   The second, iii. 5, connects the Spirit with Baptism as the source of regenerating power: 'Except a man be born of water and the Spirit, he cannot enter into the kingdom of God'. The third, iii. 34, 'For he giveth not the Spirit by measure', explains why Christ, whom God 'sent', speaks the words of God.   He does so because God bestowed on Him the fulness of the Spirit.[2]   The alternative explanation,[3] that it is Christ who does not give the Spirit by measure, seems less in harmony with the context.   The passage is part of a section (iii. 31–6) in which the Evangelist comments on the discourse with Nicodemus (iii. 16–21).   The fourth passage, vii. 39, is also a comment of the Evangelist, in this case upon the saying, 'He who believes on me, as the scripture has said, out of his body shall flow rivers of living water'.   'This', says St. John, 'he spoke of the Spirit, which they that believed on him were to receive', and to this comment he adds, 'for the Spirit was not yet; because Jesus was not yet glorified'.   Here the Evangelist introduces his distinctive idea of the death and exaltation of Jesus as His 'glorifying', thus making this divine event

[1] Many commentators interpret this saying of the Holy Spirit.   Cf. Hoskyns, *The Fourth Gospel*, 340;   C. K. Barrett, *The Gospel according to St. John*, 251.

[2] Cf. J. H. Bernard, *The Gospel according to St. John*, 125;   W. Temple, 'He received the Spirit in all the fulness of the divine gift', *Readings in St. John's Gospel*. 55.

[3] Cf. M.-J. Lagrange, *Évangile selon Saint Jean*, 98f.

the dividing-line between two periods, that of the Son during His earthly existence, and that of the Spirit in the life of the believer and in the Church. The teaching gives expression to ideas found in the Synoptic sayings regarding the future operations of the Spirit[1] and prepares the way for the Paraclete-sayings in xiv–xvi. The fifth and last passage is xx. 22. It tells how the Risen Christ breathed on His disciples, and said, 'Receive the Holy Spirit'. The gift is interpreted in relation to the forgiveness of sins. The passage is an adaptation of the Matthaean sayings on binding and loosing (xvi. 19, xviii. 18), and reflects the practice of the primitive communities in circumstances like the case of incest at Corinth described by St. Paul in 1 Cor. v. 1–5.

It will be seen that, apart from characteristic adaptations like the reference to the glorifying of Christ, the ideas in these five Johannine passages resemble those in the Synoptic Gospels and the Acts which connect the Holy Spirit with baptism and the bestowal and reception of divine power. Christ Himself is endowed with the Spirit, and therefore speaks the words of God, and after His death believers are to receive the same gift, although nothing is said in these passages of witness-bearing and of duties to be fulfilled apart from the reference to the remission of sins. It cannot be said that Johannine teaching concerning the Spirit, outside the Farewell discourses, contributes anything distinctive to the Evangelist's Christology. What he writes is primitive Christian teaching.

The situation is entirely different in the Paraclete-sayings. These sayings stand apart from anything else in the Gospel and therefore merit the closest study. The passages in question are xiv. 15–17, 25f., xv. 26f., xvi.

[1] Mk. xiii. 11, Lk. xxiv. 49, Ac. i. 8.

5–11, 12–15. These five passages stand so loosely articulated in their contexts that with some reason H. Windisch[1] has claimed that they do not belong to the original text of the Farewell discourses. They belong, he suggests, to a 'Doctrine concerning the Paraclete' composed of short logia, which the Fourth Evangelist has taken over and interpreted by identifying the Paraclete with the Holy Spirit and applying His testimony to Christ as He bids farewell to His disciples.

This interesting suggestion has not attracted the attention it deserves.[2] It may be doubted if the Farewell discourses ever existed without the five passages in question, but they may well have been inserted by the Evangelist in the process of compiling the Gospel. W. F. Howard[3] is justified in saying that Windisch's service has been to show that they form a unity. 'The rest of the farewell discourse', he says, 'is complete, self-contained, and consistent without them. They interrupt the sequence of thought and represent a different conception'. It is quite possible that the Evangelist has used contemporary teaching concerning the Paraclete and has given it a new turn by applying it to the work of the Spirit. The phrase 'even the Spirit of truth' has the appearance of such an adaptation, and the Holy Spirit, as described in these passages, exercises some of the functions otherwise fulfilled by the Paraclete of Rabbinical speculation.[4]

The word παράκλητος describes one who is called to the aid of another to speak on his behalf, an advocate. In

---

[1] *Die fünf johanneischen Parakletsprüche* (*Festgabe für Adolf Jülicher*, 1927), 113.

[2] It is rejected by C. K. Barrett, *op. cit.*, 75f., but not, I think, on adequate grounds.

[3] *Christianity according to St. John*, 74.

[4] See the important note of Billerbeck on Jn. xiv. 16, *Kommentar zum Neuen Testament aus Talmud und Midrasch*, ii. 560–2.

this sense it is used in 1 Jn. ii. 1, and the idea, but not the word, appears in Rom. viii. 34 and Heb. ix. 24. Παράκλητος is transliterated in the Rabbinic literature in the form p⁽e⁾răqlēt, 'intercessor', and more frequently the s⁽e⁾gēgōr, συνήγορος, 'accuser', is mentioned. The terms are used of the intercessory angel who pleads the cause of men and of Moses who speaks for Israel. Billerbeck[1] says that, although the Holy Spirit is not described as the Paraclete, the conception of the Spirit as Israel's intercessor was not unknown within the Old Synagogue.

It is useful to record these usages, but in the five Johannine sayings the Spirit-Paraclete appears in a different role; not as 'the friend at Court', to use B.W. Bacon's phrase, but as the Helper, Counsellor, 'the friend from Court'.[2] Attempts have been made to trace this conception to the *Elijah-redivivus* expectation, and similar functions have been pointed out in the figure of the Shepherd in *The Shepherd* of Hermas,[3] in the witness-bearing ministry of the Baptist, and the envoys from the world of light described in the Mandaean writings.[4] Windisch[5] suggests that the idea of a Paraclete-angel sent to the earth and ruling on earth was already present in Judaism, and that this figure can have coalesced with that of *Elijah-redivivus*, who was expected to explain the Torah and to solve disputed questions of interpretation. It is not likely that the Evangelist's debt can be traced to Philo,[6] since he uses the word of the Logos, but his language may reflect Jewish ideas.

---

[1] *Op. cit.*, ii. 562.
[2] *The Expositor*, 1917, ii. 274–82.
[3] Cf. Windisch, *op. cit.*, 123–33.
[4] Cf. W. Bauer, *Das johannesbuch der Mandäer*, 60f., 69f.
[5] *Op. cit.*, 136.
[6] *Vita Mos.*, ii. 134. For Philo's usage see C. K. Barrett, *The Journal of Theological Studies*, N.S., vol. i. 1–15.

The points I have mentioned are speculative, and no assured results have been reached.[1] It is not unlikely, however, that the Evangelist has taken over the idea of the Paraclete, and has applied it to' the Holy Spirit,[2] just as he has used the Logos-conception in order to interpret the Person of Christ. For our immediate purpose, however, the question of importance is the use he has made of the idea of the Spirit-Paraclete and how his teaching affects his Christology.

For this purpose it is necessary to examine the five sayings in xiv–xvi. There are none, it should be noted, in xvii. In considering these sayings I propose to use the term 'Paraclete' rather than 'Helper' which is too general or 'Advocate' which, although appropriate in 1 Jn. ii. 1, is not a suitable rendering of παράκλητος in Jn. xiv–xvi in view of the functions described.

The first saying announces the gift of the Paraclete:

'If you love me, you will keep my commandments, and I will pray the Father, and he will give you another Paraclete, that he may be with you for ever, even the Spirit of truth: whom the world cannot receive; for it beholds him not, neither knows him; you know him; for he abides with you and shall be in you' (xiv. 15–17).

Every reader notes the phrase 'another Paraclete', suggesting, as it does, that hitherto Jesus had been to His disciples a Paraclete, as their counsellor, guide, and protector. Now that He is about to depart from them, He tells them that at His request the Father will give them Another to be with them for ever. This Paraclete, as in the case of Jesus Himself, the world cannot receive, since it neither sees nor knows him, but the disciples know him, for he is with them and in them. He is 'the Spirit of

[1] The whole question calls for further study.

[2] C. H. Dodd suggests that παράκλητος may have become a fixed title for the Holy Spirit in the Church, so that the Evangelist uses it even where the specific functions of the advocate are not in view, *op. cit.*, 415.

truth'; that is, he imparts truth, and eternal reality is the mark of his being.

The second saying describes his functions:

'These things have I spoken to you, while yet abiding with you. But the Paraclete, even the Holy Spirit, whom the Father will send in my name, he shall teach you all things, and bring to your remembrance all that I said to you' (xiv. 25f.).

The Paraclete is sent in Christ's name, as a successor to Him, and his work is that of a teacher and remembrancer. It is probable that the work described is not merely that of recalling to mind something forgotten, but of bringing out the true meaning of what Jesus had said (cf. ii. 22, xx. 9), and that St. John may have understood his own work as an evangelist in this light (cf. xvi. 13). The Spirit's functions are those of a person. This fact is also apparent in the third saying.

The third saying speaks of witness-bearing:

'But when the Paraclete is come, whom I will send to you from the Father, even the Spirit of truth, which proceedeth from the Father, he shall bear witness of me: and you also bear witness, because you have been with me from the beginning' (xv. 26f.).

Sent by Christ, the Paraclete bears witness of Him, as the Baptist did during the earthly ministry. The 'eternal procession' of the Spirit is a later doctrine based on this passage. The immediate implication is that the Spirit goes forth for the purpose of witness-bearing at the command of Christ. The apparent conflict between the statement that Christ will send the Paraclete and xiv. 16 and 25, where he is sent by the Father, lies upon the surface and would hardly have been recognized as such by the Evangelist in view of the unity of love which in his teaching exists between the Father and the Son. The saying recalls Mk. xiii. 11, 'Whatsoever shall be given you in that hour, that speak: for it is not you that speak, but the Holy Spirit', but here the Spirit speaks through the disciples. In the Johannine saying both bear witness side by side. If the Evangelist is adapting current teaching about the Paraclete, he must mean that previously the Spirit-Paraclete has been with the Father from whom he is now to go forth, not as an influence or emanation, but as a person and on a personal mission.

The fourth saying describes the Paraclete as the accuser of the world:

'Nevertheless I tell you the truth; It is expedient for you that I go away: for if I go not away, the Paraclete will not come to you; but if I go, I will send him to you. And he, when he is come, will convict the world in respect of sin, and of righteousness, and of judgement: of sin, because they believe not on me; of righteousness, because I go to the Father, and you behold me no more; of judgement, because the prince of this world has been judged' (xvi. 7–11).

No clearer statement could be given of the distinction between Christ and the Spirit-Paraclete. In no sense are the two identified. The ministry of the one begins when that of the other ceases. In respect of the world the Spirit's ministry is not that of an advocate, counsellor, or helper, but that of an accuser, a prosecuting counsel, who claims a verdict of 'Guilty' against the world on three counts; of sin arising from unbelief in Christ, of righteousness because, in going to the Father, Christ has left 'a complete exhibition of righteousness in relation to God and man',[1] and of judgement because men are subjects of 'the prince of this world' who is judged already in the glorifying of Christ (xii. 31, xiii. 31). As in xv. 26 the Spirit-Paraclete is sent by Christ.

The fifth saying is the most far-reaching of all; it describes the ministry of the Paraclete in relation to truth:

[1] Westcott, *The Gospel according to St. John*, 229.

'I have yet many things to say to you, but you cannot bear them now. Howbeit when he, the Spirit of truth, is come, he shall guide you into all the truth: for he shall not speak from himself; but what things soever he shall hear, these shall he speak: and he shall declare unto you the things that are to come. He shall glorify me; for he shall take of mine, and shall declare it unto you' (xvi. 12–15).

The Spirit's mission is to complete the revelation Christ has brought, which is incomplete only because as yet the disciples cannot grasp it in its fulness. Christ is the ultimate reality (xiv. 6); and it is the work of the Spirit to guide men into the possession of reality. He does this not of himself, but as sharing the knowledge which belongs to a divine fellowship. The content of the teaching is twofold: things to come, an eschatological phrase; and all that glorifies Christ, that is, 'makes Him known in His full majesty by gradual revelation'.[1] As the Son glorifies the Father (xvii. 4), so the Spirit glorifies the Son.

If we take this teaching as a whole, we cannot fail to see how much the Church owes to it for her understanding of the meaning and implications of Christianity. I fully endorse the statement of W. F. Howard when he says: 'Though with St. John we are still in the pre-dogmatic stage of the Trinitarian teaching, the sayings about the Paraclete carry us a degree farther than any other writing in the development of the New Testament doctrine of the Godhead'.[2] C. K. Barrett observes that none of the earlier references in the Gospel to the Spirit show the same measure of 'personalization' as do the last discourses. 'It is true', he says, 'that even in these no doctrine of the Trinity is formulated; but the materials are present out of which such a doctrine might be formulated. The three divine Persons are mentioned side by side, distinct from one another, yet akin to one another as they are not akin to man'.[3]

---

[1] Westcott, *op. cit.*, 231.   [2] *Op. cit.*, 80.   [3] *Op. cit.*, 77.

I

The teaching concerning the Holy Spirit crowns and completes the Evangelist's conception of the Person of Christ. Based upon traditional teaching and reflecting a knowledge of the sayings of Jesus, it boldly appropriates and develops ideas which give to the Spirit a distinctive place alongside the Father and the Son. Without this teaching it is possible, so far as one can see, that the doctrine of God might have developed upon binitarian rather than trinitarian lines, with the result that the Holy Spirit might have been conceived as no more than the power of God operative in the Church and in the world. Thanks to the Evangelist's inspiration a much richer conception of God has prevailed, so that the Father, the Son, and the Holy Spirit can be distinguished as Persons within the unity of the One God, thus making it possible to receive the gifts and the benedictions of the triune God in individual experience and in the worship of the Church, in praise, sacrament, and offering. The implications of Johannine teaching are that, as loved by the Father, we share also in the blessed ministrations of the Son and the Holy Spirit; that as redeemed by the Son we enjoy a reconciliation with God in which the Father and the Holy Spirit are also vitally concerned; and that as guided, taught, and strengthened by the Holy Spirit we have at our disposal all the fulness of God. Our immediate concern is with the Person of Christ. In the teaching of the Fourth Evangelist it is a Christ with all these holy relationships of love who is presented and offered to us.

V. THE IMPLICATIONS OF THE WORK OF CHRIST

As in other New Testament writers the Fourth Evangelist's treatment of the work of Christ has important bearings upon his Christology. A detailed account of his soteriology cannot be given here,[1] but even a summary statement is enough to show its importance in our inquiry.

Christ's work is conceived by the Evangelist as the fulfilment of the divine purpose in order that, through faith in Him, men may receive the gift of eternal life. 'God so loved the world, that he gave his only begotten Son, that whosoever believes on him should not perish, but have eternal life' (iii. 16). Here and now, as well as in the Age to Come, life in its fulness is revealed by Christ and offered to men by His life and death. He came that 'they may have life, and may have it abundantly' (x. 10). As the Son of Man, He is lifted up 'that whosoever believes may in him have eternal life' (iii. 14f.). His self-offering is conditioned by sin; it is vicarious in character (x. 11, xi. 50, xv. 13) and sacrificial in its expression (i. 29, 36, vi. 53–8, xii. 24, xvii. 19). The Lamb of God bears away the sin of the world (i. 29). His Sacrifice is the supreme proof of the love of God (iii. 16); it is dedicated to the highest moral and spiritual ends (vi. 51, 56), and is universal in its scope (iv. 42, xi. 51, xii. 32). Christ is the Lamb of God (i. 29) and the Saviour of the world (iv. 42).

This teaching adds no new element to the Evangelist's doctrine of the Christ, but it deepens and enriches all that he has to say concerning Him. The greatness of His Person is necessary to His Work.

VI. THE CHRIST-MYSTICISM OF THE EVANGELIST IN RELATION TO THE PERSON OF CHRIST

The same conclusion must be drawn from the Evangelist's Christ-mysticism.[2] Repeatedly he speaks of

---

[1] I have attempted to do this in *The Atonement in New Testament Teaching*, 130–61.

[2] See *Forgiveness and Reconciliation*, 119–21, 192.

'abiding' and 'being in Christ', and by the use of many figures he presents Christ as meeting the deepest needs of men in the attainment of communion with God. Herein lies the importance of the seven 'I am' sayings. Christ is 'the Bread of life' (vi. 35), 'the Light of the world' (viii. 12), 'the Door of the sheep' (x. 7), 'the Good Shepherd' (x. 11), 'the Resurrection and the Life' (xi. 25), 'the True Vine' (xv. 1), and 'the Way and the Truth, and the Life' (xiv. 6). He is all these things to the believer because of the revelation which He brings and because of the communion He makes possible between men and Himself. Especially significant in this respect is the eucharistic teaching of Jn. vi, for while the Evangelist does not describe the institution of the Eucharist and warns his readers against quasi-materialistic ideas by insisting that 'it is the spirit that quickens; the flesh profits nothing' (vi. 63), he designedly connects sacramental teaching with the miracle of the feeding of the five thousand in the wilderness. 'I am the living bread', says the Johannine Christ, 'which came down out of heaven: if any man eat of this bread, he shall live for ever: yea and the bread which I will give is my flesh, for the life of the world' (vi. 51); and again, 'Verily, verily, I say unto you, Except you eat the flesh of the Son of Man and drink his blood, you have not life in yourselves' (vi. 53). No argument is needed to show that this teaching is in full accord with the Evangelist's Christology. Spiritual communion of the kind he describes is possible only with the Word made flesh, the eternal Son of God.

VII. SUMMARY

We have seen how high a Christology the Fourth Gospel presupposes and teaches: a doctrine of incarnation illuminated by the Logos conception, but essentially a doctrine of divine Sonship, which by its association with the idea of the Spirit-Paraclete implies distinctions within the Godhead afterwards worked out in the theology of the Church. The question of its truth and authority presses. If we were able, as our fathers were able, and as many Christians still believe, to accept the Johannine sayings as the *ipsissima verba* of Jesus, our question would be readily answered. This blessing is less easily claimed by those who accept as valid the results of modern criticism and who, in consequence, find the presence of interpretation, that of the Evangelist and of the Ephesian community, in the sayings. The Johannine sayings and discourses are a challenge to us and will remain a challenge to the end. Nevertheless, acceptance of their teaching is not, and need not be, a blind leap. The sayings are indeed interpretations, but, as we have seen, interpretations based on tradition, and often on Synoptic sayings, by one who believed that he was guided by the Spirit. Three considerations bear upon the question of the validity of his work: first, the impression which the Evangelist and his Gospel make upon us after years of brooding study; secondly, the endorsement which the Church Catholic has given to the teaching in doctrine and worship; thirdly, the degree to which the teaching, especially that which concerns communion with Christ, finds an echo in our personal experience. The order in which we place these tests, and the strength of each, will vary with the individual believer according to his training and temperament; but each way of approach is open to us and can be followed patiently and resolutely. In this endeavour the Gospel gives us the assurance that, if any man is willing to do His will, he shall know of the teaching whether it be of God (vii. 17).

IX

THE JOHANNINE EPISTLES

THE Christological teaching of 1 John must now be examined and compared with that of the Fourth Gospel. 2 and 3 John are too brief and too occasional in purpose to be of value in this connexion, apart from 2 Jn. 7, 'For many deceivers are gone forth into the world, even they that confess not that Jesus Christ comes in the flesh'. A difference of aim must be recognized in considering 1 John; for while the Gospel is written to show that Jesus is the Christ, the Son of God, 1 John is composed to strengthen the faith of the readers and to guard them from the perils of false teaching. I propose to take up the themes already treated in studying the Gospel and to observe how far, and in what way, they are represented in the Epistle.

1. The humanity of Jesus is emphasized in the strongest possible manner. That which was from the beginning 'concerning the Word of life', it is insisted, was 'heard', 'seen', 'beholden', and 'handled' 'That which we have seen and heard', the writer affirms, 'declare we unto you, that you also may have fellowship with us' (i. 3). 'Every spirit which confesses that Jesus Christ is come in the flesh', he says, 'is of God: and every spirit which confesses not Jesus is not of God' (iv. 2f., cf. 2 Jn. 7). And again, 'This is he that came by water and blood, even Jesus Christ' (v. 6). Denial of the reality of the Incarnation is 'antichrist' (iv. 3). As he says in 2 Jn. 7b, 'This is the deceiver and the antichrist'. The writer is manifestly attacking some early form of dualistic Gnosti-

cism, although not one of the Gnostic systems of the second century. Pagan in character, with an emphasis on knowledge (*gnosis*), the false teaching was docetic in its doctrinal emphasis; it denied the reality of the coming of Christ in the flesh. The false teaching was also antinomian. Hence the writer's emphasis upon the keeping of the commandments (ii. 4–6) and the reality of sin (i. 7–10). In meeting this teaching his method is to insist on the historical basis of the Christian revelation and to affirm that it offers the true *gnosis* (ii. 20, 27).

2. The name 'the Lord' is not used in the Epistles. This difference from the usage of the Gospel is more apparent than real, for of the nine examples found there, six are traditional statements of the disciples and of Mary Magdalene in connexion with the Resurrection. Only in Jn. xx. 20b, 'The disciples therefore were glad, when they saw the Lord', does the Evangelist himself use this title, and again in Jn. xxi. 7 and 12 if the Appendix is from his pen. In the Gospel and in 1 John this title gives place to 'the Son' and allied names. This contrast with the Acts, the Pauline and Pastoral Epistles, the rest of the Catholic Epistles, and the Apocalypse, is remarkable. It is a highly characteristic agreement between the two writings, which perhaps has not been sufficiently esteemed. It marks the writer's preoccupation with the conviction that Jesus is the Son of God. He is not satisfied with primitive Christianity to say 'Jesus is Lord'.

3. In proportion to their length, the Epistles use the terminology of Sonship more frequently than the Gospel. The names 'the Son of God', 'the Son', 'His Son', 'His only begotten Son', 'the Son of the Father' are found no less than twenty-four times,[1] often in conjunction with references to 'the Father'. This frequency is to be ex-

[1] See *The Names of Jesus*, 58.

pected in writings which are hortatory in character. Two passages in particular give us the heart of Johannine teaching concerning Christ: v. 11f., 'And the witness is this, that God gave unto us eternal life, and this life is in his Son. He who has the Son has the life; he who has not the Son of God has not the life'; and v. 20, 'And we know that the Son of God has come and has given us an understanding, to know him who is true, and we are in him that is true, in his Son Jesus Christ. This is the true God[1] and eternal life'. In the Epistles there is no occasion to speak of that subordination in love which marks the Son's relation to the Father, but three times the Son is described as 'sent' (iv. 9, 10, 14). More surprising is the absence of references to the mutual love between the Father and the Son, since love amongst believers is commended. The supreme manifestation of love is seen in the sending of the Son, but this love is God's love for us (iv. 10). Nevertheless, as in the Gospel, the Son is presented in the closest relationship with the Father. The fellowship of believers is 'with the Father, and with his Son Jesus Christ' (i. 3), and to deny or confess the Son determines whether a man has, or has not, the Father also (ii. 23). Higher claims could hardly be made.

3. How far the Logos conception is implied in 1 John is not easy to determine. In their interpretations of 'the Word of life' (i. 1) the commentators are divided; some finding in it a reference to 'the life-giving Word' or Logos,[2] others explaining the genitive ('of life') as one of definition, 'the revelation concerning life'.[3] C. H. Dodd[4] compares the phrase 'word of life' in Phil. ii. 16 and the

---

[1] The reference is to God, not to Christ. Cf. A. E. Brooke, *op. cit.*, 151.

[2] Cf. A. L. Humphries, Peake's *Commentary*, 917; R. Law, *The Tests of Life*, 44f., 370.

[3] So Westcott, *The Epistles of St. John*, 6f.; A. E. Brooke, *op. cit.*, 5.

[4] *The Johannine Epistles*, 4f.

expression 'the words of this life' in Ac. v. 20, and takes the writer to mean 'the life-giving Word of God which came to men through Christ and is embodied in the Gospel'. If the writer is the Evangelist it is natural to find a backward glance in the phrase to Jn. i. 1; but in any case the Logos conception is not a regulative idea in the Epistle. All the emphasis is upon Sonship.

4. The doctrine of the Spirit is not brought into connexion with the Person of Christ by means of the Paraclete conception; but in v. 6–8 the Spirit bears witness to Christ along with the water and the blood, that is, the baptism and crucifixion of Jesus as historical events and the two sacraments by which the witness is continued. Elsewhere in the Epistle the Spirit is the seal of God's abiding presence (iii. 24) and the proof of our abiding in Him (iv. 13). In each passage the Spirit is God's gift. He is also the object of knowledge (iv. 2). The teaching is of a more primitive character than that contained in the Gospel, but not more traditional than it is in the sayings outside Jn. xiv–xvi.

5. The work of Christ as described in 1 John bears directly on the doctrine of the Person of Christ, and indeed more fully, since it contains teaching concerning expiation not found in the Gospel apart from Jn. i. 29. Christ Himself is our Paraclete, or Advocate, with the Father and is the expiation for our sins (ii. 1f., iv. 10). 'He laid down his life for us: and we ought to lay down our life for the brethren' (iii. 16). 'The blood of Jesus', says the writer, 'cleanses us from all sin' (i. 7), and sins are forgiven 'for his name's sake' (ii. 12). This vicarious, intercessory, and sacrificial work invests His Person with the highest significance. It is, in the author's view, the purpose of His coming into the world. 'You know', he writes, 'that he was manifested to take away sins' (iii. 5,

cf. Jn. i. 29). It ought not to be accounted strange, or inconsistent with the theory of a common authorship, that this aspect of Christ's Person and Work is prominent in the Epistle, but not in the Gospel. A difference of aim in the two writings seems a sufficient explanation.

6. Finally, the increased use of the idea of 'abiding' in Christ in the Epistle[1] as compared with the Gospel underlines all the high claims that are made for Christ. Devotional in tone, the teaching is Christological in its implications. 'In the Gospel it is used only of Christ, but in 1 John of Christ and of God. In both writings the relation is mutual: Christ or God abides in man, and man abides in Christ or God'.[2] This marked emphasis upon communion is natural if Christ is the Son of God.

We must conclude that, in spite of important differences, the Christological teaching of the two writings is fundamentally the same. If the writer of 1 John is a disciple of the Fourth Evangelist, he has absorbed his master's teaching to an outstanding degree and shares fully with him the belief that Jesus is the Son of God. If, as seems more probable, the two writings are the work of a single author, we are permitted to see how in a later composition he applies the significance of the earlier portraiture to the practical needs of believers assailed by incipient Gnosticism. Unwavering is his insistence that 'God gave to us eternal life, and this life is in his Son' (v. 11). The importance of this teaching for doctrine and worship cannot be measured. It supplements all that we learn from Hebrews and the Epistles of St. Paul, opening up new perspectives for subsequent Christian thinking and commending itself still to the believer as a Spirit-inspired witness of the abiding and eternal significance of Christ.

[1] Cf. 1 Jn. ii. 6, 24, 27f., iii. 6, 24, iv. 12f., 15f.; also ii. 5f., v. 20.
[2] V. Taylor, *Forgiveness and Reconciliation*, 119–27.

X

THE PASTORAL EPISTLES

In the study of the Christology of the New Testament the Pastoral Epistles are often neglected because they make no distinctive and original contribution to the doctrine, and because, in considering them, attention tends to be absorbed by the problems of authorship, the ecclesiastical situation they presuppose, and the false teaching they so vigorously attack. This neglect is to be regretted. These Epistles not only supply valuable testimony to the Christological beliefs in the period A.D. 70–100, but also reflect the traditional views of a much earlier time. As through a glass darkly we can see how the Person of Christ was interpreted in circles in which practical and ecclesiastical interests were uppermost, and the beliefs which they inherited. The Pastoral Epistles furnish impressive testimony to the ideas of primitive Christianity which lived on in spite of the contributions of the great New Testament writers.

1. The names of Christ used in the Epistles show that Messianic interests had almost disappeared under the stronger influence of liturgical and ethical motifs. *Christos*, when used by itself or in combination with other names, has become a personal designation charged with religious meaning. It is, of course, difficult to decide in what tone names are used in ancient writings, but unless I am mistaken, it is possible to detect in the use of these titles an attitude of religious veneration. This appears to be true of the names 'Our Lord', 'Our Lord Jesus Christ', and 'Christ Jesus our Lord', each of which

appears twice, 'the Lord', which is found twelve times, and perhaps most of all the name 'Saviour', which is used of Christ in 2 Tim. i. 10, Tit. i. 4, ii. 13, and iii. 6.[1] We have reason to find such a tone in the reference to 'the appearing of our Saviour Christ Jesus' when He is said to have 'abolished death, and brought life and incorruption to light through the Gospel' (2 Tim. i. 10), when the Holy Spirit is declared to have been poured out richly by God 'through Jesus Christ our Saviour' (Tit. iii. 6), and again when 'Christ Jesus' is described as 'our hope' (1 Tim. i. 1). In sum, we have not done justice to the Pastoral Epistles unless above and beyond discussions about the character of bishops and elders and spirited denunciations of heresy we hear resounding echoes of praise and worship.

In one important respect Messianic ideas are still present, in the vivid expectation of the Parousia in the exhortation to keep the commandments 'without spot, without reproach, until the appearing of our Lord Jesus Christ' (1 Tim. vi. 14); and in the Pauline note embedded in 2 Tim. iv, which speaks of 'the crown of righteousness, which the Lord, the righteous judge, shall give to me at that day: and not to me only, but also to all them that have loved his appearing' (2 Tim. iv. 8). The eschatological hope is the expectation of the coming of the divine Lord.

2. The traditional element in the Pastorals appears clearly in the allusions to the Jesus of history. These are more numerous than might be expected. Thus, 'his appearing', in the sense of His incarnation, is mentioned several times (2 Tim. i. 10, Tit. ii. 11, and iii. 4). It is said expressly that 'Christ Jesus came into the world to

[1] The name 'Saviour' is used of God in 1 Tim. i. 1, ii. 3, iv. 10, Tit. i. 3, ii. 10, and iii. 4.

save sinners' (1 Tim. i. 15), and His humanity is unambiguously expressed in the word 'man' in 1 Tim. ii. 5.
There are references in the Pastorals to the Davidic
descent of Christ (2 Tim. ii. 8), to His confession before
Pontius Pilate (1 Tim. vi. 13), His long-suffering (1 Tim.
i. 16), His Resurrection (2 Tim. ii. 8) and Ascension (1
Tim. iii. 16). The saying of Jesus in Mk. x. 45 about
giving Himself 'a ransom for many' is interpreted in 1
Tim. ii. 6 in the phrase 'a ransom for all' (ἀντίλυτρον ὑπὲρ
πάντων).[1] Manifestly the faith of the readers is vested in
One who in His grace and mercy had appeared in flesh
upon the field of history. In a passage of great beauty
the writer refers to the time when 'the kindness and love
of God our Saviour' appeared in Jesus Christ (Tit. iii. 4–7).

3. Already, in the manner in which the coming of
Christ is described, it is clear that in the teaching of these
Epistles He is regarded as divine. This belief is further
indicated by the references to the blessings which men
obtain through Him: 'life and incorruption' (2 Tim. i.
10, Tit. iii. 7), 'mercy' (1 Tim. i. 2, 2 Tim. i. 2, 18),
'grace' (1 Tim. i. 2, 2 Tim. i. 2, Tit. i. 4, iii. 7), 'peace'
(1 Tim. i. 2, 2 Tim. i. 2, Tit. i. 4), 'godly living' (2 Tim.
iii. 12, iv. 8),[2] and 'salvation' (1 Tim. i. 15, 2 Tim. ii.
10, iv. 18, Tit. ii. 14). Tit. ii. 13, 'looking for the blessed
hope and appearing of the glory of our great God and
Saviour Jesus Christ', has often been interpreted as a
direct assertion of the deity of Christ. This rendering,
which is that of the RV supported by the RSV, describes Jesus Christ as 'our great God and Saviour', in
contrast with the translation 'the great God and our
Saviour Jesus Christ' of the AV and RSVm, which distinguishes the two Persons. The former is confidently

[1] So many commentators. Cf. F. D. Gealy, *The Interpreter's Bible*, xi.
400.   [2] Cf. Moffatt, 'the crown of a good life'.

defended by Ellicott,[1] and with great hesitation by J. H.
Bernard,[2] and has recently been adopted by C. F. D.
Moule[3] and F. D. Gealy.[4]   It is the traditional interpretation of the Greek Fathers, and is supported by the absence
of the definite article before the name 'Saviour', the use of
the epithet 'great' with 'God', and the fact that ἐπιφάνεια
is used in the Pastorals of the appearing of Christ.
Moreover, there is evidence from seventh-century papyri,
admittedly late, which attest the phrase 'our great God
and Saviour' as current among Greek-speaking Christians,
and similar evidence from the second century that
language of this kind was applied to deified kings.[5] These
are persuasive arguments.   But they are not conclusive.
The grammarians admit that a second article is not
necessary since 'Saviour' is sufficiently qualified by the
word 'our'.[6] Further, the writer appears to use θεός of
the Father only (1 Tim. i. 1f., Tit. i. 4, etc.), and the reference to the glory of God in association with the Parousia
is illustrated in Mk. viii. 38 and its parallels.   Again,
most of the ancient versions agree with the AV in distinguishing two Persons in the clause.   Finally, one is
inclined to think that the writer would have expressed the
idea of Christ's deity more clearly, if against his practice
elsewhere he had meant to assert it.   It is probable, therefore, that we ought to translate the passage, with Moffatt,
and in agreement with the AV, RVm, and RSVm, 'the
appearance of the Glory of the great God *and* of our
Saviour'.[7] Bultmann's observation, that, in describing

---

[1] *In loc.*   [2] *The Pastoral Epistles*, 173.
[3] *An Idiom Book of New Testament Greek*, 110.
[4] *The Interpreter's Bible*, xi. 539f.   [5] J. H. Moulton, *Prolegomena*, 84.
[6] Winer-Moulton, *Grammar of New Testament Greek*, 162: F. Blass,
Grammar of New Testament Greek, 163.
[7] So Scott, Jeremias, Moffatt, N. J. D. White, C. A. Anderson Scott,
and others.

Christ as 'God', the New Testament 'still exercises great restraint', has already been quoted. 'Ignatius on the contrary', he says, 'speaks of Christ as God as if it were a thing to be taken quite for granted'.[1]

If Tit. ii. 13 is ambiguous, the writer is frequently on the verge of affirming Christ's deity and certainly holds Him to be divine. This distinction, which is sometimes contested, is particularly relevant in the Pastoral Epistles because to speak of Christ as 'divine' brings Him within the orbit of deity at an undefined point which in the thought of the period could have been made precise only at the expense of suggesting the idea of a Second God. Time was to elapse before an enriched conception of mono-theism made it possible to speak of Christ as 'God', and even to-day many devout minds hesitate to use the name. The Pastoral Epistles illustrate this situation. Thus, the author frequently mentions Christ in the closest asso-ciation with God the Father (1 Tim. i. 2, v. 21, vi. 13, 2 Tim. i. 2, iv. 1, Tit. i. 1, 4, ii. 13). He presents Christ as the object of faith (1 Tim. i. 16, iii. 16, 2 Tim. iii. 15) and quotes 'hymns' addressed to Him in adoration (1 Tim. iii. 16, 2 Tim. ii. 11–13). He gives Him the place of God without the use of the name. His silence is not hesi-tation to affirm deity, but the fear of being misunderstood. We may say with justice that these Epistles represent a practical and unspeculative type of primitive Christianity in which Christ is tacitly assigned the powers and func-tions of God. They imply more than they say. In this respect they reflect the mind and spirit of a Christianity which lived on to the close of the first century broken only by the, as yet, unassimilated teaching of the great New Testament writers.

---

[1] *Op. cit.*, i. 129. See earlier, p. 55.

XI

ST. JAMES, ST. JUDE,
AND SECOND PETER

THE Johannine Epistles and 1 Peter have already been examined, and it now remains for us to consider the teaching of the rest of the Catholic Epistles, St. James, St. Jude, and the Second Epistle of Peter. Each of these writings is of late date, extending from the end of the first century to the middle of the second century in the so-called Second Epistle of St. Peter. They have little to contribute to the doctrine of the Person of Christ. Usually they receive scant attention in summaries of New Testament teaching, since, in contrast with the great writers, they are silent about Christological issues. Their interests are concentrated upon ethical admonitions, opposition to false teaching, and the hope of the Parousia with its problems. The relatively few allusions to Christ centre upon His Lordship and the truth that He is 'the Saviour'. Once more, as in the case of the Pastoral Epistles, they supply valuable testimony to the virility of primitive Christian beliefs.

In the Epistle of St. James the title 'Lord' appears in every reference to Christ. In the opening salutation He is named 'the Lord Jesus Christ' (i. 1), and in ii. 1 He is spoken of as 'Our Lord Jesus Christ'. In both cases 'Jesus Christ' is a personal name. No reference is made to His Messianic dignity. More surprisingly He is not mentioned again by this name. The great emphasis is laid upon the fact that He is 'Lord'. It is remarkable, however, that in at least eight of the fourteen passages in

which this name appears the reference is to God (i. 7,
iii. 9, iv. 10, 15, v. 4, 10, 11 (*bis*)). Only in i. 1, ii. 1, v. 7,
8, 14, 15 is the name 'Lord' applied to Christ.

In St. Jude the situation is similar. 'Lord' is used of
God in verses 5, 9, and 14, and the title is applied to
Christ in the phrases 'Our (only Master and) Lord Jesus
Christ' (4 and 17), 'Our Lord Jesus Christ' (verse 21), and
'Jesus Christ our Lord' (verse 25). As in St. James
'Jesus Christ' (verse 1 (*bis*)) is a personal name.

The same usage appears in 2 Peter. 'The Lord' in
ii. 9, 11, iii. 8f. is God, but denotes Christ in iii. 2, 10, and
15, and 'Our Lord', with added designations ('Jesus',
'Jesus Christ', and 'Saviour') describes Him in i. 2, 8,
11, 14, 16, ii. 20 and iii. 18. Once more 'Jesus Christ' is a
personal name. A striking feature common to 2 Peter,
1 Jn. iv. 14, and the Pastoral Epistles is the use of the
name 'Saviour', ten[1] times in all as compared with only
six[2] examples in the rest of the New Testament. In *The
Names of Jesus* I suggested that the use of the designation
in Greek religion and in Caesar-worship restricted and
delayed its currency in the primitive tradition.[3]

The value of this statistical summary is at once apparent. The dominating usage of these late Epistles is
the use of the name 'Lord' when speaking of Jesus. The
terminology of Sonship appears only once in the reference
to the Transfiguration in 2 Pet. i. 17 where the words of
the divine voice are recalled. 'This is my beloved Son, in
whom I am well pleased'. This allusion is manifestly
traditional. How, then, is the failure to use such titles as
'the Son of God' and 'the Son' to be explained. I have
previously discussed this problem when treating the

[1] Cf. 2 Pet. i. 1, 11, ii. 20, iii. 2, 18; 2 Tim. i. 10; Tit. i. 4, ii. 13, iii. 6;
1 Jn. iv. 14.

[2] Lk. ii. 11, Jn. iv. 42, Ac. v. 31, xiii. 23, Phil. iii. 20, and Eph. v. 23.

[3] *Op. cit.*, 109.

Pauline use of these titles;[1] but the question is so important and the usage of the Pastoral and Catholic Epistles is so remarkable that it needs to be raised again.

It is manifestly not enough to rest content with the negative observation that the higher Christology of the great New Testament writers is wanting in these Epistles, and even the fact that these writers seek to teach their readers is not a complete explanation. The significant point is that, in spite of their powerful contribution to Christology, primitive usage lived on for many decades. Primitive Christology, it appears, is not a stage merely antecedent to St. Paul, which quickly passes into a stage more impressive; it is the Christianity of the common man both before and after the time of the great writers. Dr. L. S. Thornton has observed that the most arresting fact in the history of doctrine is the contrast between the richness of Johannine Christology and 'the, comparatively speaking, meagre thought of Christian writers upon this subject during the second century A.D.'.[2] The soundness of this observation must not be allowed to obscure the fact that the Christology of the Pastoral and later Catholic Epistles is richer than the terminology used might suggest. It is difficult to miss the accents of veneration in Ju. 4, 17, 21, 25, and in the phrase 'Our only Master and Lord' in Ju. 4. The passages which speak of Jesus as 'Lord' are not distant echoes, but peals of devotion from the worship of this late period. 'Our Lord Jesus Christ' is the ringing and sustained Christian confession. This does not mean that the description of Jesus as 'the Son of God' in the Pauline and Johannine writings, and in the Epistle to the Hebrews is forgotten, or is only a phase of New Testament teaching. It means

[1] See earlier, p. 44.
[2] *The Incarnate Lord*, 303

that this teaching was not absorbed quickly in the Christianity of the ordinary believer to the extent of replacing the earlier terminology of religious devotion. 'The Lord' is a different, but not necessarily a lower, Christological designation; it voices the passionate worship of gathered communities of believers both early and late. It comes from the conventicle and the altar rather than the school, and it was destined to live on through later centuries down to the present day.[1]

This discussion naturally raises the question of the abiding value of the teaching of the great New Testament writers. This issue must be deferred until Part II where the Christology of the primitive communities and the special contributions of St. Paul, the writer of Hebrews, and St. John are summarized and evaluated.[2]

---

[1] The fact that the three Johannine Epistles do not use the term 'the Lord' is only an apparent objection to this conclusion. As previously maintained (see p. 125f), these Epistles, and 1 John in particular, are preoccupied with the Sonship of Jesus. 1 Peter describes Christ as 'Lord' in i. 3, ii. 3, 13, and iii. 15.

[2] See pp. 190–244.

XII

THE APOCALYPSE OF ST. JOHN

To a greater degree than in any writing we have examined, the Apocalypse is remarkable for the way in which it combines primitive elements with a lofty Christology. H. R. Mackintosh[1] quotes the opinion of W. Bousset, that apparently it is the most advanced Christology in the New Testament. Mackintosh denies that this is due to Pauline influence. 'It may represent', he says, 'a late independent branch of primitive faith'. Since by wide consent the Apocalypse was probably written during the reign of Domitian (A.D. 81–96),[2] it supplies impressive evidence for the virility of primitive Christian Christology and suggests its far-reaching implications.

1. In a writing of this apocalyptic character we might not expect features which recall the historical Jesus, and yet undoubtedly they are present. The name 'Jesus' is found nine times,[3] more frequently in fact than 'Jesus Christ' (3 times), 'Lord Jesus' (once), and 'the Lord Jesus' (once). The name 'Christ' is Messianic in xi. 15 and xii. 10 and personal in xx. 4 and 6. In v. 5 He is described as 'the Lion that is of the tribe of Judah'. Reference is also made to the Crucifixion (xi. 8), the Resurrection (i. 5), and the Exaltation (iii. 21). The writer has no doubt that Jesus is a historical figure.

2. In the reference to Exaltation we have passed from

---

[1] *The Doctrine of the Person of Jesus Christ*, 88.
[2] Cf. R. H. Charles, *The Revelation of St. John*, xci–xcvii.
[3] i. 9 (*bis*), xii. 17, xiv. 12, xvii. 6, xix. 10 (*bis*), xx. 4, xxii. 16.

the standpoint of history to that of worship and doctrine. Pre-eminently the Apocalypse is a book of worship and of song. Christ is seen as the Exalted Lord, and it is upon this conception that all the emphasis lies. Thus, in language which recalls Dan. vii. 13 and 1 Enoch xlvi. 1, He is twice described as 'one like unto a son of man' (i. 13, xiv. 14), and the context shows that no human figure is meant, but a being of superhuman majesty. Many striking phrases are used to describe the Exalted Christ. Thus, He is spoken of as 'the faithful witness, the firstborn of the dead, and the ruler of the kings of the earth' (i. 5), and again as 'the Living One' who has 'the keys of death and of Hades' (i. 18). In the Seer's opening vision He walks in the midst of the seven golden candlesticks, holding the seven stars in His right hand, and He sends messages of warning and promise to the Churches of Asia (i. 13, ii–iii). He is the future ruler of the nations, who 'shall rule them with a rod of iron, as the vessels of the potter are broken to shivers' (ii. 27, xii. 5), out of whose mouth a sharp sword proceeds (xix. 15), and who 'treads the winepress of the fierceness of the wrath of Almighty God' (xix. 15). 'Lord of lords, and King of kings' (xvii. 14, xix. 16), He is the divinely appointed agent of the Messianic judgement (i. 7, xiv. 14, 18–20, xix. 11–16, xxii. 12).

All these dignities and prerogatives are assigned to the One whom the Seer loves to describe as 'Jesus'.

3. There can be no doubt that the Exalted Christ is pictured as the divine Son of God. The actual phrase 'Son of God' is used once only: 'These things says the Son of God, who has his eyes like a flame of fire' (ii. 18); but Sonship is implied in the frequent references to the Father. Thus, the writer speaks of 'his God and Father' (i. 6). In sayings ascribed to Him He speaks of 'my Father'

, 21), and in xiv. 1 the hundred and forty-four
and with the Lamb on Mount Zion and are
ed as 'having his name, and the name of his
Father' written on their foreheads. In xix. 13 He is
spoken of as 'the Word of God', by which name we are to
understand, not the Logos, but the warrior figure described in Wisdom xviii. 15f.:

'Thine all-powerful word leaped from heaven out of the
royal throne,
A stern warrior, into the midst of the doomed land,
Bearing as a sharp sword thine unfeigned commandment'.

A pregnant phrase is used in iii. 14, when Christ is
said to be 'the beginning of the creation of God'. R. H.
Charles interprets this to mean that He is 'the active
principle in creation'.[1] He thinks that the author was
probably acquainted with the Epistle to the Colossians
and may be indebted to Col. i. 18 where Christ is said to
be 'the beginning' and to Col. i. 15 which speaks of Him
as 'the firstborn of all creation'. Christ, however, is not
designated the Creator, for this function is assigned to
God (iv. 11, xiv. 7). How high is His dignity is seen in
passages which describe Him as sitting upon God's
throne (iii. 21, vii. 17, xxii. 1, 3) and as receiving worship
(v. 12f.) like the worship addressed to God (iv. 11). We
have only to recall the horror with which St. Paul contemplates the thought of Antichrist exalting himself 'so
that he sits in the temple of God, setting himself forth as
God' (2 Thess. ii. 4) to appreciate the height of the
Seer's Christology. The same divine rank is assigned to
Christ when He is pictured as the High Priest 'clothed
with a garment down to the foot, and girt about at the
breasts with a golden girdle' (i. 13), and when He is
described no less than twenty-eight times as 'the Lamb',

[1] *Op. cit.*, 94.

at once the sacred Victim (v. 6, 12, xii. 11, xiii. 8) and the divine Leader of men (vii. 17, xiv. 1, 4, v. 6).

Significantly, Old Testament passages which refer to God are applied to Christ, including the description of the Ancient of Days in Dan. vii. 9 (i. 14f.), and Jer. xvii. 10 and Psa. lxii. 9 in the saying of ii. 23, 'I am he who searches the reins and the heart'. Further, the Spirit, mentioned in ii. 7, 11, 17, 29, iii. 6, 13, 22, is in some sense the Spirit of Christ. The Exalted Christ speaks, but the message is 'He that has an ear, let him hear what *the Spirit* says to the Churches' (ii. 7). All these indications show that Christ occupies in the writer's thought a transcendent place as compared with that of men and of angels. His Person is divine.

4. High though the Christology of the Apocalypse is, it is transitional in character, in the sense that it raises questions to which the Seer gives no answer, and which may not have been present in his mind. The doctrine of the Spirit is a case in point. Is the Spirit, for example, identical with the Exalted Christ? Or, on the other hand, is the apparent identity due to the fact that the relationship between the two has not yet been made the subject of reflection? So far as we know the Seer from his writing, we should conclude that the latter is the case. He is a religious genius, but not a theologian, and the implications of his Christology still await discussion. The same conclusion is suggested by the element of subordination in the relationships of the Son to the Father. Although a divine status is ascribed to Christ, the revelation which the Seer sees and records is the revelation 'which God *gave* to him to show to his servants' (i. 1). Christ has sat down with His Father on His throne; but the reason given is that He has *prevailed*: 'As I also overcame, and sat down with my Father in his throne'

(iii. 21). Further, while the Exalted Christ is 'the beginning of the creation of God' (iii. 14), God Himself is the Creator (iv. 11, xiv. 7) as He is also the Judge (xx. 11–15). We should wrong the Seer if we described these features in his writing as contradictions; they are unresolved tensions in his religious thinking comparable to those we may find in our own thought and worship. Worship, in particular, is always theology in solution, and it may be continued long before the hour of crystallization draws near. Rich as the Christology of the Apocalypse is, it cries out for a still richer Christology which faces the problem of the doctrine of God raised by its claims concerning Christ.

APPENDIX:
THE CATEGORIES OF
LORDSHIP AND SONSHIP

Our investigation has shown how markedly the categories of Lordship and Sonship stand out in New Testament teaching concerning Christ. It will therefore be of advantage to set out in tabular form a summary of the uses of the names 'Lord' and 'Son' in all the New Testament writings together with the combinations into which these names enter. In this way it will be possible to set the facts of distribution before the eye, and to see how far suggestions already made are illustrated and what further inquiries remain to be considered.

Complete accuracy in the tables is not possible in view of textual uncertainties in a number of cases and difficulties of interpretation in others. This limitation applies especially to the name 'Lord'. Sometimes 'Christ' or 'God' appears as a variant reading, and especially in St. James, St. Jude, and Second Peter it is not easy to determine whether the name is being used of God or of Jesus Christ. Fortunately in the final results some of these disabilities cancel themselves out, with the result that the tables may be used with confidence in studying the issues that are involved. The value of this method of approach is great. A welcome degree of objectivity is provided in a field in which subjectivity and imagination are often given too free a rein.

Several comments upon this table must be made.

1. The number of these designations, amounting in all to 345, is remarkable. They are manifestly primitive

THE USE OF THE NAME 'LORD' IN THE NEW TESTAMENT WRITINGS

	The Lord	The Lord Jesus	The Lord Jesus Christ	Our Lord	Our Lord Christ	Our Lord Jesus Christ	Jesus Christ Our Lord	Christ Jesus Our Lord	Jesus Our Lord	Our Lord Jesus
Mt.	1									
Mk.	1									
Lk.	19?									
Jn.	9									
Ac.	26	13	2			1				
Rom.	16	1	2		1	4	3	2	2	1
1 Cor.	46	2	1			6	1	1	1	2
2 Cor.	17	2	2			2				1
Gal.	2		1			2				
Eph.	16	1	2			4		1		
Phil.	10	1	3					1		
Col.	10	1			1	1		1		
1 Thess.	12	3	1			4				3
2 Thess.	7	2	5			4				2
Phm.	2	1	2							
1 Tim.	1			1		2		2		
2 Tim.	11			1				1		
Tit.										
Heb.	2			1						1
Jas.	4		1			1				
1 Pet.	3					1				
2 Pet.	3		1			5				
1 Jn.										
2 Jn.										
3 Jn.										
Jude						3	1			
Apoc.	4	1								
	222	28	23	3	2	40	5	9	3	10

Christian names, and in their use St. Paul fully shares. Yet, while primitive, they do not belong to the period covered by the life and ministry of Jesus. The evidence in favour in Mark and Matthew is tenuous, if it exists at all. In Luke the use of the name is editorial and in John it is traditional. It springs into existence at the Resurrection and spreads far and wide throughout the Christian communities.

2. Almost three-fifths of the record in the table covers the use of the name 'the Lord'. The bareness of the name has perhaps not sufficiently been esteemed. When used of kings and pagan divinities the personal name is commonly added, although this is not always the case; but in relation to Jesus the title in the vast majority of cases stands by itself. Everywhere Christians knew who was meant by 'the Lord' in spite of the fact that in the Septuagint it so frequently designates God. Had it been simply taken over from Greek religion we should expect a fuller use of personal characterizations in order to distinguish, for example, 'the Lord Jesus Christ' from 'the Lord Sarapis' and other divinities.

3. The personal designations actually used are of much interest. 'Jesus' altogether outnumbers 'Christ', being found forty-one times without the addition of 'Christ', while 'Christ' without 'Jesus' appears but twice. This 'human' name derives cultic significance by its association with 'Lord', and this is also true of the seventy-seven cases in which 'Jesus Christ' or 'Christ Jesus' is used. That these designations breathe the atmosphere of worship is probable. Their strongly communal character is suggested by the frequency of the pronominal adjective 'Our' which appears seventy-two times. Christians knew that, as He belonged to them, so they belonged to Him, and that this common relationship belonged to all the members of the community.

4. The distribution of these names among the New Testament writers is a matter of much interest and importance. In this volume St. Paul's frequent use of this terminology has been noted repeatedly. In his ten Epistles he uses 'the Lord' 138 times and this name in other combinations 84 times. The terms are also common in 1 and 2 Timothy, although their complete ab-

sence from Titus is surprising. Less common in 1 Peter in consequence of the writer's preference for more personal names, they appear with relative frequency in the later Catholic Epistles, St. James, St. Jude, and 2 Peter, thus providing an impressive proof of their popularity well on into the second century. Far and wide and both early and late the terminology of Lordship persists in the Primitive Church. All the more astonishing is the marked break in the record, to which attention has already been drawn, in the Epistle to the Hebrews and the Johannine writings. The four examples in the former and the complete absence of this terminology in the Johannine Epistles stand out in the table; and, as previously maintained, the Fourth Gospel is in virtual agreement with the Epistles since its references to 'the Lord' are traditional and belong to the post-Resurrection period. The same situation appears in the Apocalypse. Here there are only five examples over against the many full and descriptive phrases used of Christ.

The significance of the facts here recorded can be fully esteemed only when a complementary table illustrating the terminology of Sonship is supplied. This table is given below. It must, however, be added, even at the risk of repetition, that the vocabulary of Lordship, although less colourful in appearance, is anything but colourless in content. For those who have ears to hear it is also full of echoes, the Hallelujahs of personal devotion and the peals of corporate worship.

1. The table shows how delusive statistics can be without adequate consideration of all the relevant facts. No examples are listed in 2 Thessalonians, Philippians, and Philemon, and only one each in Ephesians, Colossians and 1 Thessalonians. The fact that St. Paul uses this terminology seventeen times, especially the phrase 'His

THE USE OF THE NAME 'SON' IN THE NEW TESTAMENT WRITINGS

	The Son of God	The Son	His Son	A Son	My Son	The Only Begotten Son	His Only Begotten Son	Thy Son
Mt.	9	4			2			
Mk.	5	1			2			
Lk.	6	3			2			
Jn.	8	16				2	1	1
Ac.	1				1			
Rom.	1		6					
1 Cor.		1	1					
2 Cor.	1							
Gal.	1		3					
Eph.	1							
Col.		1						
1 Thess.			1					
2 Thess.								
Phil.								
Phm.								
1 Tim.								
2 Tim.								
Tit.								
Heb.	4	1		5	2			
Jas.								
1 Pet.								
2 Pet.					1			
1 Jn.	7	6	8				1	
2 Jn.		2						
3 Jn.								
Jude								
Apoc.	1							
	45	35	19	5	10	2	2	1

Son' (11 times), shows that it is a marked characteristic feature in his usage and at the same time illustrates further that dependence upon primitive Christianity already revealed in the number and variety of names belonging to the category of Lordship.

2. It would be a mistake to infer that, because there are no examples of the terminology of Sonship in the Pastoral Epistles, 1 Peter, St. James, and St. Jude, and only two

in the Acts, and one each in 2 Peter and the Apocalypse, the first Christians did not think of Christ as 'the Son of God'. The communal origin of some of the Pauline examples, notably Rom. i. 3f., is highly probable. Moreover, editorial passages in the Synoptic Gospels, in Mt. viii. 29, xiv. 33, xvi. 16, xxvi. 63, xxvii. 40, 43, and xxviii. 19, in Mk. i. 1 and iii. 11, and in Lk. i. 35, iv. 41, and perhaps also in the phraseology of Mk. v. 7, xv. 39, xiv. 61, and their parallels, suggest that these titles had long been current at the time when the Gospels were written.

3. Nevertheless, the paucity of these references to Christ's Sonship in the writings mentioned strongly supports the positive evidence supplied by the first table that 'Lord' in its various combinations was by choice and preference the habitual usage of primitive Christianity both early and late. Christians in general knew that Christ was 'the Son of God', but they preferred to call Him 'Lord'.

4. 'The Son' and its cognate expressions are distinctively, although not exclusively, the designations of the great New Testament writers. Hebrews has these names twelve times as compared with four examples of 'Lord'. The Fourth Gospel, with twenty-eight examples of the former as against nine, and the Johannine Epistles, with twenty-four as compared with none, reveal a strong preference for the terminology of Sonship. The Apocalypse stands nearer primitive usage, but it reflects the theology of the Johannine 'school' by its abundant and high-sounding Christological phrases. St. Paul's usage is transitional and significant. As we have seen, he has 'Lord', in agreement with primitive custom, 222 times, as compared with 17 passages in which he speaks of Christ as 'Son'. But these passages register a contrast

with primitive usage. He shows a desire to insist that 'the Lord' is also 'the Son of God'. His use of the phrase 'His Son' breathes a sense of awe, as in Rom. viii. 32, 'He that spared not his own Son, but delivered him up for us all, how shall he not also with him freely give us all things'. An explanation of this emphasis by the New Testament writers upon Sonship has already been suggested in the need for fuller teaching. Many problems, however, arise which will manifestly demand further consideration in Part II, when the special contribution of St. Paul, St. John, and the writer of Hebrews is under discussion.

5. One point of the greatest importance must be noted. The table does not supply the full evidence for the New Testament use of the idea of Sonship. The items listed amount to no more than 119 as compared with 345 in the first table. But it would be highly misleading to say that in the New Testament Lordship is ascribed to Christ three times as often as Sonship is predicated of Him. To the direct uses cited we must add the tacit evidence supplied by the name 'Father' in cases where this name suggests 'Son' as its correlative. This evidence is summarized in the third table given below.

6. Meantime one contrast must be mentioned with the use of the name 'the Lord'. After full allowance is made for the presence of editorial passages in the Synoptic Gospels, it is clear that, according to our earliest sources, Q and Mark, Jesus spoke of Himself as 'the Son' (Mk. i. 11, xiii. 32, Lk. x. 22 = Mt. xi. 27). This question also will be considered in Part II. Meantime it is a fact of importance that, if the genuineness of these sayings is accepted, Sonship has a dominical basis. Lordship is ascribed to Him because He rose from the dead: Sonship because of what He was and taught.

THE USE OF THE NAME 'FATHER' IN THE NEW TESTAMENT WRITINGS

	The Father	My Father	Father (voc.)	Abba Father	His Father	Our Father	Thy Father	Your Father	Their Father	One Father
Mt.	4	14	4		1	1	5	14	1	
Mk.	1			1	1			1		
Lk.	3	4	6					4		
Jn.	82	25	9		1		1	2		1
Ac.	3									
Rom.	2			1		1				
1 Cor.	2					1				
2 Cor.	3					1				
Gal.	2			1		1				
Eph.	7					1				
Phil.	1					2				
Col.	3					1				
1 Thess.	1					3				
2 Thess.	1					2				
Phm.						1				
1 Tim.	1									
2 Tim.	1									
Tit.	1									
Heb.	1									
Jas.	2					1				
1 Pet.	3									
2 Pet.	1									
1 Jn.	12									
2 Jn.	4									
Jude	1									
Apoc.		3			2					
	142	46	19	3	5	16	6	21	1	1

1. Of these 260 examples many of those in the first five columns are relevant for our purpose. 'My Father', 'Father' in the vocative, 'Abba Father', and 'His Father', 73 in all, seem to imply 'Son' as a correlative. Of the 142 passages which speak of 'The Father' some also mention the Son. Of those which do not expressly refer to Him not a few imply that Christ is the Son, especially in salutations in the Epistles, in the Fourth Gospel, and 1 and 2 John, but it is impossible to enumerate these cases

since identification is conjectural. What can be asserted with confidence is the probability that Christ is often regarded as 'the Son' in many passages where He is not expressly designated as such.

2. It is further apparent from the table as a whole that the question of the Fatherhood of God bears intimately upon Christ's Sonship both as regards His own teaching and the beliefs of the New Testament writers. These points with many others must be taken up and discussed in Part II.

some determination is conceivable. What can be asserted with confidence is the probability that Christ is often regarded as the Son, in many passages where He is not expressly designated such.

2. It is further apparent from the table as a whole that the question of the Fatherhood of God bears intimately upon Christ's sonship, both as regards His own teaching and the Reports of the New Testament writers. These points, with many others, must be taken up and discussed in Part II.

PART II
HISTORICAL AND THEOLOGICAL

INTRODUCTION

In Part II the main interests will be historical and theological. An attempt will be made to discuss the implications of the exegetical conclusions reached in Part I. Historical questions are necessarily bound up with this inquiry, but the principal aim is to consider what the teaching of the New Testament means and the nature of its contribution to the doctrine of the Person of Christ.

Our first task must be to examine, within the limits open to us, the emergence of the divine consciousness of Jesus. What did He mean when He described Himself as the Son of God, and in what manner did this consciousness arise? Secondly, we must look more closely at the Christology of the primitive Christian communities and attempt to estimate its limitations as well as its strength. Thirdly, and against this background, it will be necessary to discuss the importance of the contribution of the great New Testament writers, St. Paul, the writer of Hebrews, and St. John, the bearings of their teaching concerning Christ's Work upon His Person, and the consequent effect of both upon the doctrine of God. Fourthly, this purpose will compel us to consider the Christological aspects of the Trinity, particularly in the light of recent discussions, and, further, to examine the hypothesis of the Kenosis, its merits and the objections which have been brought against it. Finally, a modern statement of the doctrine of the Person of Christ cannot be avoided, in spite of the fact that in this matter our reach must always exceed our grasp, in order to state the hypothesis which seems most in harmony with New Testament teaching as a whole.

XIII

THE DIVINE CONSCIOUSNESS
OF JESUS

I

I HAVE chosen this title with some care. The older subject for these discussions is 'the Messianic Consciousness of Jesus', as we may still see in Bultmann's *Theology of the New Testament*. This title, however, is open to objection. We have seen how little Jesus esteemed current Messianic ideas and was never happy with the name 'Christ'. He had, it is true, His own conception of Messiahship, but it was so totally different from anything which had been conceived under that designation that a better approach is called for. He tacitly accepted the title 'Christ' when it was addressed to Him by Peter, and when challenged by Caiaphas, but in the former case He replaced it by the name 'Son of Man' and in the latter He said, in effect, 'That is how you put it'. 'You will see', He said, 'the Son of Man sitting at the right hand of power and coming with the clouds of heaven' (Mk. xiv. 62). I propose, therefore, to abandon the phrase 'Messianic Consciousness', except in so far as it is included in the bolder and more comprehensive expression 'the Divine Consciousness of Jesus'. By this phrase I mean the sense in which He was conscious of being more than a man, of sharing during His earthly existence in the life of Deity itself. This putting of the question has the advantage of raising the central issue.

The difficulty of the inquiry is apparent from the outset. Every man's personality has its mysteries. It is only approximately, and with inevitable differences of opinion, that we can understand the mind of any great figure of the past. When, however, we consider a personality which, while truly human, transcends human categories, the attempt to describe His self-consciousness seems desperate. It is certainly foredoomed to failure if we expect to do more than apprehend a mystery we cannot solve. Many New Testament scholars hold that the difficulty is increased by the fragmentary character of the historical sources in the Gospels. I have repeatedly faced this problem,[1] and here can only repeat my conviction that this difficulty is over-rated, and that we possess in the Gospels material which ultimately rests on the testimony of eyewitnesses. The evidence is interpreted, but not distorted, by the life and worship of the earliest Christian communities, although naturally the tradition has suffered in discernible respects from the inevitable consequences of exposition and transmission. In the sayings and parables of Jesus we possess much more direct information than is available for the study of the personality of Socrates. It is, of course, fair to reply that for belief in a divine-human personality we require far more compelling testimony than is necessary to establish the greatness of Socrates, but this testimony we possess in the Gospels and in the Epistles which reflect the life and worship of the primitive Christian communities. Outstanding in the early sources are the sayings which speak of the divine Sonship of Jesus: the assurance which came to Him at His Baptism that He was God's beloved Son (Mk. i. 11, cf. ix. 7), the saying concerning the mutual knowledge of the Father and the Son (Lk. x. 22 = Mt. xi. 27), and the saying in which Jesus denies knowledge of the day or hour of His Parousia (Mk. xiii. 32).

[1] Recently in *The Life and Ministry of Jesus* (1954), 25–34.

These important sayings will be considered in due course, but it is mistaken procedure to isolate them, since their genuineness is contested by many critics. In these circumstances it is better to examine them in a wider context of ideas. Chief among these are the significance of the use by Jesus of the name 'Son of Man' with reference to Himself; His consciousness of being at victorious odds with Satan and the powers of darkness; His sovereign use of the Old Testament, including His majestic 'But I say unto you'; His 'mighty works'; His teaching concerning the Spirit; and, above all, His conception of His redemptive ministry as the Suffering Servant of the Lord. It is in such a context as this that the sayings about His divine Sonship appear in a true and convincing light.

1. The title 'Son of Man' was discussed in *The Names of Jesus*,[1] and in *The Life and Ministry of Jesus*[2] an attempt was made to expound its historical significance. Here our interest is centred, not so much in its communal aspects, but rather in its Christological implications when it describes Jesus as the Head of the Messianic community and the Future Judge and Lord of mankind. What is meant when He declares that He will be seen sitting at the right hand of God and coming with the clouds of heaven (Mk. xiv. 62)? It is probable that too little consideration has been given to the eschatological implications of Christ's lordship. He is the Head of the elect community, not merely as its president and leader, but as its Lord and King, a conception fully grasped by the first Christians when in worship they cried, '*Marana tha*', 'Our Lord, come' (1 Cor. xvi. 22). The suggestion of a future superhuman dignity essentially belongs to the idea of the Son of Man as an eschatological figure, and

[1] Pp. 25-35.   [2] Pp. 70-7.

when the genuineness of the sayings in which it is expressed is accepted, a divine consciousness to this extent must be attributed to Jesus. The same suggestion is conveyed in Mk. xii. 35–7 when, in reply to His own question, 'How say the scribes that the Messiah is the Son of David?', Jesus quotes Psa. cx. 1, 'The Lord said to my lord, Sit thou on my right hand until I make thy enemies the footstool of thy feet', as words spoken by David 'in the Holy Spirit', and then presses the question, 'And whence is he his son?' The implication is that He is infinitely more. As David's Lord He is not merely David's son. This polemical question is no mere exegetical wrangle: it is a glimpse into the mind of Jesus Himself and is a testimony to His sense of Sonship.

2. A more than human consciousness is further suggested if Jesus is the binder of Satan, the One who has entered into the house of the strong man and spoiled his goods (Mk. iii. 27, cf. Lk. xi. 21f.). Commentators[1] are divided upon the question whether God or Jesus Himself has bound 'the strong man', but the opinion is probably right that in the context in which the saying stands (cf. Lk. xi. 20) Jesus Himself has bound Satan before He frees his victims by His exorcisms.[2] It does not seem justifiable to attribute this conception to the later Christian community.[3] The exorcisms themselves, however we explain their nature, bespeak this consciousness of victory, just as Lk. xxii. 53 and the story of the Temptation reveal the sense of a death grapple with the powers of evil. It is difficult to believe that in this conflict the experience of Jesus is comparable with that of Luther in his cell or with the struggles of the hermits of the Egyptian deserts. In

[1] Cf. V. Taylor, *The Gospel according to St. Mark*, 241.
[2] Cf. E. Percy, *Die Botschaft Jesu*, 182.
[3] Cf. Percy, *op. cit.*, 185.

this warfare He is active, the attacker as well as the attacked, the foe of Satan and all his powers. Since in eschatological thought the downfall of Satan is the act of God, the activity of Jesus against evil powers is involved in His sense of Sonship. It is a part of His mission as the Son of Man.

3. Another aspect of the consciousness of Jesus is revealed in His attitude to the Law of Moses. He does not hesitate to attribute the teaching of the Law regarding divorce to the hardness of men's hearts and to speak, contrary to Jewish teaching, of adultery against the wife (Mk. x. 5, 11): and St. Mark brings out the implications of His teaching concerning things clean and unclean by the laconic comment, 'This he said, making all meats clean' (Mk. vii. 19). Above all, in the Sermon on the Mount He sets over against what had been said in the Law to men of old time His royal word, 'But I say unto you' (Mt. v. 21–48). The older exegetes made much of this phrase, and with the fuller knowledge of the Rabbinic literature in modern times it has lost nothing of its force. Although He held the Law in high regard (cf. Mt. v. 17), Jesus was bold to exercise on occasion the functions of a second Moses, an attitude which is reflected both in the Synoptics and in the Fourth Gospel (Jn. vi. 32 f.). The exercise of this prerogative is prophetic, but in degree it transcends the normal functions of a prophet and is harmonious with other aspects of His personality under discussion. He speaks with an authority recognized with astonishment by His hearers as different from that of the scribes (Mk. i. 22, cf. Jn. vii. 46), an authority seen in deed as well as in word (Mk. xi. 28). It is an authority grounded in His Person.

4. The same unearthly quality is seen in His 'mighty works'. We are grateful for all the evidence supplied by

modern psychotherapy[1] pointing to the power of mind over body, which is so abundant that the credibility of the healing miracles is no longer disputed. But the differences are more striking than the similarities. Jesus heals with a word (Mk. i. 41) and a touch (Mk. i. 31), and even when His garment is grasped (Mk. v. 28f.). The Evangelists find it natural to think of power (*dynamis*) proceeding from Him. St. Luke says expressly, 'The power of the Lord was with him to heal' (v. 17), and St. Matthew finds it appropriate to cite the Servant passage, 'Himself took our infirmities, and bore our diseases' (viii. 17, cf. Isa. liii. 4). These judgements are credible, for the healings are acts of power and not merely cases of suggestion. Scholars who accept the historical character of the so-called 'nature-miracles' (Mk. iv. 35–41, vi. 35–44, 45–52, etc.) and of the narratives of the raising of the dead (Mk. v. 35–43, Lk. vii., 11–17, Jn. xi. 1–44) explain these incidents also as works of divine power. Those, on the other hand, who interpret these narratives as embellishments of the original tradition, not for theological reasons but on grounds of literary criticism, cannot make this claim, but even they must concede that the stories attest the powerful impression which Jesus left on the minds of eyewitnesses as a worker of miracles. The older apologetic, which based upon miracles, as also upon prophecy, the proof that Jesus was divine, tended to ignore the real critical difficulties, but the modern approach, which dismisses the stories as products of mythological fancy, is no more satisfactory unless it presses on to inquire the meaning of the narratives.[2] Jesus accomplished mighty works, to which adequate parallels have not been found, with an ease and certainty which bespeak a consciousness

---

[1] Cf. E. R. Micklem, *Miracles and the New Psychology* (1922).
[2] Cf. Bultmann, *Kerygma and Myth*, ed. H. W. Bartsch (1954), 11.

transcending the ordinary powers of human personality.

5. What is to be said of the relationship of Jesus to the Holy Spirit? The question is not easy to answer. In *The Holy Spirit and the Gospel Tradition* C. K. Barrett argues that the eschatological thought of Jesus, so far as this may be known, accounts for His silence regarding the Spirit.[1] To speak of His own plenary inspiration, or unmistakably reveal it, he maintains, would have meant the betrayal of the Messianic secret.[2] As the Messiah, Jesus was 'the bearer of the Spirit', but in Him its presence was veiled.[3] There is much force in this suggestion, for on the whole British scholarship has acted too negatively to the challenge of W. Wrede in *Das Messiasgeheimnis in den Evangelien*.[4] Jesus had His own Messianic secret. This fact may account for the paucity of His references to the Spirit, whose outpouring was to be a sign of the dawn of the Messianic Age. It is difficult, however, to believe that He made no references to the Spirit in relation to Himself and the future of His disciples, since He held that in a measure the Kingdom was already present in Himself and in His mighty works. The deepseated conviction of the Christian community that at His Baptism the Spirit descended upon Him is best explained if the tradition is traced to Himself, and, further, His saying, 'If I by the finger of God cast out devils, then is the kingdom of God come upon you' (Lk. xi. 20), is a veiled allusion to the Spirit, as St. Matthew's variant, 'by the Spirit of God', suggests. It is also credible that He should have promised the aid of the Holy Spirit to His

[1] *Op. cit.*, 160.   [2] *Ibid.*   [3] *Op. cit.*, 159.

[4] I have discussed this question in two articles in *The Expository Times*, lix. 146–51, lxv. 246–50. See also *The Gospel according to St. Mark*, 122–4.

disciples when brought to judgement before a hostile tribunal, bidding them not to be anxious in advance about what they should say, and declaring, 'It is not you that speak, but the Holy Spirit' (Mk. xiii. 11).[1]

For our immediate purpose, however, the genuineness of the sayings is not of first importance. The relevant matter is that Jesus was Spirit-filled, 'the bearer of the Spirit'. In Otto's phrase He belongs, as His miracles and exorcisms show, to the 'charismatic type': His personality is 'pneumatic'.[2] We cannot say that in this respect He was unique, since St. Paul also is a 'charismatic' person,[3] but we can say that, as compared with prophets and apostles, the degree to which He is possessed by the Spirit is unique. Whether it is *sui generis* depends on our estimate of His personality as a whole. These considerations must be added to those discussed above when we seek to apprehend the nature of His consciousness.

6. We take a very decisive step when we consider His sense of vocation, His deep conviction of fulfilling a redemptive ministry as the Suffering Servant of the Lord. I have previously discussed the critical problems connected with the sayings in Mk. viii. 31, ix. 12, 31, x. 33f., 45, Lk. xvii. 25, and other passages, especially Mk. xiv. 22, 24,[4] but I should like to mention the kind of submission I have made in *New Testament Studies* on

[1] As every commentator knows, the saying on blasphemy against the Holy Spirit (Mk. iii. 28f., Mt. xii. 31f., Lk. xii. 10) raises greater exegetical difficulties, and the same is true of the post-Resurrection sayings (Mt. xxviii. 19, Lk. xxiv. 49) which reflect the beliefs of the Christian community.

[2] Cf. *The Kingdom of God and the Son of Man*, 333–81; Barrett, *op. cit.*, 113–19. Otto writes: 'That Jesus ascribed his deeds to a numinous power, and that this power, the Holy Spirit, was present in His person, can be regarded as good tradition', *op. cit.*, 380.

[3] Cf. Otto. *op. cit.*, 337–41.

[4] Cf. *The Names of Jesus*, 36f., *The Life and Ministry of Jesus*, 142–5.

'The Origin of the Markan Passion-Sayings'.[1] In this article I have suggested that the sayings ought to be considered, not only by themselves, but also against the background of New Testament teaching as a whole concerning the doctrine of the Suffering Servant. When this is done, we find that this teaching was at its height during the earliest period of primitive Christianity and that, although it continues to appear as a traditional formulation in the Pauline Epistles and in later New Testament writings, it has receded steadily into the background, except in 1 Peter, and may be said to be in eclipse. This consideration raises formidable objections against the view that the Servant passages in Mark, written about A.D. 65, are not authentic utterances of Jesus, but 'prophecies after the event' read back into the Gospel tradition. Against the opinion that it was an early addition to the teaching of Jesus stands the objection that it is more credibly explained as reflecting His own views rather than those of unknown teachers in the decades immediately following His death. Instead of pursuing this critical discussion further I propose to ask what significance it has for the Person of Jesus.

The suggestion of the Passion-sayings is that Jesus went to His Cross believing that it was an inalienable part of His Messianic vocation. His mission, as He conceived it, was that as the Son of Man He had come not to be served, but to serve, and to give His life a ransom for many (Mk. x. 45). At the Last Supper, when His disciples drank of the Cup, He said, 'This is my blood of the covenant, which is shed for many' (Mk. xiv. 24). Jeremias[2] well interprets these and other sayings when he writes, 'Such is the efficacy of the death of Jesus, for it is

---

[1] Vol. 1, no. 3, 159–67.
[2] *The Parables of Jesus* (Eng. Tr. 1954), 152f.

the vicarious death of the sinless for the sinful, a ransom (Mk. x. 45, Mt. xx. 28) and a sacrifice (Mk. xiv. 24) for the innumerable host of the redeemed'. He brings out the meaning of the Last Supper when he says, 'On the night before his death he took the opportunity of the common meal to perform the last symbolic act of his life, by offering to his own a share in the atoning efficacy of the death that awaited him'.[1]

As the history of the doctrine of the Atonement shows, many hypotheses have been put forward to explain the nature of this redemptive ministry. These do not call for discussion in our present inquiry. The point of importance for us is that, if Jesus did conceive His ministry to be vicarious, representative, and sacrificial, His consciousness is unique amongst men. No one else, no prophet, no founder of a great religion has thought of His vocation in this way. And if He thought of the elect community of the Son of Man as sharing in its atoning efficacy, as filling up, in St. Paul's words, 'that which remains over of the afflictions of Christ' 'for his body's sake which is the church' (Col. i. 24), it is not as equals or co-partners that they participate therein. Their privilege is to know the fellowship of His sufferings (Phil. iii. 10). There is in the suffering of the Son of Man a deep, mysterious, and incommunicable element, as the prayer of Gethsemane (Mk. xiv. 36) and the cry of desolation on the Cross (Mk. xv. 34) disclose, a sense of destiny which sets Him apart as the loneliest and most central figure of human history. This vocation He chose, accepted, and fulfilled. And the astonishing thing is that the idea of a destiny which in others could only be described as megalomania appears in Him as natural because it is in keeping with His whole personality. He is most Himself when

[1] *Op. cit.*, 158.

He does that which no other can contemplate. His Person and His Work are one. Here, more than anywhere else, we must recognize a consciousness not of this world, a quality of being which, however human in its manifestation, is divine.

II

Our views regarding the aspects of the life and personality of Jesus examined above cannot fail to influence our judgement concerning the sense of Sonship which is implied in His sayings. I have endeavoured not to claim for each more than it will bear in order to gain a background against which Mk. i. 11, Lk. x. 22 = Mt. xi 27, and Mk. xiii. 32 may be judged, but I recognize that the inferences I have drawn do not amount to demonstrative proof. No such proof is possible. Jesus will always remain a challenge to be met rather than a problem to be solved. One thing at least is clear; the sayings mentioned above do not stand alone. They harmonize with the tradition as a whole. This relationship I have endeavoured to illustrate, and in my submission it is so close as to suggest that in the Christ of the Gospels we are challenged by a divine Person. In order to complete this argument it is necessary to examine the sayings in which the consciousness of Sonship is directly expressed.

1. For well-known reasons I have not included Mt. xxviii. 19 in the sayings listed above. This is the saying which speaks of baptizing disciples 'into the name of the Father and of the Son and of the Holy Spirit'. By wide consent it is agreed that this terminology is that of the Evangelist's time.[1] As such, the passage is of the greatest importance, but it cannot be used as a testimony to the consciousness of Sonship possessed by Jesus. It shows

[1] Cf. *The Names of Jesus*, 55.

how He was regarded in the closing decades of the first
century.

2. Mk. i. 11, 'Thou art my beloved Son, in thee I am
well pleased', describes in language drawn from Psa. ii.
7 and Isa. xlii. 1, and in terms of an 'I-Thou' relationship,
the filial status and vocation of Jesus as God's beloved
Son.   I have maintained elsewhere[1] that the words are
best understood as an assurance, or confirmation, of this
relationship, and that the ideas are fundamentally Jewish.
The same announcement is made in the narrative of the
Transfiguration, although here in the third person (Mk.
ix. 7).   How deeply embedded in the tradition this revelation of Sonship is can be seen from the fact that it is
echoed, not only in the Synoptic parallels, but also in Ac.
xiii. 33, Heb. i. 5, v. 5, and 2 Pet. i. 17.   It is, of course,
possible to trace this tradition to the activity of the
Christian community, but this interpretation does not
rise above the level of conjecture, and the better explanation is that it reflects the experience of Jesus Himself.
He began His ministry with the conviction that He was
God's beloved Son.   If we accept, as I think we may, the
evidence of Lk. ii. 49, 'Did you not know that I must be
in my Father's house?', this knowledge, although in a form
suitable to the experience of a boy, had been His in boyhood and youth, but in His baptism it was authenticated
by God.   His thoughts were countersigned by the revelation, as He believed, of the divine voice.

3. The Q saying, Lk. x. 22 = Mt. xi. 27, speaks of the
mutual knowledge of the Father and the Son, and of the
fact that the Son can reveal the Father to others.   Only
the Son knows the Father and only the Father knows the
Son.   The text, authenticity, and meaning of this saying

[1] Cf. *The Gospel according to St. Mark*, 162; *The Life and Ministry of
Jesus*, 50f.

M

have been discussed again and again.[1]   In a recent study
Ernst Percy[2] recognizes that this logion as a whole has
no real analogies.   He says that the Hymn of Echnaton,
which contains the words, 'Thou art in my heart, no
other knows thee except thy Son, Echnaton: thou hast
initiated him into thy thoughts and into thy power', although it is the closest parallel, presents only a partial
analogy.   He suggests that, if the Logion is the authentic
expression of a unique consciousness of fellowship with
God, Jesus is the pioneer (ἀρχηγός) and forerunner
(πρόδρομος) of His people, in the sense of Heb. ii. 10 and
vi. 20, and that through Him all the elect are to share in
His Sonship.   We may doubt if this interpretation
reaches the heart of the saying, although it goes much
farther than many other evaluations of it.   The kind of
Sonship implied is more than that of a leader of men.   As
many commentators have recognized, both those who
accept and those who reject the genuineness of the saying,
it implies a Sonship which ultimately is one of nature and
being.   Whether the Sonship of Jesus is of this character
is the ultimate decision we are compelled to make.   The
terminology of the saying, however, is not philosophical,
and the suggestion that it is of Hellenistic origin has not
been established.   The ideas are Jewish and religious, but
they describe a filial relationship to which human experience furnishes no adequate parallel.

4. This view is confirmed by Mk. xiii. 32 which in
contrast with men and angels describes Christ as 'the
Son' and yet denies that He knows the day or the hour of
the Parousia.   This conjunction of ideas strongly supports the authenticity of the saying and makes the
alternative conjecture of scribal interpolation wholly improbable.

[1] Cf. *The Names of Jesus*, 60–4.   [2] *Die Botschaft Jesu*, 259–71.

5. The Synoptic sayings discussed above reveal part of the historic foundation upon which the Fourth Evangelist builds in his greatly enhanced emphasis upon the Sonship of Jesus.[1] Moreover, it is probable that he makes use of other sayings of the kind which we can no longer identify. Although his work is that of theological interpretation, it is based ultimately upon authentic utterances of Jesus. If this is so, we are entitled to use his testimony to the divine consciousness of Jesus even though we cannot determine just when he is recording, or when he is developing, historic tradition. Indeed, his work compels us to revise our conception of what historic tradition is, and not to assume that it is limited to the best attested sayings of Mark and Q. Further, in estimating the testimony of Jesus to His divine Sonship, we have also to take into account Synoptic sayings in which He speaks of 'the Father' and 'My Father', with the direct implication that He is His Son, as well as the extended emphasis upon the divine Fatherhood which is characteristic of St. Matthew and St. John.[2]

6. From the evidence as a whole we are entitled to conclude that His consciousness of divine Sonship is the key to the presentation of Jesus we find in all the Gospels. His divine consciousness is expressed in words and in deeds. It lies behind the high dignity of His role as the Son of Man, and is the presupposition of His death-grapple with evil. It accounts for the confidence with which He affirms, 'But I say unto you', His sovereign exercise of 'mighty works', His sense of being the bearer of the Spirit, and His acceptance of the vocation of the Suffering Servant of the Lord. All these things are true of Him because He knows Himself to be the Son of God.

[1] See Table 2 in the Appendix to Part I, pp. 146–51.
[2] See Table 3 in the Appendix, p. 150f.

III

Many questions arise in the mind concerning the divine consciousness of Jesus. In what manner did it emerge during the conditions of His earthly existence? Was His sense of Sonship subject to development? Was it consciously and directly operative in all that He said and did? Or was it rather the undertone and secret spring of His activity? How far did it arise by intuition and how far through revelation from on high? Was His divine consciousness always at its peak, or were there times when the great moments of revelation had to be recalled, times when for a season it was in eclipse?

Theologians have sometimes to ask questions to which they know that no complete answer can be given because they lead to realms of ultimate mystery. Not to ask these questions, however, shows a failure to face relevant issues. The origin of our Lord's consciousness of Sonship, together with the problems connected with it, is one of these.

It is easily possible to short-circuit the problems of Christology. Christians who accept the authority of Scripture and the constant witness of the Church throughout the centuries may unwittingly do this very thing. The Son, we may argue, knows who He is because He is the Son. His consciousness of Sonship is grounded in Himself; it is the inevitable expression of His divine nature. I shall return to this view later because I believe that in the end it is a conclusion to which we must come. If, however, we are to apprehend the reality of Christ's Sonship, it is important to recognize that, however great its force may be, this way of thinking reaches its conclusion too quickly and too easily because it does not give sufficient consideration to the reality of Christ's humanity.

We have seen again and again how fully the Gospels

and the Epistles attest Christ's humanity; His emotions, His fears, His disappointments, His exposure to temptation, and the limitations of His knowledge in matters not essential to His ministry. He shared traditional Jewish beliefs and uttered predictions concerning His Parousia which, in the form in which they were uttered, have not been fulfilled.

These facts are not to be accepted in a spirit of resignation. They are part of the Gospel itself concerning Him who for our sakes became poor. The facts, however, are too easily forgotten, or are insufficiently weighed, in the anxiety to insist upon the divinity of Christ; so much so that in all periods, and even to-day, docetism, the belief that the humanity was but a semblance or phantom, is the constant peril of the Church. Luther powerfully expresses the truth when he writes: 'He ate, drank, slept, waked; was weary, sorrowful, rejoicing; He wept and He laughed; He knew hunger and thirst and sweat; He talked, He toiled, He prayed ... so that there was no difference between *Him* and other men, save only this, that He was *God* and had no sin'. Emil Brunner, who cites this passage, goes so far as to say, 'The Son of God in whom we are able to believe, must be such a One that it is possible to mistake Him for an ordinary man'.[1] This opinion, I think, is an exaggeration, but it is the exaggeration characteristic of an epigram.

If the reality of the humanity, and of the limitations attendant upon it, are recognized fully, the questions we are considering cannot be ignored. Granted that Christ knows Himself to be the Son of God because of His divine nature, it must still be asked, 'In what way did this consciousness emerge, and what factors and circumstances contributed to its emergence?'

[1] *The Mediator*, 341.

XIV

THE EMERGENCE OF THE DIVINE CONSCIOUSNESS OF JESUS

GENERAL considerations and the testimony of Lk. ii. 52 suggest that the divine consciousness of Jesus was subject to growth and development. He 'advanced in wisdom and in stature, and in favour with God and men'. He can speak of 'my Father' at the age of twelve (Lk. ii. 49) in words which reveal a sense of Sonship, but it would be difficult to believe that this relationship has the depth and intimacy of later years and to deny that it was preceded by still simpler thoughts and by a period during infancy when there was no knowledge of Sonship at all. If this is so, the question of the emergence of His divine consciousness is a legitimate field for meditation. Even if no more than tentative suggestions can be offered, the problem itself cannot be brushed aside, since it is bound up with the factual situation presented to us in the Gospels of a divine Sonship associated with a truly human life. Under what circumstances, we may ask, did this consciousness disclose itself upon the historical plane?

I

1. Certain negative observations must first be made. It is unthinkable that Jesus spoke of Himself as 'the Son' under the influence of Greek religious ideas. No one indeed has suggested any such thing, since at no point during His ministry was He in contact with the Hellenistic spirit apart from the architecture of the Herods and

the pagan associations of Tiberias and the Gentile popu-
lations beyond Galilee. Improbable also, as a formative
factor in His unique consciousness, is Jewish religious
teaching. It is for this reason that some scholars claim
that the title 'the Son' has only Messianic significance
and is equivalent in content to the name 'the King of
Israel'. In later times the name 'Son' in Psa. ii. 7, 'Thou
art my son; this day have I begotten thee', was interpreted Messianically by some of the Rabbis,[1] but even
if this view was current in the first century, the filial consciousness of Jesus has no real parallel in Jewish thought.
'No evidence is forthcoming', writes Jeremias, 'for the
application of the title "Son of God" to the Messiah in
pre-Christian Palestinian Judaism'.[2]

In these circumstances one of two conclusions must be
drawn. Either the title was read back into early Gospel
tradition from the theology of the Christian community,
or its use by Jesus was original and creative. The former
possibility I have discussed and rejected as unjust to the
sayings on exegetical grounds. That the thought of
Jesus was creative is in harmony with His re-interpreta-
tion of Jewish teaching and is probable in itself if good
reasons can be given for its presence in His sayings. If
this view is taken, it becomes necessary to inquire, so far
as we can, how the consciousness of Sonship arose within
the limitations of our Lord's humanity. In this inquiry
it will be helpful to distinguish different levels in the
consciousness, the knowledge of a unique Sonship attested
in Mk. i. 11 and Lk. x. 22 = Mt. xi. 27 and the Sonship
implied in Lk. ii. 49 and perhaps also in Mk. xiii. 32, that

---

[1] Cf. Billerbeck, *Kommentar*, iii. 19f.
[2] *The Parables of Jesus*, 57. Jeremias points out that Eth. Enoch 105,
2 is an interpolation and that *filius meus* of the Latin version of 4 Ezra vii.
2i f., xiii. 32, 37, 52 is a rendering of παῖς μου, 'my servant'.

is to say, in the less ecstatic and more usual experiences of Jesus. This hazardous path we must tread even though it leads to the bounds of ultimate mystery.

2. The suggestion that lies most readily to hand is that the sense of Sonship in the thought of Jesus is intimately connected with His knowledge of the Fatherhood of God and was mediated by frequent and deep communion with Him during hours of prayer and meditation. It might, of course, be argued that He was influenced by such Old Testament passages as Ex. iv. 22 and Hos. xi. 1, where the name 'son' is used of Israel, and 2 Sam. vii. 14 and Psa. lxxxix. 26f., where it is applied to kings. The idea of Messianic kingship, it might be suggested, was the path which led to a richer and more intimate sense of Sonship. Evidence to support this suggestion, however, is wanting. It suffers also from the objection that the implied process of thought is exegetical rather than personal and religious. The consciousness of Sonship was reached in experience rather than by argument and inference. It was a discovery, not a deduction.

At first sight it might appear that the doctrine of the Fatherhood of God does not hold out much promise of progress in the inquiry we are undertaking. Did not Jesus take over, doubtless with a deeper emphasis, contemporary Jewish teaching concerning God as 'Our Heavenly Father', and was not His ampler presentation of this doctrine the constant element in His message? As is well known, Harnack included 'God the Father and the infinite value of the human soul' as one of the three major themes of Jesus' teaching.[1] Speaking of the name 'Father' Dalman wrote, 'Jesus adopted this term for God from the popular usage of His time'.[2] This view is widely taken for granted. So much so that most readers

[1] *What is Christianity?*, 52. [2] *The Words of Jesus*, 188.

of the Gospels, influenced above all by the Matthaean Sermon on the Mount and the Gospel of St. John, are convinced that from first to last Jesus repeatedly spoke of God as 'the Father' or 'Your heavenly Father', although not, by including Himself in the designation, as 'Our Father', a fact, of course, which is highly significant. I suggest that, without important qualifications, neither the statement of Dalman nor the common assumption will stand close investigation, and still less the submission of Harnack.[1] There was a unique element in the teaching of Jesus regarding the Fatherhood of God, and it was much less a familiar theme in His sayings than we have been led to suppose.

3. The observations of T. W. Manson upon this question in *The Teaching of Jesus* (1931) and *The Sayings of Jesus* (1949)[2] have not received the attention by theologians, which they deserve, for they bear intimately upon the problem we are considering. Dr. Manson does full justice to Jewish teaching about the Fatherhood of God, but he shows from a close study of the Gospel sources how distinctive the usage of Jesus was. In *The Teaching of Jesus* he supplies very significant statistics bearing upon the use of the name 'Father' by Jesus. He summarizes the examples as follows: 'Mk. 4; Q 8 or 9; M 23 at the outside; L 6; John 107'.[3] Along with these examples he lists 39 in the Pauline Epistles, 16 in 1 and 2 John, and from 1 to 4 in each of the other books of the New Testament. 'It is the Johannine writings primarily', he observes, 'which have made "Father" the natural name of God for Christian people'.[4] As regards 17 examples in

<hr />

[1] Cf. Professor H. F. D. Sparks, *Studies in the Gospels* (ed. D. E. Nineham), 260.

[2] First published in *The Mission and Message of Jesus* (1937).

[3] *Op. cit.*, 99.   [4] Ibid.

the Sermon on the Mount he points out that some of them are plainly editorial. He concludes that the constant emphasis in Matthew and in John on the divine Father-hood is 'an attempt to bring out clearly what appeared to these writers to be the essence of the Gospel'.[1] They do not introduce a new doctrine; 'They rather proclaim from the housetops what, in the more primitive documents, is whispered in the ear'.[2] Mark and Q reveal a disinclina-tion on the part of Jesus to speak of the Fatherhood of God at all except during the latest period of the ministry, and then only to a limited circle of hearers.[3] This re-ticence, it is claimed, arises out of the fact that for Jesus the doctrine was not 'a theological commonplace'; it points to the intense reality and deep sacredness of the experience itself and to the true humanity of Jesus.[4]

These submissions of Dr. Manson are, or ought to be, familiar to us, but I fear we have not yet realized their Christological importance. Any deductions from the pre-sentation of the facts, which may be thought necessary, do not destroy their significance. For example, it may be contended that the Synoptic sources are of limited range and that previous to Caesarea Philippi other sayings of the kind may have been current in oral tradition, some of which are reflected in Matthew and John. Even so the gap between the relatively few examples of the use of the name 'Father' in Mark, Q, and L and the flood of sayings in John remains.

No less important are Dr. Manson's comments on Mt. vi. 9, 'Our Father which art in heaven' in *The Sayings of Jesus*.[5] Acknowledging his indebtedness to G. Kittel,[6] he points out that in speaking of God Jesus used the Ara-

---

[1] *Op. cit.*, 100.   [2] *Op. cit.*, 100.   [3] *Op. cit.*, 101.
[4] *Op. cit.*, 108.   [5] *Op. cit.*, 168.
[6] *Die Religionsgeschichte und das Urchristentum*, 92–5.

maic word *Abba*, but in an unusual way. *Abi*, 'my father' and *abinu*, 'our father', are used of some one else's father, but *abba* of one's own father. In Jewish usage, however, *abba* is not used of God: it was felt to be unfitting to use a mode of address suitable for one's earthly father. 'Jesus abolished this distinction. He used *abba* of God and taught His followers to do the same'.[1] In this usage we see a sign of the depth and intensity of His realization of the Fatherhood of God.[2]

4. In agreement with Kittel and Manson, Professor Jeremias has expressed similar views. In *The Parables of Jesus* he refers to the statement of Chrysostom, Theodore, and Theodoret that *abba* was the word used by a young child of its father. 'It was', he writes, 'an everyday family word, which no one had ventured to use in addressing God. Jesus did so. He spoke to his heavenly Father in as childlike, trustful, and intimate a way as a little child to its father'.[3] This fact, of course, might be applied in a humanistic way. That much more is involved is seen from a recent note on *Abba* by Professor Jeremias in the *Theologische Literaturzeitung*,[4] which is all the more important because it deals with the usage of Jesus in relation to contemporary and later Jewish teaching. In pre-Christian Palestinian Judaism, he observes, the designation of God as Father, although used in the Old Testament to express the certainty of His choice of Israel, is only quite rarely attested. Later, from the first century A.D. onwards, examples increase, especially in the use of the phrase 'Heavenly Father', but for the use of the phrase 'My Father' in Jewish Palestinian literature, he submits, there is no proof until the Middle Ages. Jesus so speaks in the prayers attributed to Him, employing the word

[1] *Op. cit.*, 168.   [2] Ibid.
[3] *Op. cit.*, 134.   [4] Nr. 4 (1954), 214.

Abba (cf. Mk. xiv. 36) a diminutive from the daily speech of children.

Like Dr. Manson, Professor Jeremias maintains that the common opinion, that Jesus spoke often of God as 'Father' and made it a principal element in His teaching, will not stand examination. Jesus applied the name to God only rarely and with the greatest reserve. His use of 'My Father' (*abba*), he claims, is without analogies. He goes further and submits that an analysis of Lk. x. 22 = Mt. xi. 27, a logion remarkably Semitic in its language forms, shows that its meaning is Christological. 'This means', he says, 'that the word *abba* is a very important characteristic of the esoteric message of Jesus'.[1]

These views are not necessarily in conflict with the evidence of the Rabbinical writings regarding the place of the Fatherhood of God in early Judaism.[2] 'The term "Father"; writes S. Schechter,[3] 'or "Our Father who is in heaven" or "My Father who is in heaven", is one of the most frequent in the Jewish Prayer Book and the subsequent liturgy'. We may say as much of the later New Testament writings. The difficulty is to establish beyond dispute the usage and thought of Judaism in the opening decades of the first century. The Editors of *The Beginnings of Christianity* rightly observe that the doctrine is characteristically Jewish, but they add, 'It is only by a natural and intelligible inconsistency Jewish writers spoke of any particular individual or any special class as God's son or children'.[4] The significant point for Christology is, we have seen, the peculiar intimacy of Jesus' knowledge of God as 'My Father'. On this question I. Abrahams writes, 'Jesus indeed was animated by a strong, one may

[1] *Op. cit.*, 214.

[2] Cf. G. F. Moore, *Judaism*, ii. 201–11; W. D. Davies, *Paul and Rabbinic Judaism*, 11f.

[3] *Some Aspects of Rabbinic Theology*, 54f.   [4] Vol. I. 401f.

even say unique, sense of his own relation to and unbroken intercourse with God'.[1]   It is on this fact that our present argument turns.

In the light of these interesting discussions we may infer that the striking and distinctive use of the name 'My Father' by Jesus, with all the depth of meaning He put into it, is part of the secret of His parallel use of the phrase 'the Son'. It is also the justification of the Evangelist's choice of the name 'the Son of God'. These names, and the ideas they express, developed in use *pari passu*.

5. Nevertheless, we should still lack an essential point of connexion between the names 'Father' and 'Son' if the Gospels did not supply evidence of the resort by Jesus to long hours of prayer and meditation.   It was through prayer, as well as by revelation and intuition, that He came to know Himself as 'the Son'.   The medium was religious.   We cannot think that St. Luke was mistaken when he prefaced his version of the Q saying, 'I thank thee, O Father, Lord of heaven and earth' (x. 21), with the words, 'In that same hour he rejoiced in the Holy Spirit, and said'.

In *Communion with God in the New Testament* (1953) A. R. George has discussed the theme, 'Jesus as a Man of Prayer',[2] reminding us of His constant habit of private prayer, when He withdrew from His disciples, sometimes for whole nights.[3]   His recorded prayers are few,[4] and are of the prophetic rather than the mystical type. 'They show a spirit of intimacy which among the Jews

---

[1] *Studies in Pharisaism and the Gospels*, I. 142. This passage is significant because Dr. Abrahams adds, 'But this sense of nearness is weakened for all other men when the intercourse with God is broken by the intrusion between them and God of the person of Jesus'.

[2] *Op. cit.*, 31–57.

[3] Cf. Mk. i. 35, vi. 46, Lk. iii. 21, v. 16, vi. 12, ix. 18, 28.

[4] Cf. Mt. xi. 25f.=Lk. x. 21, Mk. xiv. 36, Lk. xxiii. 34. 46.

had been unusual, but there is no trace of mystical ab-
sorption'.[1] Characteristic of these prayers is the vocative
'My Father', for 'Father' in the English version too
literally translates the Greek rendering of *abba*. M.
Black observes that it is possible that 'the Father' in the
Johannine sayings and speeches of Jesus 'reflects the
ambiguous Aramaic *abba*, "the Father" or "my Father"',
and adds, 'The latter was probably original'.[2] It may
also well be that the vocative πάτερ in the three prayers of
Jesus found in the Fourth Gospel (xi. 41f., xii. 27, xvii. 1)
is used in the sense of *abba*, 'My Father'.[3]

Apart from particular exegetical questions, upon
which opinions notoriously differ, the broad conclusion
seems justified that, in the conditions of His human
existence, it was through His knowledge of God as 'My
Father', deepened and enriched by experiences of prayer
and communion with Him, that Jesus came to know
Himself as 'the Son'. This explanation applies to the
emergence of this consciousness; it manifestly does not
account for its origin, and to this question it will be
necessary to return. Meantime, in order to have all the
available facts before us, we must take up the question of
the manner in which this consciousness manifested itself
in the earthly life of Jesus.

II

We shall best appreciate the importance of the question
how the divine consciousness of Jesus manifested itself if
we compare the evidence of the Synoptics with that of the
Fourth Gospel.

1. In the Fourth Gospel the sense of divine Sonship is
presented as a permanent and abiding experience re-

---

[1] *Op. cit.*, 57.   [2] *An Aramaic Approach to the Gospels and Acts*, 218.
[3] Cf. M.-J. Lagrange, *Évangile selon Saint Jean*, 439.

flected by the use of the term 'the Son' even in controversies with the scribes and Pharisees. In the Synoptic
Gospels, on the contrary, it is manifested for the most part
in crucial experiences, at the Baptism, during the Temptation in the wilderness, on the Mount of Transfiguration,
and in the hour when He cried, 'I thank thee, O Father,
Lord of heaven and earth' (Lk. x. 21). It emerges, that
is to say, in times of special insight and exultation of
spirit. St. Luke's statement, 'He rejoiced in the Holy
Spirit', is surely an inspired editorial comment. We need
not, of course, limit the presence of the sense of Sonship
to these four examples. It is reasonable to infer the
probability of like experiences in those hours of prayer and
of lonely communion with the Father to which reference
has already been made. They may also have been
associated with His 'mighty works'. Nevertheless, the
impression we receive from the Synoptics is that there
were times when, as it were, the curve of His filial consciousness suddenly swept above the normal experiences
of His conscious life. These outstanding events have the
twofold character of divine revelation and of spiritual
intuition. The Father reveals Himself as pre-eminently
His Father and Jesus perceives that He is *His* Son and
that He is acknowledged as such by the Father. So far as
we are able to judge from the Synoptic narratives, these
experiences are occasional. They leave an abiding sense
of Sonship which is the undertone of the work of Jesus as a
healer, exorcist, and teacher, and above all of His mission
as the Suffering Son of Man. But they do not always
throb at their highest intensity, and Jesus rarely speaks of
them. They are His secret, part of the incognito which
He chooses to preserve. Moreover, as we have claimed,
this consciousness of Sonship is subject to development.
If we are right in interpreting His Baptism as the authenti-

cation of His filial consciousness, we shall think of 'the hidden years' as a growth in this knowledge (Lk. ii. 52), sealed and confirmed when the divine voice declares, 'Thou art my beloved Son; in thee I am well pleased' (Mk. i. 11). It will seem natural that His temptations turn upon the issue, 'If thou art the Son of God' (Lk. iv. 3, 9), that the narrative of the Transfiguration stands midway in the ministry (Mk. ix. 2–8), and that the cry, 'I thank thee, O Father, Lord of heaven and earth' (Lk. x. 21), is set in the same period. The knowledge that Jesus is the Son of God is present from the beginning of the ministry, but it flames out in climacteric moments which illuminate the whole. In this respect the Synoptic account, especially that of Mark and Luke, differs from the sustained emphasis which distinguishes the Johannine record.

2. If we have to choose between the Synoptic and the Johannine representations of the Sonship of Jesus in its earthly manifestation, we are compelled on historical grounds to give preference to the Synoptic account as a truer picture of events that happened. This judgement does not imply any disparagement of the Fourth Gospel, since the author avows a doctrinal purpose when he says, 'These are written, that you may believe that Jesus is the Christ, the Son of God; and that believing you may have life in his name' (xx. 31). On the contrary, we cannot be anything but grateful that in this Gospel we have a profound interpretation of the Person of Jesus, and equally because in the Synoptics we stand nearer to the facts interpreted. It is often held that Mark is also a doctrinal composition, and in important respects this opinion is true. According to the best texts St. Mark begins his Gospel with the caption, 'The beginning of the Good News about Jesus Christ, the Son of God', and in these

words he states his belief and that of the Church for which
he wrote. Further, he puts into the mouths of daemons
the confession, 'Thou art the Son of God' (iii. 11, cf. v. 7),
and he reads the confession of the centurion at the Cross,
'Truly this man was the Son of God' (xv. 39), in the full
Christian sense. But while this Gospel contains doctrine,
this fact would not supply an adequate explanation of its
actual account of the Sonship of Jesus. A Gospel which
mentions the theme so sparingly, limiting its expression
to high moments, and for the most part contenting itself
with hints, suggestions, and intimations, seems far removed from a doctrinal composition. Doubtless, in
expounding its teaching, the expositor inevitably brings
his own insight into play, and, even if aware of the peril, he
may bring out of the record more than it implies. But
his claims can always be checked by the views of others, so
that an agreed, but not undisputed, interpretation is
gained. It is not likely that any just interpretation will
quarrel with the submission that in the Synoptics the
Sonship of Jesus, with permanent consequences, stands
out like the tall crests on a relief map, and that in the
Fourth Gospel it appears continuously like high points
studded upon a broad plateau. Which of these representations stands closer to the facts of history is the decision which every reader must make for himself.

It is a strong argument in favour of the Synoptic
account that it describes a consciousness of Sonship in
harmony with the humanity of Jesus. We may well
wonder if His life could have been lived in its stark reality
if His self-consciousness had been such as the Fourth
Gospel presents it. Would not unbroken and sustained
knowledge of a unique relation to the Father have con-
sumed the frail tenement of flesh and blood, as perhaps in
the end it did? Would it have been compatible with ex-

N

periences of temptation, suffering, and conflict? I have earlier maintained that, while this Gospel is insistent upon the fact that the Word became flesh and actually appeared upon the plane of history, its emphasis upon this truth is mainly doctrinal, and that significantly the Evangelist does not record the stories of the Baptism, the Temptation and the Transfiguration, and replaces the narrative of the Agony by the less realistic allusion in xii. 27f. In this Johannine counterpart to the story the possibility of a petition is mentioned and immediately and resolutely set aside.

In the Synoptics the tension is both heightened and relaxed. In the Temptation story the revelation at the Baptism is recalled and examined; in the saying about the Parousia (Mk. xiii. 32) Sonship is quietly assumed. In this saying we are far from the ecstatic feeling with which the cry of joy in Lk. x. 22 must have been uttered. In the cry of dereliction (Mk. xv. 34) Sonship is temporarily obscured, except for those who interpret the utterance, 'Why hast thou forsaken me?', as an utterance of supreme faith. The story of the daughter of Jairus (Mk. v. 21–43) lacks a confession like that of Martha, 'I have believed that thou art the Christ, the Son of God' (Jn. xi. 27), and the prayer of Jesus, 'Father, I thank thee that thou didst hear me' (Jn. xi. 41), and reflects a sense of exalted, but sober, realism. And in general we may say that the Synoptic narratives are not dominated by an overwhelming consciousness of divine Sonship.[1] They disclose to us the form of Jesus of Nazareth and it is from the Christian tradition as a whole that we know that this is the Son of God. In short, the Synoptic revelation is not continuously tuned to the same pitch. The treatment ranges

[1] One recalls the phrase of Dibelius, 'a book of secret epiphanies', *From Tradition to Gospel*, 230.

from a first movement to a finale heard in the Synoptics in Peter's confession (Mk. viii. 29) and in the Fourth Gospel when Thomas cries, 'My Lord and my God' (Jn. xx. 28).

It might be contended that, if the revelations of Sonship recorded in the Synoptics were remembered by Jesus, the difference between these Gospels and the Fourth Gospel is sensibly reduced. All testify to an abiding consciousness of Sonship. This argument has weight, and, so far as it goes, it justifies the Johannine representation. But only up to a point, for this Gospel smoothes out the tension present in the Synoptics. It does not distinguish between a revelation received in all its compelling power, and as it must appear in retrospect, and by omitting the cry of desolation—one must say with intention—it tacitly rejects the idea that the sense of Sonship had its nadir as well as its zenith. In the Fourth Gospel Sonship is always in its noon-day splendour. Perhaps no saying is so significant for Christology as 'My God, my God, why hast thou forsaken me?' But it is from the Synoptics that we learn that Jesus said this.

3. So far as a conclusion is possible it would seem that the consciousness of Sonship emerged in the mind of Jesus in the manner described in the Synoptic Gospels. The Synoptics reveal the form of its manifestation; the Fourth Gospel its quality.

If this view is accepted, its effect upon Christology must be profound. In the third and fourth centuries the greater influence upon theology was exerted by the Fourth Gospel. To-day, if any deeper understanding is to be gained, it will be obtained not by devaluing this Gospel, but by weighing its teaching along with the testimony of all the Gospels, and particularly the Synoptics. If this opinion is sound, it will be necessary to expand the provisional results already gained in the light of the answer given to the question discussed above. Restated, the conclusion is this: Within the limitations of the human life of Jesus His consciousness of Sonship was gained through the knowledge that God was His Father, mediated by prayer and communion with Him in a process of growth and development which begins before the opening of the historic ministry and is consummated in decisive experiences of revelation and intuition. It is upon this historical foundation that Christological thinking must build.

4. The conclusion just stated appears to represent the farthest point to which historical criticism can go, and I am not forgetful of the fact that it extends much farther than many New Testament scholars are prepared to go. This hesitation is natural. If a deeper understanding of the Sonship is sought, we are compelled to return to the theological opinion mentioned in chapter XIII,[1] the claim of many theologians that it was because Jesus is the Son by nature that He came to know Himself as such. The critic naturally wishes to exclude such questions. They disturb that poise and detachment which are proper to scientific investigation, and they introduce values which may be estimated, but cannot be precisely weighed. Nevertheless, it must be recognized that unless we are willing to consider the theological issues, we must confess that the problem of Christ's divine consciousness is insoluble. For reasons already given, especially the danger of underestimating His humanity, we were justified in leaving these issues in suspense. We must now examine their relevancy.

[1] See p. 170f.

III

In the older forms of Christological discussion it was debated whether or not the divine Sonship of Jesus was metaphysical in character. In reaction against the philosophical associations of this word, the tendency during the last fifty years has been to say that the Sonship of Jesus is 'ethical and spiritual' and to overwork the word 'unique' in describing its character. This wilderness period, I think, has ended. The words 'ethical and spiritual' are painfully inadequate to describe a 'unique' sense of Sonship, and the term 'unique' is meaningless unless it describes a supra-human consciousness. What we need to ask is whether the Sonship which the Gospels reveal is grounded in the very being of Christ. Was He in fact the Son of God?

It is still too soon to answer this vital question fully, since any conclusion to which we come must be based, not only on the Gospels, but upon the teaching of Scripture as a whole and upon the historic witness of the Church. It must also be sustained, if it is to gain compelling power, in the experience of the individual Christian by that inner testimony of the Holy Spirit, without which it remains a doctrine accepted by external authority. At the present stage of the inquiry a humbler but necessary question must be asked: Is the emergence of the consciousness of Sonship which the Gospels attest such as to suggest, or point to, an origin grounded in being? Has it a character and a quality which suggest essential divinity? Can we give to it a credible explanation within the limits of historical criticism, or are we driven to transcend these limits and so to consider the possibility that it has its origin in the nature of Christ's Person?

In these high matters one can only express convictions

open to challenge, but grounds can be given for these opinions and an estimate formed of their strength. I suggest that the account I have given of the emergence of the consciousness of Sonship in the experience of Jesus demands a still deeper explanation of its origin. The emergence of a conviction and a description of factors which have contributed to it do not explain its origin. It is necessary to trace the one and equally imperative to seek the other. For reasons already given we are justified in thinking that the Sonship of Jesus developed step by step with His knowledge of God as His Father, and that it was deepened in His consciousness by prayer and communion with Him. But one is left with the feeling that, in saying this, less than half has been told. We are bound to remember that others, prophets, apostles, and saints, have not claimed to be Sons of God from the knowledge of God as Father. In this matter there is a great gap between Jesus and the best of His followers. This fact would be generally admitted. It would also be conceded that the gap is widened by the intensity of His filial knowledge and the warmth of His communion with the Father. But is the gap one of quality, and not only of degree? We have still to answer the question, 'Why does He believe Himself to be the Son of God?' Moreover, as we have seen, His recorded sayings imply the idea of a revelation received from the Father, and not only an intuition of Sonship. He hears the assurance, 'Thou art my beloved Son'. He rejoices in the Holy Spirit because all things have been delivered to Him of His Father. Unless He is deceived there is no parallel to His consciousness of Sonship. It appears, grows, and burns in a life which is truly human, and amid limitations which do not hide its glory. This is the picture given in the Gospels, and it is hard to believe that it is a product of human imagination, and so of man's devising. It is, admittedly, a challenge and a judgement. One must appreciate the great insight of the Fourth Evangelist when he writes: 'And Jesus said, For judgement came I into this world, that they which see not may see; and they which see may become blind' (Jn. ix. 39). But there is no compulsion in this challenge. Every man's decision is his own, and rejection is better than easy acquiescence. For my own part I cannot but think that the consciousness of Jesus bears the signature of its truth, and that it agrees with the testimony of the Epistles and the constant witness of the Church; that, in human language, He comes from God and is the Word of God to men.

This testimony we have now to scrutinize, no longer only as it appears in writings, but as it lives in history; first as it is found in the life, thought, and worship of the primitive Christian communities, and then as it emerges in the distinctive teaching of the great New Testament writers. The former is the theme of the next chapter.

XV

THE CHRISTOLOGY OF THE PRIMITIVE CHRISTIAN COMMUNITIES

How did the early Christian communities think and speak of Christ? Did they recognize that divine element which we have seen reason to ascribe to the consciousness of Jesus during His earthly ministry? What effect had the Resurrection upon their thought and religious practice? Were they decisively influenced by contact with Greek thought or was the deeper and more permanent impression made by Jesus Himself and the testimony of eyewitnesses and preachers?

Some of these questions have already confronted us in considering the names of Jesus, especially those of 'Lord' and 'Son of God', and also in our study of the New Testament writings. I do not propose to approach these problems of Christology by going over the same ground a second time, and I feel at liberty to use the results already reached, particularly those which concern the use of the title 'the Lord' as it was applied to Jesus. With reference to this title and the combinations into which it enters, 'the Lord Jesus', 'the Lord Jesus Christ', and 'Our Lord Jesus Christ', which are the most frequent designations of Jesus in primitive Christianity and in the usage of St. Paul, I have maintained that, although the religious atmosphere of the Hellenistic world fostered the use of the title, its adoption by the first Christians is to be explained by factors in the Christian movement itself.[1]

[1] Cf. *The Names of Jesus*, 47-51.

These factors include the influence of the Resurrection upon Christian thought, the use of the term 'Lord' by Jesus in His parables and His teaching concerning David's Son (Mk. xii. 35–7), the use of the Old Testament in primitive Christian exegesis, the effects of the invocation of Christ in worship, exorcism, and confession at baptism, and above all the sense of union with Christ experienced at the Eucharist in 'the breaking of bread'. Along with the first preaching of Christ as 'Lord' the believing response of hearers, sealed by teaching and worship, made the Christian confession 'Jesus is Lord' inevitable and lasting. In this chapter I shall devote myself to the attempt to show how this basic conviction found expression in the life of the first communities. The markedly less use by these communities of the names 'the Son of God' and 'the Son' is due partly to the dominating place of the titles of Lordship in their thought and worship, and at the same time is a sign of the limitations in their Christology which will be the subject of Chapter XVI.

I

Before discussing the various aspects of primitive Christian teaching it is necessary to refer more fully to two facts which have been already mentioned, the persistence of this teaching in the Pauline, Pastoral, and Catholic Epistles, and the marked degree to which it is independent of the influence of the distinctive ideas of St. Paul, the writer of Hebrews, and St. John.

1. We have seen that the readiness of modern New Testament scholars to attach greater importance to primitive Christianity is a feature of contemporary research. Greater evidence for its range is found than was customary a generation ago. Much that appears in the great New Testament writers is not in any way peculiar to their

teaching, but is part and parcel of the common faith of primitive Christianity itself. Further, our own study of the Christology of the Pastoral and Catholic Epistles has shown that this common faith lived on to the end of the first century and the beginning of the second. It is the Christianity of multitudes of believers, fervent in spirit and loyal in worship, but without any marked inclination to explore the intellectual implications of their faith. This fact enhances the importance of primitive Christianity for our inquiry.

2. Closely bound up with this situation is the absence of any deep influence exerted by the great New Testament writers upon primitive Christianity in general. Their writings were read and prized, as we see from Col. iv. 16[1] and as their preservation proves, but at first their influence was purely local. Only to a small degree is this influence visible in the period in question. From the middle of the second century it can be traced with increasing clarity, doubtless as the result of the formation of the Pauline Canon[2] and the teaching of Ignatius, Polycarp, and Justin Martyr in the period A.D. 110–50, and it assumes decisive importance in the writings of Irenaeus and Tertullian and the Fathers of the third and fourth centuries. Deepened by the theology of Augustine, the influence of the great New Testament writers continues in the mediaeval period and takes fire in the theology of the Reformation, with the result that it has dominated Christian thinking down to the present day. In the early period under discussion it thus appears that the doctrinal

---

[1] 'And when this epistle has been read among you, cause that it be read also in the church of the Laodiceans; and that you also read the epistle from Laodicea'.

[2] Cf. C. L. Mitton, *The Formation of the Pauline Corpus of Letters* (1956.)

influence of St. Paul, the writer of Hebrews, and St. John
is a striking example of what, without impropriety, might
well be called the power of 'delayed action'.

Great efforts have been made in the past to find
'Paulinism' in the Synoptic Gospels and the Acts, but it
cannot be said that the results are impressive. Even in
the Pastoral Epistles its presence is secondary; St. Paul
is echoed but not understood. In St. James, St. Jude,
and Second Peter, as well as in the Apocalypse, it is
almost non-existent. All these writings reflect traditional primitive Christianity. Indeed, it may be said that
some of them write almost as if St. Paul had never lived
or written. St. James has a confused knowledge of his
teaching on faith; the author of the Pastorals knows, but
has not grasped, the profundity of his thought; the
writer of Jude has something of St. Paul's spirit, but none
of his doctrinal insight; the author of the Apocalypse
belongs to another world of thought; the late writer of
Second Peter in referring to the wisdom given to 'our
beloved brother Paul' pathetically refers to things in his
letters which are 'hard to understand' and which 'the
ignorant and unsteadfast wrest, as they do also the other
scriptures, to their own destruction' (iii. 15f.). Hebrews
was almost still-born. In the East it was received from
the end of the second century, but with hesitations about
its authorship; in the West, although prized by Clement
of Rome, it was accepted at a late period under the influence of Jerome and Augustine. The Gospel and
Epistles of St. John have marked affinities, amid striking
differences, with the language and doctrinal ideas of the
Apocalypse, but exert no influence upon St. James, St.
Jude, and Second Peter. These observations, it need
hardly be said, imply no disparagement of the principal
New Testament writers. On the contrary, they throw

their greatness into relief, since they point to their ultimate triumph in spite of contemporary neglect.

The twin facts noted, the persistence of primitive Christianity and the independence of the writings by which it is reflected, reveal its historical and doctrinal importance. The writings show the tenacity of a common well-established faith, on which they depend and to which their writers contributed more by their exertions and counsels than by original ideas. They are instructive both by their strength and by their limitations. Primitive Christianity is the matrix out of which a greater faith was born. It is not to be supposed that everywhere it was the same in its expression, but it is marked by broad common aspects to which attention must now be given.

II

It will be useful to discuss the Christology of the primitive period as it is reflected in the life and worship of the early communities in respect of preaching, teaching, worship, Baptism, the celebration of the Eucharist, and the common experience of believers. These activities will now be examined in detail. The point of interest is the Christological ideas involved in each.

1. *Preaching.* In treating this subject it is usual and necessary to draw upon the early chapters of the Acts. Here we find the kind of message which was preached in the open street and in the earliest days. In Part I we have seen that the emphasis lies upon the Resurrection.[1] The burden of the preaching is that by His Resurrection Jesus is seen to be 'both Lord and Christ' (ii. 36), 'a Prince and a Saviour' (v. 31). He was 'delivered up by the determinate counsel and foreknowledge of God' (ii. 23), and in Him the ancient prophecies were ful-

[1] Ac. ii. 24, 32, iii. 15, v. 31, xiii. 30.

filled.[1]   He is the Servant of the Lord[2] and now sits at the right hand of God.[3]   He is the Holy and Righteous One (iii. 14), the Prophet like unto Moses (iii. 22).   These and other designations show how shallow is the contention that the first Christians held an adoptionist Christology. The Resurrection did not make Jesus 'Lord and Christ', but declared Him to be such (Rom. i. 4).   No deified man could have been fitted into the role assigned to the Stone of Old Testament prophecy (iv. 11) or have been preached as the object of faith (iii. 16), the Christ who would return (iii. 20f.) and who was ordained of God to be the Judge of the living and the dead (x. 42).   Baptism 'in' or 'into his name' is mentioned from the beginning,[4] and He is proclaimed as the sole medium of salvation (iv. 12).

If the Form Critics are right in suggesting that pronouncement-stories were used as illustrations in sermons, we have further light upon early Christian preaching, but at a later time, since they presuppose hearers to whom Jesus is already known.[5]   They imply that Christians were anxious to know, and preachers were ready to give, pronouncements of Jesus upon moral, religious, and doctrinal questions.   Some of these stories bear upon the significance of Jesus Himself and to this extent have Christological importance.[6]   They suggest a deep in-

---

[1] Ac. ii. 16–21, 25–8, iv. 11, x. 43, etc.

[2] Ac. iii. 13, 26, iv. 27, 30.

[3] Ac. ii. 34f., vii. 56.

[4] Ac. ii. 38, viii. 16, xix. 5, xxii. 16.

[5] Cf. Fascher, 'In the beginning was the sermon', *Die formgeschichtliche Methode*, 54, Dibelius, *From Tradition to Gospel*, 9–69. Bultmann also admits the constructive influence of preaching, but also, and rightly, stresses the importance of other factors. Cf. *Die Geschichte der synoptischen Tradition*, 64.

[6] As for example the Baptist's Question (Lk. vii. 19ff. = Mt. xi. 2ff.), Cornfields on the Sabbath Day (Mk. ii. 23ff.), the Man with the Withered Hand (Mk. iii. 1–5), the Beelzebul Controversy (Mk. iii. 22ff., Lk. xi. 14ff., Mt. xii. 22ff.), the Question about Authority (Mk. xi. 27ff.),

terest in His Messiahship, His attitude to the Sabbath, His authority as an exorcist and teacher, His use of signs, and His Sonship. These stories are told with the assumption that Jesus was more than a teacher, that He spoke with an authority which astonished His hearers (Mk. i. 22). Their connexion with preaching, however, is conjectural, and it may be that they were associated rather with teaching and the discussions which arose therefrom. A sharp line cannot be drawn between preaching and teaching as we see from the credal formula in 1 Cor. xv. 3–7 which summarizes the kerygma which St. Paul delivered 'as of first importance (ἐν πρώτοις)' to the believers at Corinth. Other fragments of creeds and hymns, to be mentioned later, are more naturally connected with worship and the common life of the communities.

Our clearest light, then, upon the substance of early preaching is found in the passages in the Acts already noted. To these we must add the missionary addresses based by St. Luke upon early tradition: that of St. Peter to Cornelius and his friends (Ac. x. 34–43) and those of St. Paul at Pisidian Antioch (Ac. xiii. 16–41) and at Athens (Ac. xvii. 22–31).

The term 'Lord' as we find it in these sermons and addresses is not necessarily a lower designation than 'Son of God'. Flexible in application, it could carry and express the highest tributes of religious devotion. When St. Peter declares that God has made the Crucified One 'both Lord and Christ' (Ac. ii. 36), he puts a meaning upon these names which hitherto they had not borne. A deeper meaning is present also in the phrase 'the name of

the Temptation (Lk. iv. 1–13 = Mt. iv. 1–11), David's Son (Mk. xii. 35–7), the Demand for a Sign (Mk. viii. 11f.). For similar Resurrection-stories see C. H. Dodd, *Studies in the Gospels* (1955, ed. D. E. Nineham), 9–35.

Jesus Christ', since the Apostle goes on to speak of repentance and of baptism leading to the remission of sins and the gift of the Holy Spirit (Ac. ii. 38). In the context in which the phrase appears it has a divine content, although this is not brought out. The same also may be true of the command of St. Peter to the lame man at Jerusalem, 'In the name of Jesus of Nazareth, walk' (Ac. iii. 6). Indeed, we may say that the names used in the early preaching hide rather than reveal a meaning they are forced to bear. Conviction precedes expression. This is exactly what might be expected in the history of the proclamation of a new message. Values appear first, adequate names later.

It is in the light of this situation that the failure to use the terminology of Sonship illustrated in Table II in the Appendix to Part I must be explained. We recall the fact that 'Son of God' was not a Jewish Messianic designation. It is not therefore to be expected in sermons to Jewish crowds. That St. Paul proclaimed Jesus as 'the Son of God' at Damascus is exceptional, and the locality is significant, unless we assign the phrase to the writer, a view not easy to accept since ix. 20 is the sole example in the Acts. If we had examples of primitive preaching from a later period the evidence might be different, but this suggestion is conjectural. We must accept the testimony of our sources that it is the Lordship of Christ to which prominence was given, and infer that the idea is far richer in Christological meaning than the name 'Lord' might itself suggest. If, as we have maintained, the consciousness of Sonship was the deepest conviction of Jesus, we must regard the absence of the name in primitive Christology as a mark of its limitations, and its re-emergence in the great New Testament writings as a natural and necessary contribution to Christian thought.

2. *Teaching*.   At a very early stage catechesis, or teaching, assumed a very important place in primitive Christianity.   *Kerygma* and *didache* stand side by side. Immediately after his reference to baptism on the day of Pentecost St. Luke tells us that the first believers 'continued steadfastly in the apostles' teaching', and the word stands first followed by 'fellowship', 'the breaking of bread', and 'the prayers' (Ac. ii. 42).

The first converts appear to have been baptized almost at once in consequence of the manifest gift of the Spirit. Even at a later stage the Philippian jailor and his household were baptized 'immediately', although it is said that St. Paul and Silas spoke the word of the Lord to him, with all that were in his house' (Ac. xvi. 32f.).   But very soon it must have been found that instruction was imperatively necessary.   One would give much to gain precise information concerning the teaching, but it is safe to suppose that it consisted of instruction arising out of the basic elements in the kerygma, including Old Testament prophecies now seen to be fulfilled in the ministry, death, and resurrection of Jesus, His exaltation to the right hand of God as Messiah and Lord, His expected return, the gift of the Holy Spirit, and the call to repent and receive forgiveness.[1]

The assembling and use of Old Testament prooftexts, which we know from the Acts were drawn upon in preaching, must also have characterized instruction, not only for catechumens, but also for more mature Christians. Teaching of this kind may lie behind the statement that Priscilla and Aquila expounded to Apollos 'the way of God more carefully' (Ac. xviii. 26).   The Old Testament, it has often been observed, was the Bible of Primitive

---

[1] Cf. C. H. Dodd, *The Apostolic Preaching and its Development; According to the Scriptures.*

Christianity; it was read with avidity and with new eyes. At a time which we cannot date written *testimonia* were probably compiled,[1] but before this stage and from the beginning oral teaching of this nature was at the disposal of the first Christians.[2] Along with other features the 'testimonies' must have contained a strong Christological element. That they did so is clear from the evidence supplied by the Acts, the Pauline Epistles, 1 Peter, and Hebrews. From these writings we can infer that many Old Testament passages caught the eyes of the first teachers, including Deut. xviii. 15, 18, Psa. ii. 7, viii. 4–6, xxii, lxix, cx. 1, cxviii. 22f., Isa. viii. 14, xxviii. 16, liii, lxi. 1f., Dan. vii. 13, and Zech. ix. 9. Some of these passages had arrested the attention of Jesus, and, taught by the Resurrection, the first Christians gave to them eager and sustained study. The Beroeans, we may be sure, were not the only community which readily received the preached word 'examining the scriptures daily, whether these things were so' (Ac. xvii. 11). The passages which appear to have made the deepest impression were Psa. ii. 7, 'Thou art my Son; this day have I begotten thee'; Dan. vii. 13, with its picture of one like to 'a son of man'; Isa. liii, with its description of the Suffering Servant; Psa. cx. 1, which suggested the session on high; and Psa. cxviii. 22f. coupled with Isa. viii. 14 and xxviii. 16, which describe the stone rejected of the builders or use similar imagery. This intellectual activity is not one which can naturally be associated with the followers of a human prophet; it is an exegetical impulse felt and obeyed by the worshippers of a revered and exalted Lord.

A parallel activity connected with the primitive teaching is the compilation of collections of the sayings of Jesus.

---

[1] Cf. J. R. Harris, *Testimonia*, I, II.
[2] Cf. C. H. Dodd, *According to the Scriptures*, 23–7.

o

The process is older than Q and M, for these sources probably grew out of earlier and shorter collections of sayings and parables. St. Mark's Gospel also pre-supposes a parallel collection. This Markan collection is important because the catch-words and repeated phrases in ix. 37–50 point to compilation for didactic purposes.[1] Christians were expected to learn and re-member the words of the Lord. The intention which guided the making of these collections was wider than that pursued in the assembling of proof-texts. It em-braced the teaching of Jesus concerning the Kingdom of God and the demands of the new life to which disciples were called. We see this from the sixfold cycle, con-structed from material in M and Q, which is woven into the Sermon on the Mount in v. 21–48,[2] where that which had been said of old time is replaced by what Jesus says now. In the primitive collections sayings of deep Christo-logical importance, of which Lk. x. 22 = Mt. xi. 27 is the most conspicuous example, show how powerfully they served the purpose of revealing who Jesus was. Besides the collections, Passion-narratives and groups of pro-nouncement-stories were used in teaching. The group in Mk. ii. 1–iii. 6 was probably compiled in order to show how it was that He who went about doing good came to His tragic end through the hostility of the scribes and Pharisees.

All these and other indications disclose how many-sided the teaching activity of the primitive communities was. Not without good reason was Jesus described as 'the Lord'. Albertz has maintained that the primitive

---

[1] *The Gospel according to St. Mark*, 408–10.

[2] Cf. M. Albertz, *Die synoptischen Streitgespräche*, 146–9. Attention paid to the more radical Form Critics has tended to overshadow the sound and sober views of Albertz.

collections show that He was regarded as more than a prophet, a wisdom-teacher, and a rabbi, that, as He Himself says, He was the One who fulfils and completes the Law absolutely (*der Erfüller und Vollender schlechthin*).[1]

3. *Worship.*   In estimating the nature of primitive Christology the worship of the early communities is of decisive importance.   That it centred in the figure of the Exalted Lord is undoubted.   In itself this fact is highly significant since the object of worship is always regarded as divine.

Much that is connected with the earliest worship is unfortunately obscure, but our sources make certain facts clear.   We know that both Baptism and the Eucharist were closely associated with Christian worship from the first.   These rites will call for separate treatment in view of their complexity.   In addition, the earliest worship, modelled on that of the synagogue, included prayers, the reading of the Old Testament, and praise to God.   Ac. ii. 42 tells us that the first Christians continued steadfastly in 'the prayers', and these we know had probably already assumed a liturgical form in the worship of the synagogue.   But free prayer was not excluded.   This fact is attested by the prayer of the Jerusalem community in Ac. iv. 24–30, as well as by the prayer of Stephen addressed to the 'Lord Jesus' in Ac. vii. 59f.   A direct invocation of Jesus is present in the cry *'Marana tha'* 'Our Lord come' (1 Cor. xvi. 22, cf. Apoc. xxii. 20), and again by St. Paul's use of the words of Joel ii. 32 in Rom. x. 13, 'For whosoever shall call upon the name of the Lord shall be saved' (cf. Ac. ii. 21).   It need hardly be said that this action of invoking the name of Jesus in prayer matches the highest names used of Him in the tradition.   To pray to Him and to invoke His name is to

[1] *Op. cit.*, 164.

embody the conviction that He shares in the exercise of divine powers and prerogatives.

The same conviction is only less conspicuously expressed by the hymns which the primitive communities used in worship. Their use is indicated when St. Paul writes, 'Speaking one to another in psalms and hymns and spiritual songs, singing and making melody with your heart to the Lord' (Eph. v. 19, Col. iii. 16, cf. 1 Cor. xiv. 26). In addition to the Lukan canticles and the songs of the Apocalypse fragments of early Christian hymns can be seen in Eph. v. 14,

> 'Awake, thou that sleepest,
> And arise from the dead,
> And Christ shall shine upon thee',

in 1 Tim. iii. 16,

> 'He who was manifest in the flesh,
> Justified in the spirit,
> Seen of angels,
> Preached among the nations,
> Believed on in the world,
> Received up into glory',

and in other passages.[1]

We do not know when Christian hymnody began, but there is no reason to doubt that it was early. Pliny the Younger's reference[2] to the custom of Christians meeting together on a fixed day before it was light and singing in alternate verses 'a hymn to Christ, as to a god' is late, but one can hardly think that he was describing a recently established practice. Lohmeyer, we have seen, and others explain Phil. ii. 6–11 as a pre-Pauline hymn to Christ, and the suggestion has force even if we prefer to

---

[1] Cf. A. M. Hunter, *Paul and His Predecessors*, 41–51; E. G. Selwyn, *The First Epistle of St. Peter*, 273–7; G. B. Caird, *The Apostolic Age*, 113–15.   [2] *Epp.* x. 96, 97.

think that the passage was composed by St. Paul himself before the Epistle to the Philippians was written. In sum, we may say that sufficient indications exist to show that the praise and adoration given to God were addressed in early Christianity to Christ. If so, the practice reflects the divine status He was instinctively accorded.

4. *Baptism.* The marked interest of 1 Peter in Baptism was noted in Part I. This interest is also to be seen, not only in many passages in the Acts, but equally in Rom. vi. 4, Col. ii. 12, Eph. v. 26, Heb. vi. 2, x. 22, and Tit. iii. 5. St. Paul reminds his Corinthian converts that, in contrast with their former evil way of life, they had been 'washed', 'sanctified', and 'justified' in Christ and in the Spirit (1 Cor. vi. 11). Recent studies[1] have brought home to us the immense importance ascribed to Baptism in early Christianity; its decisive character marked by the confession, 'Jesus is Lord', and the experience of incorporation with Christ described in Rom. vi. 4. 'We were buried therefore with him through baptism into death; that like as Christ was raised from the dead through the glory of the Father, so we also might walk in newness of life'. No Pauline novelty, this teaching reveals how realistically baptized Christians interpreted their immersion into the baptismal waters and their rising therefrom to share in the risen life of Christ.

The rite itself, and the teaching which preceded it, had by general consent a marked doctrinal content, and it is with good reason that early credal statements have been traced back to the questions put to the baptized and the answers given by them.[2] The Western reading which

---

[1] Cf. W. F. Flemington, *The New Testament Doctrine of Baptism* (1948); O. Cullmann, *Baptism in the New Testament* (Eng. Tr. 1950); G. W. H. Lampe, *The Seal of the Spirit* (1951).

[2] Cf. J. N. D. Kelly, *Early Christian Creeds* (1950), 40–61.

appears in the AV text as Ac. viii. 37, although rightly omitted by the RV and the RSV, reflects a custom which must have been of long standing. According to this ancient reading, when the Ethiopian eunuch said, 'See, here is water; what hinders me to be baptized?', Philip replied, 'If you believe with all your heart, you may', and the eunuch said, 'I believe that Jesus Christ is the Son of God'. On this reading Professor F. F. Bruce comments, 'It reflects common Christian practice, and its insertion seems due to a feeling that Philip could not have baptized the Ethiopian without so much as a confession of faith'.[1] The fragments of early creeds which scholars find in 1 Cor. xv. 3–7, Rom. i. 3f., viii. 34, 1 Tim. ii. 5f., iii. 16, 2 Tim. ii. 8, 1 Pet. iii. 18–22, and other passages,[2] must have extended to other forms of communal worship than those connected with Baptism.

It is not possible here to discuss many interesting questions connected with Baptism. Of its Christological significance there can be no doubt. 'Is Christ divided? was Paul crucified for you? or were you baptized into the name of Paul?' the Apostle indignantly asks the disputing factions at Corinth (1 Cor. i. 13). By these words it is implied that the first Christians were baptized into the name of Christ and that incorporation with Him carried with it the necessity of fellowship one with another within the Christian community. The argument of St. Paul is unintelligible unless the Exalted Christ was believed to be the divine Lord of the community, revered and confessed by all.

5. *The Eucharist.* The frequent celebrations of the Eucharist in the primitive communities testify to the

---

[1] *The Acts of the Apostles,* 194.
[2] Cf. O. Cullmann, *The Earliest Christian Confessions;* J. N. D. Kelly, *Early Christian Creeds,* 13–23.

same high Christology. The phrase 'the breaking of bread', an action in which the first Christians 'continued steadfastly' (Ac. ii. 42), celebrating it 'from house to house' (Ac. ii. 46), appears to describe a table fellowship which culminated in the Eucharist. It has been described as a cryptogram concealing its meaning from non-Christian readers.[1] Certainly the accounts of the institution of the rite in Mk. xiv. 22–5, Lk. xxii. 14–20, and 1 Cor. xi. 23–5 are very early indeed, independently reflecting Palestinian liturgical tradition already current in Aramaic in the decades following the death of Jesus. These questions are discussed with much force by Professor J. Jeremias in *Die Abendmahlsworte Jesu* (2nd ed. 1949), now translated into English in *The Eucharistic Words of Jesus* (1955). 'The sources', Professor Jeremias declares, 'compel the conclusion that it is unthinkable for Jesus not to have thought about the atoning effect of His death'.[2] 'His death', he adds, 'is the vicarious death of the Servant, which atones for the sins of the πολλοί, the whole world, and ushers in the beginnings of final salvation'.[3] The Christological significance of the rite is unmistakable. In pleading and in sharing in the power of Christ's Sacrifice the primitive communities *ipso facto* recognized Him as Messiah, Lord, Servant, and Son of God. The terminology of the records is doctrinal. St. Paul tells his readers that he received from 'the Lord' that which he delivered to them (1 Cor. xi. 23). It was on the night that He was delivered up that 'the Lord Jesus' took bread, and broke it, and said, 'This is my body, which is for you: this do in remembrance of me' (1 Cor. xi. 24); and, he declared, as often as they ate this bread and drank the cup, they proclaimed 'the Lord's death' until

[1] J. Jeremias, *The Eucharistic Words of Jesus*, 84.
[2] *Op. cit.*, 152.　　　[3] Ibid.

He should come. With verbal differences the same tradition is recorded in Mk. xiv. 22–5, and in both accounts Christ's blood is described as 'covenant' blood. In addition to the sacrificial meaning of the rite, its eschatological associations are brought out in 1 Cor. xi. 26, Mk. xiv. 25, and Lk. xxii. 16 and 18, and these impressed upon the first worshippers the fact that Christ is the central figure in the consummation of all things.

There were, of course, disorders connected with the Eucharist, just as excesses in worship arising out of the gift of speaking with tongues compromised the first assemblies in the eyes of unbelievers. In a full account of primitive worship it would be necessary to dwell upon these disorders. Here it is enough to note the doctrinal arguments by which they were met. Thus the Corinthians are warned against eating the bread or drinking the cup 'of the Lord' unworthily (1 Cor. xi. 27) and against the greed which makes it impossible to eat 'the Lord's supper' (1 Cor. xi. 20). The emphasis lies upon the fact that the Supper is His. It is His outpoured life and His very self in which believers participate (1 Cor. x. 16).

6. *The Common Life of the Primitive Communities.* Finally, we observe that the fellowship, or *koinonia*, manifest in the first communities reflects the Christian beliefs expressed in preaching, teaching, and worship. The short-lived attempt to have all things in common is made by 'all who believed' (Ac. ii. 44, iv. 32). The Corinthian community assembled to pronounce judgement on the incestuous person is pictured as exercising discipline 'in the name of our Lord Jesus' and 'with the power of our Lord Jesus' (1 Cor. v. 3–5). 'Called in the Lord' the slave is 'a freedman of the Lord' (1 Cor. vii. 22), and questions of marriage are measured, not only by the standard of good order, but by the purpose of securing

'undivided devotion to the Lord' (1 Cor. vii. 35). Christians are 'judged by the Lord' (1 Cor. xi. 32), and their generosity is sought because they know 'the grace of our Lord Jesus Christ' (2 Cor. viii. 9). These are only a few of the examples which show how profoundly the life of the first Christians was dominated by their common relationship to Christ, by their shared belief in Him and their devotion to Him. Here lies the secret of an amazing communal life which inspired the great New Testament writers to develop their richer Christological teaching and later compelled the Church of the early centuries to attempt tasks of closer definition.

It is the strength of this common life, and not merely the use of certain names and titles, which compels us to conclude that Primitive Christianity regarded Christ as divine. Worship, we have seen, was of supreme importance in Christological thought. In modern New Testament study *kerygma* and *didache* have become technical terms, but it is manifest that to these we must add *leitourgia*, 'worship', if we seek a complete picture of what was believed and confessed. In the Christian cult Jesus was invoked as Lord in passionate expectation; He was hymned in song and confessed in credal statements, especially in connexion with Baptism and the Lord's Supper when His sacrificial death was remembered and pleaded. Social and personal relationships were interpreted in the light of a common fellowship with Him; barriers of race were first shaken and then transcended, and in due time the idea of a universal mission was born embracing Gentiles as well as Jews. All this we learn without drawing upon the distinctive teaching of the great New Testament writers, and with no appeal to their testimony except as they reflect and reveal what was commonly believed. The tradition strikes deep notes before it becomes the object of reflection and interpretation.

Primitive Christianity was much richer in its implications than in its statements. Its life was more eloquent than its speech. Nevertheless, limitations in its Christology are undeniable. In the next chapter it will be necessary to consider these, not by way of depreciation, but in order to see what further developments were necessary.

XVI

THE LIMITATIONS OF PRIMITIVE CHRISTIAN CHRISTOLOGY

WE have seen how virile and many-sided Primitive Christian Christology was. We have noted the strong emphasis laid upon the Resurrection, the depth of the confession of Jesus as both Lord and Christ, the authority found in His words, the zeal with which the Old Testament was read in the conviction that ancient prophecies were fulfilled in Him, the recognition of Him as the object of faith and the centre of worship, the belief in Him as the Suffering but now Exalted Lord seated at the right hand of God who would return in the 'times of the restoration of all things' declared by God through the mouth of His holy prophets. We see how naïve and mistaken it is to suppose that the first Christians were little more than a new reformed Jewish sect and to think that the great New Testament writers, St. Paul, the author of Hebrews, and St. John, transformed it into a mystery cult. The practice of breaking bread and the dominical sayings preserved in the narratives of the Lord's Supper imply that belief in the efficacy of the atoning death of Christ was present from the beginning. Christ as Lord revered and worshipped is a primitive Christian idea before contact was made with the pagan world.

Nevertheless, in spite of its virility, primitive Christian beliefs had marked limitations largely because their implications were not as yet worked out and expressed. Among these limitations two stand out in particular:

(1) the absence of a close connexion in Christian teaching between the Person and Work of Christ, and (2) the failure to relate the high claims made for Christ and the position assigned to Him to the doctrine of God. These defects are intelligible and in some respects providential. They are made good in the teaching of the great New Testament writers; but to some extent they mark the Christianity of the ordinary Christian believer down to the present day in his sometimes expressed tacit assumption that theology is of secondary importance as compared with moral and spiritual questions and the active forms of Christian duty and enterprise. A third question to be discussed in the present chapter is the Virgin Birth tradition which appears as no more than a tradition in certain circles of primitive Christianity and whose doctrinal significance is treated nowhere in the New Testament.

I

1. We have seen that the first Christians confessed that Christ died for sins and that His mission of suffering death, and resurrection is comparable to the ministry of the Servant of the Lord described in Isa. liii. It is not therefore the case that this part of the *kerygma* is wanting in primitive Christianity. In the Pastoral Epistles and 2 Peter, which are admittedly late, Christ is described as 'the Saviour', and in the Acts He is said to have been 'delivered up by the determinate counsel and foreknowledge of God' (ii. 23) and in St. Paul's missionary preaching and his speech before Agrippa it is affirmed that 'the Christ must suffer' (xvii. 3, xxvi. 23). An essential element in the Apostolic teaching is the fact that 'Christ died for our sins according to the scriptures' (1 Cor. xv. 3).

What we miss in primitive Christian teaching is the connexion of the Work of Christ with His Person. No attempt is visible, apart from the teaching of the great writers, to define more closely the purpose of His death, its atoning character, and its significance in respect of man's relationships with God. In consequence, the question, 'Who must this Saviour be who has wrought such great things for men?' is not raised. Predominantly, although not exclusively, Christ is seen as the Exalted Lord whose Coming is the object of faith and hope.

2. The second limitation mentioned above is even more discernible. The doctrine of God has a new intensity and at the same time in preaching, teaching, and worship Christ is presented as divine. But for attempts to bring these doctrines together we look in vain. The Godward aspects of the Person of Christ first begin to be considered by St. Paul, the author of Hebrews, and St. John, and, as we shall see, even by these writers reflection is not prompted primarily by a compelling theological interest and is not pursued beyond a certain point. Indeed, we may say that this great theme has proved to be the constant preoccupation of doctors and teachers throughout the Christian centuries, and at every stage, including the theology of to-day, new horizons are opened as men brood upon the problems of Christology. Nevertheless if we are to apprehend later developments, both in New Testament teaching and in Christian theology, we must pause to reflect upon the period when the problems had hardly emerged at all.

This situation is of such importance that it must be considered in greater detail.

On the one hand, the records show that the first Christians took over and taught Old Testament beliefs concerning God as the One God,[1] the Creator,[2] and the Judge

[1] Cf. 1 Cor. viii. 4–6, Ac. xiv. 15–17, xvii. 24–7.
[2] Cf. Ac. iv. 24, xiv. 15, Rom. iv. 17, 1 Cor. viii. 6, Apoc. x. 6, xiv. 7.

of men.[1] The Thessalonians are reminded that they had
turned from idols 'to serve a living and a true God' (1
Thess. i. 9); the Corinthians of the time when they were
led away 'unto those dumb idols, howsoever you might
be led' (1 Cor. xii. 2); and the Galatians of the period
when they were 'in bondage to them which by nature are
no gods' (Gal. iv. 8). Of the strong monotheistic faith of
primitive Christianity there can be no question. St.
Paul is expressing common Christian belief when he
writes, 'Yet to us there is one God, the Father, of whom
are all things, and we unto him' (1 Cor. viii. 6).

On the other hand, as we have seen, in primitive
Christianity Christ is Lord and Son of God, the object of
faith and prayer, the centre of a cult in which He is
revered and invoked, the One into whose name believers
are baptized, whose presence is known in the breaking of
bread, and whose sacrifice is remembered before God.
He is the Head of a fellowship which transcends national
boundaries, the Risen One who sits at God's right hand,
the future Judge for whose coming men look, a 'Prince
and a Saviour' who gives repentance to Israel and remission of sins, the Stone which was made the head of the
corner, the One whose name is the only name given
amongst men wherein they must be saved. These are
some of the claims made on His behalf. They are recalled in order to illustrate the high dignity assigned to
Him in preaching, teaching, and worship.

The conjunction of a strong monotheistic faith and
the divine epithets applied to Christ is startling, even to
those to whom it is most familiar. In primitive Christian
belief the two series stand side by side, each in its own
right and both with complete clarity. But manifestly they
are not related theologically the one to the other. There

[1] Cf. Ac. xvii. 31, Rom. ii. 16, iii. 6, Heb. xii. 23, Jas. iv. 12, v. 9.

is, it is true, an implicit relationship when Christ is said to have been 'delivered up' by 'the determinate counsel and fore-knowledge of God' (Ac. ii. 23), and when God is said to have 'ordained' Christ to execute judgement on the world in righteousness (Ac. xvii. 31) and to have exalted Him at His right hand. This relationship is one of subordination, but it is not expressed in those categories which might seem natural to it. It is not embodied in a Christology of adoption or presented in terms of the pagan idea of a deified man. The negative aspects of this situation are remarkable. Apparently, it is instinctively felt that such conceptions are inharmonious with the place filled by Christ in the Christian cult; yet the need to define His relationship to God in better and more suitable terms is not perceived. The position is one in which it is tacitly accepted that the monotheistic faith of Israel and the divine dignity of Christ could peacefully co-exist, since He had come into the world in fulfilment of Old Testament prophecies.

In these matters it might seem that the adversaries of the new faith were more far-seeing. Stephen was charged with speaking 'blasphemous words against Moses, and against God' (Ac. vi. 11) and St. Paul was stoned at Lystra (Ac. xiv. 19). Yet even in these cases it is far from clear that the motive was purely doctrinal. It is remarkable that the charge against Stephen mentions Moses first. Further, when the Jews were cut to the heart and 'gnashed on him with their teeth', it was not be- cause he had spoken of 'the coming of the Righteous One', since this claim was little more than Messianic, but because he had charged them with being 'betrayers and murderers' and with failing to keep the law ordained by angels (Ac. vii. 52–4). Only when he declares that he sees the Son of Man 'standing on the right hand of God'

do they cry out and rush upon him to stone him. In the
primitive records there are in fact few references to
blasphemy other than those connected with the trial of
Christ (Mk. xiv. 64) and His claim to forgive sins (Mk.
ii. 7), and the instances of resentment and opposition in
the Acts have to do with reviling rather than with
blasphemy proper,[1] a circumstance which may confirm us
in explaining the imperfect tense in Ac. xxvi. 11 as cona-
tive, 'I tried to compel them to blaspheme', indicating an
offence into which they might be entrapped but of
which normally they were not guilty. Neither friends
nor foes appear to have seen clearly the true issues involved.

I have suggested above that the failure to relate the
Christian estimate of Christ to the doctrine of God is
intelligible. For a considerable time the first Christians
and their successors were absorbed with the task of
missionary expansion and Church consolidation, and on
the intellectual side they were preoccupied with the endeavour to show that the coming of Christ was in accordance with the Scriptures. Moreover, among them
there were 'not many wise after the flesh, not many
mighty, not many noble' (1 Cor. i. 26). The appearance
on the scene of Apollos, 'a learned man', 'mighty in the
scriptures', is noted as something exceptional, and even
he, when instructed by Priscilla and Aquila, is absorbed
by the Messianic aspects of the new message, powerfully
confuting the Jews publicly, as St. Luke says, by 'showing
by the scriptures that Jesus was the Christ' (Ac. xviii. 28).
The Christological problem has not yet emerged.

No less clearly we can see from the vantage point of
history how 'providential' this limitation of interest was.
It was essential to describe Christ, and to make the greatest

---

[1] Cf. Ac. xiii. 45, xviii. 6, xix. 37.

claims for Him, before facing the problems which these claims raised. It was even more necessary that Christians should experience the realities of worship and devotion before examining the logic of their faith. And this attitude of mind, which as we have said has persisted through the centuries and still exists to-day, in which men hold tenaciously to monotheism and the divinity of Christ without attempting to correlate the two, even regarding the doctrine of the Trinity as a doubtful legacy imposed upon Christianity by dalliance with Greek philosophy, is also not without its value. It is the basic material out of which theology builds. Popular Christianity to-day sometimes appears to the theologian to be ethical Buddhism with Islamic connexions; but it is far richer than it appears and embodies assumptions inconsistent with the modesty of its theological reservations. It is these tacit assumptions which theology attempts to clarify.

The religious situation I have described, in spite of its persistence, is one that could not remain unchallenged if Christianity was to commend itself to the mind as a reasonable and consistent faith. Sooner or later Christian thinking was compelled to rationalize its assumptions, just as to-day thoughtful men are driven to ask, 'How, if Christ is divine, can God be One God?' St. Paul, the author of Hebrews, and St. John do not pose the problem in this modern form, but they are dealing with its substance when they unfold their teaching concerning the Work of Christ and give greater prominence in their Christology to the doctrine of God. They do not solve the problems, as indeed theology has not solved them yet and will never solve them to its full satisfaction; but, in their thinking and teaching, they addressed themselves to the vital issues which are involved, and they did so in such a manner that what they say and teach has proved to be the inspiration

P

and prompting of all subsequent Christian thought.

These questions must be considered in the chapters that follow; but before this is attempted it is necessary to examine the Virgin Birth tradition. It must be considered at this point because in primitive Christianity it was current only as a tradition without any indication of its doctrinal importance. Further, unlike the other themes mentioned in the last section, its Christological significance is not discussed in the rest of the New Testament.

II

Many years ago now I made a careful investigation of the tradition in *The Historical Evidence for the Virgin Birth* (1920). I take occasion to mention this work because, while it left the historical problem open, it contains one critical suggestion which has not commended itself to many British New Testament scholars. I maintained that Lk. i. 34f., in which the virginal conception is expressly mentioned, is an addition to an earlier form of the Lukan Birth Stories made by the Evangelist himself in the last stages of the composition of the Gospel.[1] I did so mainly on the ground of the contrast between this passage and Lk. i. 30–3 in which the birth is announced by the angel Gabriel. The interpolation-hypothesis, it is felt by many, rests upon arguments which, however logical they seem to the modern scholar, may not be relevant to the situation of the Evangelist. Further, it is contended, the contrast between the annunciation to the Virgin and the announcement to Zacharias of the birth of John, suggests that the narratives of Lk. i–ii are dominated by the Virgin Birth tradition.[2] I am not sure that

---

[1] The alternative view that Lk. i. 34f. is the work of a later redactor is less cogent, since, in addition to other objections, it lacks textual support.

[2] See the important article of Dr. H. E. W. Turner, *The Expository Times*, lxviii (October 1956), 12–17, 'The Virgin Birth'.

these objections are well founded; but in any case the question of the date of the emergence of the tradition is not seriously affected, and the historical problem remains.

The question of date is important. The evidence suggests that, as a known tradition, the knowledge of the Virgin Birth belongs to the period A.D. 65–80 and was current at that time in Palestine and Syria. This is the period during which the tradition came to the knowledge of the communities for which the Birth Stories of Lk. i–ii and Mt. i–ii were compiled. If it is historical, it must, of course, have been known in certain circles earlier, and in any case it probably existed as an oral tradition before it was embodied in writing. The date mentioned is suggested by the fact that the tradition is not attested in Mark, unless it be in the phrase 'the son of Mary' in Mk. vi. 3, which is exposed to textual objections; and further, if the Proto-Luke hypothesis is accepted, by the probability that Proto-Luke began with the sixfold date in Lk. iii. 1f. and did not include the Birth Stories of Lk. i–ii. St. Matthew's Gospel, written about A.D. 85, points to the same period, since it presupposes the tradition, and implies that it had been known for some considerable time. This inference is suggested by the fact that the Matthaean Birth Stories attempt to answer questions regarding Joseph which might be and probably had been raised. The tradition is already known to St. John, as Jn. i. 13 and vii. 41f. suggest, but otherwise it is not mentioned by him and contributes nothing to his Christology. St. Paul[1] and the author of Heb-

---

[1] The argument that there is an indirect allusion to the Virgin Birth in the use of γενόμενος in Rom. i. 3 and Phil. ii. 7 (cf. Dr. Turner, *op. cit.*, 12) will not stand because both in Classical Greek and the Koine the verb is regularly used with the meaning 'to be born' as distinct from the causitive γεννάω which means 'to beget'.

rews[1] do not refer to the tradition, and one must infer, I think, that it was not known to them.

If the tradition as known is relatively late and of limited currency, its absence from primitive Christian teaching is intelligible, and the same must be said of St. Paul's Epistles. If it is historical, it is reasonable to suppose that for some time it was a guarded secret on the part of those who knew of it. If it is not historical, its origin must be sought, not in the influence of pagan stories of divine births, since its character is strongly Jewish-Christian, but in reflection prompted by Isa. vii. 14, 'Behold, a virgin shall conceive, and bear a son, and shall call his name Immanuel'. The objection that Mt. i. 18, in which the virginal conception is mentioned, 'signifies an absolute novelty for Jewish thought'[2] does not carry us far, since it is not a question of Jewish exegesis, but of how Christians read and interpreted the Old Testament passage.

It is widely, and rightly, agreed that literary and historical considerations do not settle the problem. Equally dubious, I believe, is the widespread assumption that theological arguments determine the issue. So I think we must conclude from the discussions of half a century.[3] Arguments based on the entail of original sin and the necessity of a new beginning in Christ, the Second Adam, do not turn the scale, since alternative views are possible.[4]

[1] Heb. vii. 3, 'without father, without mother' (of Melchizedek) is appealed to, but the exegesis is desperate.

[2] Billerbeck, *Kommentar*, I, 49.

[3] Cf. W. M. Ramsay, *Was Christ born at Bethlehem?* (1898); J. Orr, *The Virgin Birth of Christ* (3rd. ed. 1914); G. H. Box, *The Virgin Birth of Jesus;* (1916): J. G. Machen, *The Virgin Birth of Christ* (1930); D. Edwards, *The Virgin Birth in Faith and History* (1943). See also R. Syme, *Klio* (1934), T. Corbishley, *The Journal of Theological Studies*, xxxvi, 22ff.

[4] I therefore doubt if I was justified in saying in *The Historical Evidence for the Virgin Birth* that 'the ultimate considerations which determine a true estimate of the Virgin Birth tradition are doctrinal', *op. cit.*, 127.

This theological situation is revealed by the discussions of Emil Brunner and Karl Barth. Brunner says that the contention that the Virgin Birth was necessary because of original sin breaks down because it is difficult to see how generation through the Virgin alone could be a condition for the sinlessness of the Lord, and why a birth through two sexes should prevent the creation of a sinless God-Man.[1] Barth maintains that the Virgin Birth 'really signifies the exclusion of sin in the sense of *peccatum originalis*',[2] but he is careful to say that it is not the *cause* of this exclusion, but a *pointer* to it. He recognizes that it is unbiblical to say that sexual life is evil, but holds that it is involved in sin, and is sin, because man is a sinner from his birth, and since 'every natural generation is the work of willing, achieving, creative, sovereign man'.[3] For this reason, he contends, man in the person of Joseph must be set aside. Only by grace, and by a miracle of grace, is human nature, in spite of its corruption, made worthy to be a partaker of the divine nature.[4] How far this submission meets the arguments of Brunner, and whether it is the side-stepping of a theological fencing-master, will no doubt continue to be debated. Barth's strongest argument is the claim that 'a certain inward, essential rightness and importance' first admitted the narratives into the Gospels and out of this text introduced the doctrine into the Creeds.[5] This emphasis upon congruity, rather than upon the necessities of doctrine, appears to be the upshot of the long debate.

The wide acceptance of the doctrine in the Church is due, not primarily to the evidence in the Gospels and to doctrinal arguments, but to the fact that it is affirmed by the post-apostolic Fathers and confessed in the Apostles'

[1] *The Mediator*, 325f.   [2] *Church Dogmatics*, I, 2, 191.
[3] *Op. cit.*, 192.   [4] *Op. cit.*, 196.   [5] *Op. cit.*, 176.

and Nicene Creeds; to the unbroken tradition of the Church; and to the conviction of many Christians that it supplies a fitting and congruous account of the entrance of the Son of God into the world. This is the majority view expressed in *The Report on Doctrine in the Church of England*. The minority view is that the wonder of the Incarnation is even greater if Christ was born as other men are born. The gap which separates these views is narrower than might be supposed, since it cannot be demonstrated that the acceptance of the tradition is essential to the confession that Jesus is the Son of God. In these circumstances liberty of interpretation must be granted to those who hold different views. This opinion is not universally accepted, but it has great weight in the opinion of those who in forming their conclusions give first place to New Testament teaching as compared with the testimony of tradition and the Creeds.

One point of the greatest importance needs to be made. Whatever views we hold concerning the Virgin Birth, the existence of the tradition in the New Testament period is an impressive testimony to early Christian belief in the supernatural character of Christ's birth. Even among those who reject the tradition not a few believe that the Son of God was 'conceived by the Holy Ghost' and joyfully confess this fact in reciting the Creeds.[1] They can also confess that He was 'born of the Virgin Mary', not in the sense in which this confession is made by the Church Catholic throughout the centuries, but with the gladness of the conviction that He was 'born of a woman, born under the law'. Many Christians will think this confession to be inadequate, but these must learn to bear with the views of others who are conscious of difficulties which are not present to themselves in the same way. In

[1] Cf. Karl Barth, *op. cit.*, I, 2, 196.

his *Doctrines of the Creed*, in summarizing the arguments of both sides, Canon Oliver Quick has wisely said, 'The chief result to my mind is to suggest that on the subject of the Virgin Birth we ought to be especially tender and sympathetic towards the convictions of those who differ from ourselves'.[1] He thinks it hard for a Christian who accepts the New Testament evidence, the constant tradition of the Church, and the value of all the devotion which has been centred upon the perpetual virginity of the Lord's mother, to believe that all these things have their origin, not in the truth of historical fact 'but in a pious myth'.[2] Whether the alternative is rightly described as 'a pious myth' is open to argument, but the opinion is sound that we must hesitate to claim that the view that Christ was born as other men are born is inconsistent with the essentials of saving faith in Him. Dr. Turner speaks in similar terms of an individual who rejects the Virgin Birth, but he takes the view that for the Church as a whole to falter with regard to the doctrine would be a wholly different matter. 'Ultimately, if not immediately', he says, 'such a procedure would almost certainly undercut the gospel'.[3] The Virgin Birth, he maintains, is 'congruous with rather than necessary to the Incarnation'.[4]

III

The three questions discussed in this chapter, the Work of Christ, the doctrine of God, and the Virgin Birth, have this in common that in primitive Christianity, in both its earlier and later stages, they are not brought into doctrinal connexion with the Person of Christ. The first two, as we shall see, are treated more fully by the great New

---

[1] *Op. cit.*, 160.   [2] *Op. cit.*, 161.   [3] *Op. cit.*, 17.
[4] *Op. cit.*, 16. Here is matter for debate. Can the removal of what is congruous with, but not necessary to, the Incarnation 'undercut the gospel'?

Testament writers, but the third is not mentioned by any of them.   For reasons already given this silence ought not to occasion surprise in the case of St. Paul, and perhaps not in the author of Hebrews, but it is less easy to explain in the theology of St. John.   St. John is familiar with the tradition, but does not expound its doctrinal meaning, probably, as we have suggested, because he was pre-occupied with the doctrine of the Logos.   In point of fact, although accepted by all as a Church tradition, the doctrine of the Virgin Birth received little attention until the Middle Ages, the controversies of the Reformation theology, and the discussions of modern times.   In contrast, the distinctive contributions of the great New Testament writers to the Person of Christ regarding His Work and the relation of both to the doctrine of God set the course for subsequent discussions.   To these contributions we now turn because they are of great interest in themselves, but even more because they are of first importance in any attempt we may make to-day to apprehend the meaning of the doctrine of the Person of Christ.

XVII

THE CONTRIBUTION OF THE GREAT NEW TESTAMENT WRITERS

W E have seen that a much larger element of primitive Christology passed into the teaching of St. Paul, the author of Hebrews, and St. John than at one time it was customary to recognize, and that it lived on throughout the first century largely unaffected by the fuller interpretation of these writers. These facts might seem to detract from their greatness. This is a misapprehension of the true situation for they filled up what was lacking in traditional teaching and left behind a legacy which became increasingly precious and is not exhausted to-day.

We saw that the principal defects in the teaching the great writers inherited were twofold: a failure to appreciate the Christological importance of the Work of Christ and a limited apprehension of the bearing of the high claims made for Him upon the doctrine of God. These defects begin to be supplied by the great writers; but it is important to realize at the outset that they are not completely met. In particular, their richer Christology throws into still greater relief the need for a new conception of the being of God and it was the work of many centuries, still in progress to-day, and to the extent that human reason is adequate to the task, to discover in the Person of Christ the key to all Christian doctrine.[1] In this chapter we shall consider the connexion between

[1] It is the supreme merit of the theology of Karl Barth that he emphasizes this fact.

their Christology and their soteriological teaching and the effect of both upon their inherited conceptions of God.

I. CHRISTOLOGY AND THE WORK OF CHRIST

The connexion between Christology and the Atonement is foreshadowed in the teaching of Christ Himself regarding His death and resurrection. It is significant that in so many of His sayings regarding His Passion He speaks of Himself as the Son of Man. What He is and what He does are inseparable. The phrases 'before I suffer' (Lk. xxii. 15) and 'the cup that I shall drink' (Mk. x. 38) are exceptional in this respect, and the same is true of the sayings at the Last Supper (Mk. xiv. 22, 24). In formal teaching He connects His prophecies of suffering with Messianic and eschatological self-designations. Thus, He announces to His disciples that 'the Son of Man will be delivered into the hands of men' (Mk. ix. 31, etc.), and declares that 'the Son of Man came to give his life a ransom for many' (Mk. x. 45). This usage shows that He thought of His sufferings, not primarily as a personal experience, but mainly as a mission to be fulfilled in obedience to the Father's will and in virtue of what He was. St. Mark catches the spirit of this usage when he writes, 'He began to teach them that the Son of Man must suffer' (viii. 31). In another idiom the same connexion of ideas appears in the Johannine saying, 'Behold, the Lamb of God, that takes away the sin of the world' (Jn. i. 29), and again in the words, 'When you have lifted up the Son of Man, you will know that I am he' (Jn. viii. 28). Christ's mission is bound up with His Person; its virtue depends upon His divine dignity, and in consequence it brings that dignity into closer focus. His Sacrifice brings Him into the closest relationships with sinful men, and no less clearly its Godward aspects are manifest. It cannot be doubted that His interpretation of His suffering reacted strongly upon His consciousness of Sonship. The two are mutually influential.

It is hardly to be expected that in the earliest preaching this connexion of thought should be prominent, but it is noteworthy that names like 'the Holy and Righteous One' and 'the Pioneer of life' appear (Ac. iii. 14f.) and that Jesus is designated as 'a Saviour' (Ac. v. 31). These names are spontaneous reactions of faith to Jesus as preached and known. No less significant is the use of the name 'the Lord' in connexion with Baptism and the Eucharist, for both rites were associated with the worship of the crucified Saviour. If the name seems bare, it is because veneration cannot be measured and because time was needed to grasp the Christological significance of Christ's death. It is natural that when the great writers responded to the wonder of the Cross, and entered more fully into its meaning, their Christology was deepened and developed. One must not forget, however, that many of the ideas they developed were already present in a rudimentary form in the primitive tradition and so were not felt by their readers to be entirely new or strange.

1. What has just been said is especially true of St. Paul. Thus, he underlines and expands, but does not create, such ideas as the necessity of Christ's death in the purpose of God; its Messianic character; its vicarious, representative, and sacrificial aspects; its relation to sin; its connexion with faith and with the Eucharist; its consequences in the experience of suffering with Christ and with moral and spiritual ends.[1] Even when he affirms the universality of redemption, he is developing teaching already implicit in primitive beliefs, in spite of the hesita-

[1] These ideas are treated in *The Atonement in New Testament Teaching*, 50-2, 57-74.

tion of the early communities to countenance table-fellowship with Gentiles. Although present to a less obvious degree, this dependence on tradition can be seen in the teaching of St. John. It is less apparent in the Epistle to the Hebrews because the author concentrates his attention almost exclusively upon the high-priesthood of Christ and His mediatorial work. But manifestly these teachers transcended that which they received. Each has his distinctive emphasis.

It is not possible or necessary in this study to describe the teaching of the great writers concerning the Work of Christ in detail.[1] It must be enough to mention the main elements in order to illustrate the influence of their Soteriology upon their Christology and the degree to which the doctrine of God was affected.

In St. Paul's teaching the elements relative to this purpose are the fuller attention he gives to the connexion of the Work of Christ with sin, justification, and reconciliation, to the representative character of His redemptive ministry, the love of God, and man's appropriation of it in faith.

Believing as St. Paul does that sin is rebellion against God, as well as the acts in which it is expressed, his strong insistence that Christ is Redeemer and Lord was inevitable. He was compelled to think of Christ's Work within the largest possible dimensions. That is why he describes His coming into the world as consummated in 'the fulness of the time' and as initiated by God. Born of a woman and under the Law, the Son of God was sent forth by God in order that He might redeem men under the Law and that believers might receive the adoption of sons (Gal. iv. 4f.). The Work of Christ takes the form of a cosmic drama in which Christ and men take part. Thus, he

[1] *Op. cit.*, 54–166.

speaks of Christ as 'having blotted out the bond written in ordinances that was against us' and he adds, 'He has taken it out of the way, nailing it to the cross'. 'Having despoiled the principalities and powers', he continues, 'he made a show of them openly, triumphing over them in it' (Col. ii. 14f.). With redemption he connects the work of the Holy Spirit, following the statement, 'God sent forth his Son', with the words, 'God sent forth the Spirit of his Son into our hearts, crying, Abba, Father' (Gal. iv. 6). If the Apostle himself does not work out the implications of these statements in their bearing upon the doctrine of God, it is manifest that such a development was bound to ensue in subsequent Christian thought.

The same reflection is prompted by all that he says about justification and reconciliation. 'It is God who forgives, justifies, reconciles, and sanctifies: it is with Him that man enters into peace, to Him that he has access, and from Him that he receives the gift of sonship'.[1] Sometimes he attributes these activities to the Spirit. This fact does not warrant premature attempts to identify the Son and the Spirit; it is a sign of unresolved tension in processes of thought which were to require centuries of discussion for their partial, and still incomplete, adjustment.

Again, what St. Paul says of Christ's representative ministry leads to the same conclusion. It is with reference to His saving ministry that he speaks of Him as 'the last Adam' (Rom. v. 12–21) and in connexion with the Resurrection that he describes Him as 'the second Man from Heaven' (1 Cor. xv. 47). 'Him who knew no sin', he writes, 'he made to be sin on our behalf; that we might become the righteousness of God in him' (2 Cor. v. 21). A word so sublime cannot be contemplated without

[1] *Op. cit.*, 75.

assigning to the Son the highest divine status, and ultimately without a modification of the doctrine of God. Rom. iii. 25f. is rightly described by commentators as the Apostle's classic statement concerning the Work of Christ, but for its justification it demands all that he subsequently says in Col. i. 15–17 about His Person, and when carried further it cries out for a new orientation of the doctrine of God. It is difficult to see how any other conclusion can be drawn from a passage in which Christ is set forth by God as a means of atonement, to be received by faith, in order to demonstrate His righteousness, that He may be righteous and the justifier of the man who has faith in Jesus. What Christ does reveals who He is, and what He does and is opens out far vistas of the nature and being of God.

Further, all that the Apostle says about communion with God through Christ points in the same direction. 'God is faithful', he exults, 'through whom you were called into the fellowship of his Son Jesus Christ our Lord' (1 Cor. i. 9). Here fellowship with Christ is the goal of divine calling and election. 'Reckon yourselves to be dead unto sin', he writes to the Romans, 'but alive unto God in Jesus Christ' (vi. 11). In these words union with Christ is not only the secret of redemption, but also the way to true life in God. It is not possible to deny the Christological implications of such teaching. It is to be noted that when the Apostle mentions the confession, 'Jesus is Lord', he speaks of the instrumentality of the Spirit.[1] Thus, he writes to the Corinthians, 'No man can say, Jesus is Lord, but in the Holy Spirit' (1 Cor. xii. 3). In this and in many impassioned utterances the first steps are taken towards a new conception of God and of His revelation of Himself in Christ.

[1] Or as the sphere in which the confession of Christ is made.

The high point in Pauline teaching is reached when the Apostle connects the Work of Christ with the love of God. 'God commends his own love towards us', he affirms, 'in that, while we were yet sinners, Christ died for us' (Rom. v. 8). Here St. Paul is speaking of the love of God for men. 'Observe', write Sanday and Headlam,[1] 'that the death of Christ is here referred to the will of the Father', and they quote with approval the comment of E. H. Gifford, 'The proof of God's love toward us drawn from the death of Christ is strong in proportion to the closeness of the union between God and Christ'. They then say, 'It is the death of One who is nothing less than "the Son"'. These inferences are not brought out by St. Paul himself, but sooner or later they were bound to be formulated. Those who absorb Pauline teaching start out on a journey which begins and ends with God.

2. Primitive Christian ideas are not present in the same fulness in the Epistle to the Hebrews. Some of these ideas are not taken up at all, others are but rarely mentioned. The belief that the Cross is the fulfilment of the divine purpose is expressed only in ii. 9f., the Servant conception only in ix. 28, the connexion of the Work of Christ with the Resurrection only in xiii. 20. The one reference to the love of God is the phrase, 'that by the grace of God he should taste death for every man' (ii. 9), and the sole allusions to moral and spiritual ends fulfilled in the Cross are ii. 15 and ix. 14. In contrast stand the abundant references to the representative and sacrificial ministry of Christ, the deep concern with sin, and the many allusions to Christ's priesthood. These aspects of His Work mark out the pathway of the author's distinctive interests.[2] These are seen in such moving and

---

[1] *The Epistle to the Romans*, 128.
[2] *The Atonement in New Testament Teaching*, 101–26.

sonorous passages as ii. 17, 'Wherefore it behoved him in all things to be made like unto his brethren, that he might be a merciful and faithful high priest in things pertaining to God, to make expiation for the sins of the people'; in the declaration of ix. 26, 'But now once for all at the end of the ages has he been manifested to put away sin by the sacrifice of himself'; and the statement of ix. 24, that Christ entered into heaven itself 'now to appear before the face of God for us'. It is significant that the reference to Christ tempted as we are, but without sin, is followed by the exhortation, 'Let us therefore draw near with boldness unto the throne of grace' (iv. 16). All these and other descriptions of Christ's Work must be added to the author's direct Christological utterances. They enhance the dignity he assigns to Christ's Person and demand an enlargement of his austere transcendental conception of God. As with St. Paul this step is not taken because its necessity is not yet felt. In the teaching of the author of Hebrews it is inhibited because he has so little to say of the love of God and nothing at all about faith-union, sacramental communion, and mystical suffering with Christ. We who look back, however, not with superior insight, but with the advantage of centuries of subsequent discussion, worship, and Christian experience, can see how imperative this development was. The Christ who makes expiation for sins, and appears for us before the throne of God, is either a being raised to divine dignity, an Arian conception ruled out by the writer's Christology, or else He comes from God and from the depths of the being of God. With all its theological implications this second alternative is the view which accords with the implications of the Epistle. It is as if we stood by the banks of an already considerable river, which has received tributaries from Jewish and Greek soil, and whose course is inevitably set for the open sea.

3. A still deeper anticipation of things to come is manifest in the Johannine writings. Traditional ideas are taken over in the Fourth Gospel, but less conspicuously than in the Pauline Epistles. If the doctrine of the Work of Christ is not treated in detail, the reason is that in the Gospel Christology and Soteriology are so closely combined. In 1 John the relation of Christ's Work to sin and its expiatory character are more fully emphasized, but in the Gospel also its vicarious, representative, and sacrificial aspects are clearly implied.[1] Emphasis is laid upon the divine purpose in the death of Christ; the Son of Man 'must be lifted up' (iii. 14), and the supreme proof of God's love is that He gave His only begotten Son, that through faith in Him men might have eternal life (iii. 15f.). In the Epistle it is insisted that the Father sent the Son into the world to be 'the Saviour of the world' (iv. 14), and divine love itself is His redemptive work. 'Herein is love', says the writer, 'not that we loved God, but that he loved us, and sent his Son to be the expiation for our sins' (iv. 10). In the Gospel the relationship of the Person and Work of Christ to God is implicit in the great saying concerning the Lamb of God (i. 29), and this connexion exists whether the Lamb of Isa. liii or the Paschal Lamb is in mind. The constant association of the Father and the Son in the Johannine writings points to a new conception of God, and the teaching concerning the Logos and the Paraclete-Spirit strengthen the urgency of this need. One must agree with Dr. C. K. Barrett when he writes, 'John takes seriously the sacrificial love of Christ which, though it was most clearly demonstrated in the cross, informed the whole earthly mission of the

[1] See earlier, p. 120f.

Q

Son of God',[1] and again, when speaking of the 'personalization' of the Spirit in the last discourses, he says that, although no doctrine of the Trinity is formulated, 'the materials are present out of which such a doctrine might be formulated'.[2]

Such, then, is the common direction in which the great New Testament writers move in describing the Person and Work of Christ. The Work illuminates the Person, and the Person explains the Work. So far from being a corruption of a simpler faith under alien influences, their teaching interprets undertones in primitive Christology, and sounds new notes which were to reverberate in all subsequent Christian theology. It will have been noticed that in treating this question it has been found impossible to exclude the influence of the Work of Christ upon the doctrine of God. This fact is highly significant, and later it will be necessary to return to it again. Meantime we must consider the second limitation in primitive Christian thought which the great writers supplied, namely the bearings of Christology upon the doctrine of God.

II. CHRISTOLOGY AND THE DOCTRINE OF GOD

The outstanding fact in the Christology of the great New Testament writers is the manner in which each of them brings the Person of Christ into close contact with his belief in God.

1. 'God', writes St. Paul, 'commends his own love towards us, in that, while we were yet sinners, Christ died for us' (Rom. v. 8). So too in the opening words of his Epistle the author of Hebrews says, 'God . . . at the end of these days has spoken to us in a Son' (i. 1f.), and in unforgettable words St. John sees the love of God in that He

---

[1] *The Gospel according to St. John*, 78.   [2] *Op. cit.*, 77.

'gave his only begotten Son' (iii. 16). In each of these classic statements God acts: He reveals, He speaks, He gives. And in each case the activity is on the grandest scale. He commends His love in a saving ministry; He speaks in a Person; He gives His Son that men may have fulness of life. The Giver is divine, His gifts are divine, and the One in whom they are given is divine. In these facts lies the problem of Christology in its bearing upon the doctrine of God.

In each writing there is no trace of a doctrine of adoption; no use is made of the idea of a deified man, and this in spite of the fact that both conceptions were common in the thought of their day. Instinctively the great writers feel these ideas to be wholly inadequate to express their apprehension of the fact of Christ. Even when they speak of His exaltation, it is the exaltation of One who is already conceived as divine. Each believes that Christ pre-existed.[1] He is not a man raised to a new dignity; He is a divine Person, the Son of God, who appears in the lowliness of a true humanity.

Inadequacy is not the only reason for the absence of the ideas of adoption and deification. No less powerful was the inhibiting power of monotheism. It may be doubted whether the ordinary reader of the New Testament, impressed as he is by the high claims made for Christ, realizes how tenaciously St. Paul, the author of Hebrews, and St. John were dominated and restrained by their belief in the One God. St. Paul's polemic against men who 'exchanged the truth of God for a lie, and worshipped and served the creature rather than the Creator' (Rom. i. 25), and his contemptuous allusion to those 'that are called gods' (1 Cor. viii. 5), warn us against too readily accepting the suggestion that he was deeply influenced by

[1] See earlier, pp. 56f, 95, 103f.

pagan ideas, however true it may be that he was responsive to his religious environment in the Greek world. His attitude to paganism is well expressed in Ac. xvii. 23, 'What therefore you worship in ignorance, this set I forth to you'. There is no such polemic in Hebrews. It is taken for granted. The writer thinks of himself and his fellow Christians as pilgrims who 'have not here an abiding city' but seek 'the city that is to come' (xiii. 14). His God is 'the living God', whose glory and majesty are such that the idea of a man raised to the dignity of deity beside Him is unthinkable. The same is true of St. John. No man has seen God at any time. He is made known by the only begotten Son, who is in the bosom of the Father (Jn. i. 18). The monotheism of these writers is as firmly held as their belief that Christ is divine. Each conviction is expressed by them and neither is sacrificed to the other. How then were these beliefs to be adjusted, the one to the other?

2. It is manifest that, if the great New Testament writers were to be able to represent Christ as divine under their monotheistic assumptions, two resources were open to them. They could think of Him as the divine Wisdom or Logos, and they could use as a vehicle of thought the idea of a supernatural being sent by God who descends from heaven to earth for man's salvation. Both conceptions appear in their teaching and each has parallels in terms of contemporary thought. There is, however, no ground for presupposing any process of mechanical borrowing. Their thinking does not begin with the Logos or the idea of the Heavenly Man, but with Christ Himself. He is the Subject of whom divine functions are predicated in familiar terms. And in the course of interpretation current thought-moulds are stretched and broken. As applied to Christ, and under the influence of

Old Testament teaching, the Logos is no longer an impersonal principle, immanent in the world and in man, and supremely manifested in Him, but a personal being active in creation and redemption; and the Heavenly Man is not a demi-god or mythological figure, but a type of the Son of God standing in the closest relationship with the Father whose purposes are fulfilled in Him. The ultimate results of this teaching are unmistakable. Looking back in the light of subsequent theological discussions, we can see that the development of Apostolic Christology was bound to lead to a new and enriched version of monotheism, but apart from significant foreshadowings of things to come this perception is hidden from the great New Testament writers who continue to think of God as the One God of Old Testament teaching.

3. We have seen that the Christology of the three writers is a Wisdom or Logos Christology. The distinction is not exclusive, since in the teaching of Philo Wisdom and the Logos are identified, functions of each being ascribed to the other. In the Alexandrian Book of Wisdom, a writing which St. Paul may have read,[1] Wisdom is described as 'the artificer of all things', 'a breath of the power of God', 'an effulgence from everlasting light', 'an unspotted mirror of the working of God', 'an image of his goodness' (vii. 22–6). By His wisdom God formed man, and she sits by Him upon His throne (ix. 2, 4). In the light of this teaching it is significant that in 1 Cor. i. 24 Christ is described as 'the wisdom of God' and that in Col. ii. 3 'all the treasures of wisdom and knowledge' are said to be 'hidden' in Him. Most commentators are agreed that in Col. i. 15–20 Christ is

[1] Cf. A. Robertson and A. Plummer, *The First Epistle of St. Paul to the Corinthians*, 17.

described in terms of Logos teaching.[1] Indeed the use of this teaching was one of the strongest arguments brought against the authenticity of the Epistle by F. C. Baur or the genuineness of these particular verses by H. J. Holtzmann. The objection fails because the passage is an essential part of the reply to the false teachers at Colossae who affirmed the activity of angelic mediators in creation and redemption. The great names assigned to Christ in this passage, 'the image',[2] 'the firstborn',[3] 'the head of the body',[4] 'the beginning',[5] have parallels in the Old Testament, in Philo, the Hermetic literature, and the Rabbinic writings.[6] The presence of the names in other New Testament writings show that they are not peculiar to Colossians, but in this Epistle they are massed together and connected with great claims for the work of Christ in creation and reconciliation. All things, it is said, have been created in and through and unto Him, including angelic powers. In Him as pre-existent they cohere. He is the Head of the Church, the embodiment of the fulness of God, the agent of God's purpose of reconciliation on earth and in heaven. Parallels to most of these statements concerning the Logos are certainly striking and detailed, but the language used need not have been derived from books. It may be due rather to a diffused knowledge of Philonic teaching in the world of St. Paul's day. It is even possible that this heritage reached the Apostle through Jewish channels.[7]

[1] Cf. J. B. Lightfoot, *The Epistle to the Colossians*, 141–58; T. K. Abbott, *The Epistles to the Ephesians and to the Colossians*, 209–24; E. F. Scott, *The Epistles to the Colossians, to Philemon and to the Ephesians*, 19–27; M. Dibelius, *An die Kolosser Epheser an Philemon*, 7–15.

[2] Cf. 2 Cor. iv. 4, Heb. i. 3.   [3] Cf. Rom. viii. 29, Heb. i. 6, Apoc. i. 5.

[4] Cf. Col. ii. 19, Eph. i. 22f., iv. 15, v. 23, (Rom. xii. 5, 1 Cor. xii. 27).

[5] Cf. Apoc. iii. 14, xxii. 13.

[6] See the detailed study of St. Paul's Wisdom Christology by W. D. Davies, *Paul and Rabbinic Judaism*, 147–76, in which the identification of Wisdom with the Torah is traced.   [7] Cf. W. D. Davies, *op. cit.*, 39.

A fuller use of the Logos conception appears in the Epistle to the Hebrews. The author's debt to Philo seems clear in the use of such phrases as 'the radiance of his glory' and 'the very image of his essence', in the description of the Son as 'heir of all things', the agent in the making of the worlds and the One who upholds all things by the word of His power; in the conception of Christ as the high priest and the description of the Word of God in iv. 12f. Dr. James Moffatt expresses the conviction that 'the more he differs from Philo in his speculative interpretation of religion the more I feel, after a prolonged study of Philo, that our author had probably read some of his works'.[1] 'The terminology of the Wisdom literature', he says, 'was as familiar to this early Christian διδάσκαλος as to the author of James'.[2]

The fact, however, that neither St. Paul nor the author of Hebrews uses the name 'Logos' is suggestive. Although Philonic terms are used in Heb. iv. 12, 'the Word of God' in this passage is not the Logos but a personification of the revelation of God.[3] The explanation appears to be that these writers not only perceived the usefulness of the Logos conception, but also its inadequacy to describe the Person of the Incarnate Christ. Each prefers the idea and the vocabulary of Sonship. St. John manifests the same preference, but he takes the bolder step of using the title 'Logos', while pointedly safeguarding his Christological beliefs by saying that the Word was θεός (not ὁ θεός)[4] and declaring that 'the Word became flesh'.

[1] *The Epistle to the Hebrews*, lxif.
[2] *Op. cit.*, lxii.
[3] *Op. cit.*, 55.
[4] See earlier, p. 20f. 'The difference may be indicated in English by contrasting the phrases "a divine being" and "the supreme being" ', G. L. Prestige, *God in Patristic Thought*, 144. See the discussion of C. F. D. Moule, *An Idiom Book of New Testament Greek*, 116.

This statement Philo would have rejected with horror. Many strands of teaching enter into the Evangelist's Christology, including Old Testament ideas concerning the Word of God, but it is clear that he draws upon conceptions current in the Greek world of his day in order to express his apprehension of the significance of Christ.

The influences which have shaped the Christological teaching of the great writers is a question of great interest, but the more important question for our inquiry is the bearing of this teaching upon the doctrine of God. This issue becomes even more urgent when we consider their presentation of Christ as the Divine Redeemer.

4. Each of the great writers presents Christ within a doctrinal pattern in which, as the Divine Redeemer, He is sent down to earth from heaven to be the Saviour of man. In this pattern there is both a downward and an upward movement. The Saviour is sent by God, accomplishes His work on earth, and then returns to heaven whither in due time all who find deliverance through Him themselves ascend. This pattern is foreshortened by the omission of any reference to the Parousia, the coming of the Christ in flesh, and His death for sin. Nevertheless, it includes ideas distinctively present in the New Testament Epistles. Thus, St. Paul speaks of Christ as the Man from Heaven, and both he and St. John describe Him as 'sent'.[1] Hebrews speaks of Him as 'appointed' (i. 2) and as 'made a high priest' (v. 5). In the Fourth Gospel the Son looks back to the glory He had with the Father (xvii. 5) and describes His return as His glorifying and ascension (xiii. 32, xx. 17). In 'the Hymn to Christ' St. Paul refers to His divine form, His self-emptying, humiliation, and exaltation (Phil. ii. 6–11). Hebrews names Him as 'the mediator of a better covenant' (viii. 6, etc.) and with

[1] Cf. Rom. viii. 3, Gal. iv. 4, Jn. x. 36, cf. xvii. 18–21.

primitive Christianity the author and St. Paul frequently declare that He is 'seated at the right hand of God' (Heb. i. 3, Eph. i. 20f., etc.). Believers are to be 'caught up in the clouds' and 'meet the Lord in the air' (1 Thess. iv. 17). Meantime, they are to 'wait for his Son from heaven' whom God raised from the dead, 'even Jesus, who delivers us from the wrath to come' (1 Thess. i. 10).

This pattern of doctrine has acquired a new interest by the claim of Bultmann[1] and others,[2] that in Hellenistic Christianity the Gospel 'was unfolded by means of Gnostic terminology'.[3] 'For Christian missions', he writes, '*the Gnostic movement* was a competitor of the most serious and dangerous sort because of the far-reaching relatedness between them'.[4] In agreement with Reitzenstein, Bultmann reconstructs the Gnostic myth of a heavenly redeemer, the son and 'image' of the highest god, who is sent by him from the light-world bringing the knowledge by which men, sunk in sleep and drunkenness, are reminded of their heavenly home and by means of secret pass-words are taught how they can pass to it safely through the spheres. These ideas appear in later forms of Gnostic teaching and in Mandaism, and they may well have a long history behind them. Bultmann justly points out the distinctive differences in the Christian message.[5] That message, he agrees, insisted that the creation of the world is the work of the one true God; that man too is His creation and no pre-existent spark of heavenly light; that Christ's humanity was no semblance or disguise; and that His work is to redeem men from sin

[1] *The Theology of the New Testament*, i, 164–77.
[2] Bultmann names E. Käsemann, *Leib und Leib Christi* (1933), *Das wandernde Gottesvolk* (1939), R. Reitzenstein, *Die hellenistischen Mysterienreligionen* (3rd ed. 1927), and other writers.
[3] Cf. Bultmann, *Theology of the New Testament*, i. 164.
[4] *Op. cit.*, i. 165.   [5] *Op. cit.*, i. 168.

and not only from ignorance. He maintains, however, that it is clear that Hellenistic Christianity is 'in the maelstrom of the syncretistic process'; 'the genuinely Christian element is wrestling with other elements; "orthodoxy" does not exist at this early period but is still to develop'.[1]

In principle one cannot reject the possibility that the great writers made use of a current doctrinal pattern, especially if we agree that in varying degrees they drew upon the Logos conception. We have recognized that, while the use of the Kyrios title can be explained by factors within the Christian movement, its wide adoption by St. Paul may have been encouraged by its ubiquity in Greek religion. The first missionaries found the name 'Son of God' intelligible to Gentiles, while 'Son of Man' was meaningless. They therefore used the one and dropped the other. St. Paul also describes Christ, in contrast with Adam, as the Second Man from heaven. The irony of 1 Cor. viii. 5 and the polemic against idolatry in Rom. i. 21f. do not exclude the influence of contemporary ideas upon the mind of one who confessed himself to be 'debtor both to Greeks and Barbarians' (Rom. i. 14). His attitude, moreover, to pagan audiences was by no means unsympathetic.[2] No intelligent writer can isolate himself from prevailing currents of thought, certainly not one who said that he became all things to all men in order that he might save some (1 Cor. ix. 22). If then Gnostic ideas were current, they could have been used by the great writers as a framework.

A more serious issue is raised if it is a question, not merely of the adoption of a pattern, but of ideas which transformed the tradition. In this matter exaggeration has run rife in Pauline exegesis, notably in questions

[1] *Op. cit.*, i. 171.   [2] Cf. Ac. xiv. 15–17 and xvii. 23.

connected with the mystery-religions. The Apostle's attitude to the Colossian errorists, when contrasted with the spirited denunciations of false teaching in the Pastoral Epistles, suggests that contact with the Greek world led him to expand his theology, not by direct borrowing, but by ideas superior to beliefs he rejected. The author of Hebrews and the Fourth Evangelist were more responsive to Hellenistic influences, but fundamentally, like that of St. Paul, their religious thought is Jewish.

Several considerations lead us to doubt the view that the great writers were influenced by a Gnostic myth. First, while these myths appear in second-century Gnosticism and in the Hermetic tractate *Poimandres*,[1] there is a complete absence of Gnostic literature in the first century. Gnostic ideas have a long history behind them, and they are certainly rebutted in the Johannine literature, but the myth of the descent of a divine redeemer is not attested so early. Reconstructions of its form in the first century are therefore highly speculative. It is indeed a superior hypothesis that Gnostic teaching was deeply influenced by Christianity itself. Again, the differences between the myth and New Testament teaching, as Bultmann points out, are considerable and, so far as the idea of deliverance from sin is concerned, they are insuperable, while the agreements in the pattern of the descent and ascent of the divine redeemer amount to no more than a natural and common mode of speech. Further, the form of the New Testament doctrine can be explained from Christian ideas and without any reference to the Gnostic myth. It arises naturally from the close connexion which the New Testament writers find be-

---

[1] Cf. J. M. Creed, 'The Heavenly Man', *The Journal of Theological Studies*, xxvi, 120f.; C. H. Dodd, *The Interpretation of the Fourth Gospel*, 41–53.

tween the Work and the Person of Christ.   If the Saviour
who redeems men from sin is divine, He must come from
God and return to God, and in terms of the cosmology
of the time it is natural to describe Him as 'sent', as
descending to earth, and as ascending to heaven.   The
picture is mythological, but only in the sense that heavenly
and spiritual truths are expressed in human and material
forms.   Vital differences rule out any process of borrowing;   the utmost that can be claimed is the use of a basic
pattern well understood in the contemporary world.[1]
We are entitled to conclude that New Testament teaching
about the Divine Redeemer is a valid development of the
tradition.

Sooner or later this development was bound to react
upon the Christian conception of God. Outwardly the
great writers do not modify inherited teaching concerning
God.   They speak of Him in the manner of their fathers
as the God of Abraham, Isaac, and Jacob, as the One
God confessed in the *Shema*, 'Hear, O Israel: the Lord
our God is one Lord' (Deut. vi. 4).[2]   But in speaking of
Christ as the Word and as the Divine Redeemer of men,
they foreshadow developments in which a new presentation of the doctrine of God was inevitable.   So far as we
can see, the great writers do not seem conscious of this
necessity.   They do not teach the later doctrine of the
Trinity.   As it stands, much of their teaching is binitarian in character, but where they describe the work of
the Son and the activity of the Spirit, it is trinitarian in

---

[1] A similar conclusion is reached by W. L. Knox in his essay, 'The
"Divine Hero" Christology in the New Testament', *Harvard Theological
Review*, xli, No. 4, 229–49.   Knox points out that St. Paul presents
Christ in very much the same light as some of the popular cult-figures of
the Hellenistic world, Heracles, Asclepius, and Dionysus, but that there is
no need to suppose that he is consciously imitating pagan usage.

[2] Cf. Mk. xii. 29 and 1 Cor. viii. 5f.

tendency. But, in spite of this, the new doctrinal situation is not apparent to them. There is thus a tension, some would say an inconsistency, in their teaching which is the harbinger of future developments. So far from being derogatory in its implications, this fact is the mark of a living and spiritual revelation.

III

THE DEVELOPMENT OF THE DOCTRINE OF GOD

The question arises whether teaching about the Work or that concerning the Person of Christ exerted the greater influence upon the shaping of the doctrine of God. The question is difficult since the two are so closely combined; but there can be little doubt that it was the growing appreciation of the Work of Christ, through worship and reflection, which proved decisive. Again and again, in discussing the Incarnation, Athanasius[1] dwells upon the significance of the Cross. In opposition to Apollinarianism Gregory of Nazianzus[2] makes the same appeal when, in speaking of the humanity of Christ, he says, 'That which has not been assumed has not been healed' (τὸ γὰρ ἀπρόσληπτον, ἀθεράπευτον).

The God whose Son redeems mankind is manifestly much more than the God of Jewish belief. In thinking of Him it is necessary to find room, within the riches of His being, for the love of the Father, the gift of the Son who goes forth to redeem, and for the exercise of His ministry Godwards in suffering, sacrifice, and intercession. Even the Abelardian view of the Atonement, as the supreme revelation of divine love which constrains man's answering response of love, requires a God who is more than the God of Abraham, Isaac, and Jacob. More

---

[1] *De Incarnatione*, xxi–xxv.
[2] *Epistle* 101 (*ad Cledonium* 1), Migne P. G., 37, 181 c.

insistent is this necessity when theories of satisfaction or substitution are maintained, and most of all, it may be claimed, when the doctrine of a representative sacrifice, in which men participate by faith union with the Crucified, is unfolded. The doctrine of the One Sacrifice of the Son of God demands for its consistency the recognition of internal relationships within the being of God for which Old Testament teaching and even express New Testament doctrine are not adequate without further development and expansion. The Cross of Christ is the rending of a veil from the top to the bottom so that the hidden being of God is revealed. What eye has not seen nor ear heard is shown to be true.

If the self-offering of Christ is viewed entirely from without, a fatal division is created between the Father and the Son. If it is consummated within the Godhead, not only is there no division, but a ceaseless service of giving and receiving, which is of the essence of love, is predicated of God, a truth which can be apprehended, although not fully described, by human thought. The Cross of Christ is of eternal significance available now as always for man's salvation. For a religion of this kind, and of these dimensions, a doctrine of God is needed in which love, sacrifice, and redemption have eternal meaning in the life of the Father, the Son, and the Holy Spirit. Christology and the Atonement are an inseparable part of the doctrine of God. In this persuasion I propose in the next chapter to discuss the question of Christology and the doctrine of the Trinity.

XVIII

CHRISTOLOGY AND THE TRINITY

I N this chapter it is not possible or necessary to discuss
the origins and historical development of the doctrine
of the Trinity. If, however, we desire to appreciate
the true nature of New Testament teaching concerning
the Person of Christ, and to see it in a modern setting,
we are bound to consider the relationship between
Christology and the Trinity because it was in consequence
of what was affirmed about Christ and the Holy Spirit
that the doctrine came to be formulated. The impulses
which led to the discussions in the early centuries, the
Middle Ages, and the Reformation period were not
primarily philosophical, but practical, liturgical, and religious. What Christ was believed to be is the foundation
of the doctrine.

Fortunately recent discussions put us in a better
position to examine the question than was possible a
generation ago. From being regarded as a doctrine of
second rank standing on the circumference of Christian
teaching, or viewed as an appendix to it, a return is manifest in modern theology to the earlier emphasis upon its
centrality. This importance is affirmed or implied in a
whole series of modern works.[1] There are, of course,

---

[1] Cf. C. C. J. Webb, *God and Personality* (1918), A. E. Garvie, *The
Christian Doctrine of the Godhead* (1925), L. S. Thornton, *The Incarnate
Lord* (1928), K. Barth, *The Doctrine of the Word of God* (1936) and *Die
Kirchliche Dogmatik* I (1945), J. Baillie, *Our Knowledge of God* (1939),
L. Hodgson, *The Doctrine of the Trinity* (1943), D. M. Baillie, *God was in
Christ* (1948), R. S. Franks, *The Doctrine of the Trinity* (1953), C. Welch,
The Trinity in Contemporary Theology (1953). Among older works are

important differences among the views of these writers, and to some of them attention will be given later, but in varying degrees all unite in finding fundamental meaning in the doctrine.

Along with this renewed interest in the Trinity must be mentioned the modern emphasis upon the factual character of Revelation.[1] The tendency is to find God's revelation of Himself mediated in act and deed, in the great crises of Old Testament history, the Exodus from Egypt and the Return from the Babylonian Exile, and especially in the life, death, and resurrection of Jesus Christ. Literary and historical criticism have led us to see that, in the words of Dr. L. Hodgson, 'the revelation of God is not given in words but in deeds', and that the importance of the Scriptures is that 'they bear witness to the activity in history of God our Creator, Redeemer, and Sanctifier'.[2] Revelation is in act and not in propositions.

The strength of this conception is on its positive side. The activity of God in Christ and in His gift of the Holy Spirit unquestionably belongs to His self-revelation. This view is especially helpful in considering the doctrine of the Trinity, since in this matter the teaching of Scripture is at best indirect. Moreover, it appears to give release from the uncertainties of literary and historical criticism. Two comments, however, need to be made. First, it may be doubted whether the limitation of Revelation to act and deed, to the exclusion of word and statement, can be justified. Every one recognizes that the data for the activity of God in history are obtained from the

those of J. Illingworth, *Personality Human and Divine* (1894) and *The Doctrine of the Trinity* (1907), and R. C. Moberly, *Atonement and Personality* (1901).

[1] Cf. *Revelation*, ed. by J. Baillie and H. Martin (1937). See also J. Baillie, *The Idea of Revelation in Recent Thought* (1956).

[2] *The Doctrine of the Trinity*, 19.

witness of Scripture, and it is not necessary to be a funda-
mentalist to claim that divine revelation is present in the
inspired utterances of prophets, apostles, and teachers,
and supremely in the words of Jesus as well as in His
actions.   Secondly, and because Scripture is the medium
of Revelation, freedom from the discipline of literary and
historical criticism is not possible.   There is no ivory
tower of refuge to which we can retire.   We cannot estimate and appraise the testimony of Scripture to the Revelation made in act and deed without considering questions of text, sources, and historical credibility, since
human factors have left their marks upon the primitive
records in respect both of expression and transmission.
For this reason the current depreciation of literary
and historical criticism is to be regretted.   These dis-
ciplines are no less necessary than the need to examine
the bearings of philosophy and of patristic testimony upon
the doctrine.

Nevertheless, it is true that, apart from its record of
divine revelation in act and deed, Scripture does not contain express testimony to the doctrine of the Trinity in
word and statement.   Great passages foreshadow later
developments, but do not state the doctrine.   Chief
among these are Mt. xxviii. 19, 'baptizing them into the
name of the Father and of the Son and of the Holy
Spirit'; 1 Pet. i. 2, 'According to the foreknowledge of
God the Father, in sanctification of the Spirit, unto
obedience and sprinkling of the blood of Jesus Christ';
2 Cor. xiii. 14, 'The grace of the Lord Jesus Christ, and
the love of God, and the communion of the Holy Spirit';
and Eph. ii. 18, 'For through him (Christ Jesus) we both
have our access in one Spirit unto the Father'.[1]   The
Baptismal formula, in Mt. xxviii. 19, shows that a three-

---

[1] See also 1 Cor. xii. 4–6, 2 Thess. ii. 13, Eph. iv. 4–6, Ju. 20f.

R

foldness of reference in connexion with the one name was already current in Palestinian and Syrian communities in the closing decades of the first century, but it cannot be cited as evidence for the teaching of Jesus. The words of St. Peter and St. Paul mention the Father, the Son, and the Holy Spirit together, but without agreement in order, in a manner significant and suggestive in the light of later developments. So far as direct statements are concerned, this is as far as the evidence goes. The Trinity is not an express New Testament doctrine. The importance of the New Testament for the doctrine is the decisive data it presents and the tension previously noted between the monotheism of its writers and their utterances concerning Christ and the Holy Spirit.

On the human side the doctrine of the Trinity is the product of reflection continued through the early Christian centuries in the discussions of the Fathers and expressed in their writings and in the Creeds of the Church, especially the so-called Athanasian Creed, better named from its opening words the *Quicunque Vult*. This Creed originated in Gaul in the fifth or sixth century on the basis of the teaching of Augustine. Apart from the serious and insuperable difficulties raised by its opening statement, which insists that the dogma is necessary to salvation, this Creed goes to the heart of the matter in the words: 'In this Trinity none is afore, or after other: none is greater, or less than another; but the whole three Persons are co-eternal together; and co-equal'. Of this historic symbol one may say that it is 'the ultimate intellectual implicate of the Christian faith, and the historic monument to a mystery with which some of the greatest minds have wrestled'.[1]

The belief that the Trinity is also a revealed doctrine

[1] J. S. Whale, *Christian Doctrine*, 120.

is a 'value-judgement' which has its justification in the testimony of Scripture; the convictions reached by the greatest teachers of the Church, notably Augustine, Aquinas, and Calvin; the general consent given to it in all sections of the Church; and its inherent worth as the essential bond of all Christian doctrine. It is the climax of Christian theology and at the same time the teaching by which all other doctrines are illuminated and co-ordinated. In a comprehensive treatment of the Trinity all these claims would have to be debated, as indeed they are debated in the standard writings. Here the humbler task alone can be attempted of maintaining that there is no satisfactory explanation of the Christology of the New Testament except in a trinitarian context.

I

How then is Christology related to the doctrine of the Trinity, and in particular, since Christ is confessed as the Second Person in the Trinity, what understanding of the three Persons enables us best to apprehend that divine status which the New Testament assigns to Him?

Three different views call for consideration: (1) the widely accepted view that the three Persons are not persons in the modern sense of the term, but, in accordance with the meaning of the Greek *hypostasis* and to a less extent the Latin *persona*, are personal centres or centres of consciousness within the unity of the Godhead; (2) the submission made by several recent writers that the distinctions within the Triunity of God are best described as 'modes of existence' or 'modes of being'; (3) the claim that the three Persons are persons in the modern sense of the term embraced within an organic unity which is real, although ultimately mysterious and only partially intelligible.

1. The first of these views has the supreme advantage of safeguarding the divine unity against tritheism by positing differentiations within the *ousia* or essence of God, which are more than aspects or temporal manifestations, but not persons in the modern sense of the term. Its weakness is that it does not adequately provide for the internal relationships of love and fellowship which belong to the life of God or do justice to that Sonship which is the outstanding mark of the New Testament revelation concerning Christ. 'Hypostasis', or 'substratum', comes to be used in patristic theology of that which subsists or has a concrete existence.[1] The Latin 'persona', first used by Tertullian, which originally meant 'a face', then a 'mask', and so a 'dramatic character' (*persona dramatis*), is nearer to, but still falls short of, what we mean by personality, a comparatively modern conception which we owe to Descartes and Locke. Augustine prefers to speak of three *personae* rather than three 'substances', but the fact that even the Latin term did not satisfy him is apparent in his well known observation that we say 'three persons', not because we wish to say this, but in order that we may not be reduced to silence, *Non ut illud diceretur, sed ne taceretur*.[2] Professor Hodgson goes so far as to say that 'whatever may be the etymological history of the words ὑπόστασις and *persona*, it is impossible to avoid the conclusion that St. Augustine regarded each Person in the Godhead as being personal in whatever sense the word is used of conscious, intelligent and purposive human beings',[3] and he takes a similar view of the teaching of Aquinas based upon his use of Boethius' definition of *persona* as 'the individual substance of a rational nature', *Naturae rationalis individua*

[1] See G. L. Prestige, *God in Patristic Thought*, 162–78.
[2] *De Trinitate*, v. 9.   [3] *The Doctine of the Trinity*, 155.

substantia.[1] This view is contested by C. Welch[2] and R. S. Franks,[3] and it is likely to be a matter for debate for some time to come. For our immediate purpose the question to consider is whether modern theology is justified in using such expressions as 'personal centres' or 'centres of consciousness' in describing differentiations within the Triunity of God.

These expressions are manifestly used as modern equivalents for the words *hypostasis* and *persona* with a desire to avoid the word 'person' in the sense of a separate individuality. The desire seems to be to choose an expression better than 'substance' and less concrete than 'person'. The intention is praiseworthy, although it appears to bespeak a fear of the more popular understanding of personality which might be dispelled by explanation and careful definition. After all, the idea that the three Persons of the Trinity are not self-contained individuals is not hard to grasp, especially when it is recognized that even human personality has its corporate aspects. To replace great theological words because they can be misunderstood is not always a reputable undertaking. What, however, is meant by 'a personal centre' or 'a centre of consciousness'? It does not seem possible to use either of these expressions without meaning a point, or psychological centre, at which consciousness is operative in the activities of knowing, feeling, and willing. The centres, however closely related they may be, can hardly be the distributive media of a single consciousness, but as sufficiently distinct to operate singly but in unison. If anything like this is meant, and the phrases in question are often used so vaguely that we cannot be sure, there does not appear to be any gain in not using the word

[1] *Op. cit.*, 159.   [2] *The Trinity in Contemporary Theology*, 295–302.
[3] *The Doctrine of the Trinity*, 189.

'persons', provided it is recognized that in using the term we are speaking analogically, as in all terminology applied to the doctrine of the Trinity. If this claim is accepted, the area of discussion is reduced. We can confine ourselves to the question of the comparative relevancy of 'modes of existence' or 'persons' as the appropriate way of describing internal relationships within the Godhead.

2. The designation 'modes of being' (*Seinsweisen*) is proposed by Karl Barth in *Die Kirchliche Dogmatik* (I, 1, 9) as 'relatively better' than 'persons'. He points out that it has a formal precedent in the expression τρόποι ὑπάρξεως used by Basil of Caesarea with the meaning 'modes of existence'.[1] C. Welch reminds us that it was used by I. A. Dorner and is employed by Abbé Penido to describe metaphysical personality.[2] Welch himself favours the use of the term and so apparently does D. M. Baillie in *God Was in Christ*[3] and also R. S. Franks in *The Doctrine of the Trinity*.[4] Barth and those who agree with him emphatically deny that anything like Modalism is implied. The 'modes', Barth insists, are not merely phases of manifestation, but are necessary distinctions in the Divine Essence and are eternal as God is eternal. ' "Modes of being" ', Welch says, 'does not refer to the distinctions in the content of God's activity or to God only in relation to the world, but to his inmost being, the

[1] *De Spiritu Sancto*, 43f. G. L. Prestige explains that the phrase was used from the end of the fourth century to express the belief that, in the Persons of the Trinity, 'one and the same being is presented in distinct objective and permanent expressions, though with no variation in divine content', *God in Patristic Thought*, 249.

[2] *Op. cit.*, 277.

[3] *Op. cit.*, 133–40. But in speaking of 'Two Trends of Trinitarian Thought' Baillie says, 'I do not propose to attempt a settlement between the two types of Trinitarian interpretation', *op. cit.*, 140.

[4] *Op. cit.*, 199.

"structure" of his existence'.[1]   He proposes that we should use the term 'Person' in respect of the Triune God and 'modes of being' (or 'existence') for the distinctions within His triunity.

Even from this brief summary it will be seen how great a problem is set for modern theology by these suggestions. I comment upon them only because I am compelled to do so if I am to speak of Christology and the Trinity.

It does not seem that any advantage is gained by speaking of God as 'Person' rather than by using C. C. J. Webb's phrase 'personality in God', or by using 'modes of being' instead of 'persons' for the distinctions of Father, Son, and Holy Spirit within the unity of the Divine Being.   We must accept the assurance that 'modes of being' is not used in a modalistic sense, that is as describing only the threefold *aspects* of God's self-manifestation, and Barth's statement that the 'modes' are 'modes of *being*' descriptive of 'the Godness of God'.   But at least two objections stand in the way of accepting these views.

First, despite the assurances offered, the term 'modes of being' almost incurably suggests Modalism, and when it is explained in a contrary sense, the explanations are far from being luminous.   What relationships of fellowship and love are possible between one 'mode of being' and another?   The advantage of the new terminology is its impressive emphasis upon the unity of God, but its description of the differentiations within the unity is little more than a verbal advance upon the classical use of the word *hypostasis*.   We are freed, it is claimed, from the ambiguity of the term 'persons', but the gain is dubious since it is replaced by one not less ambiguous, and less capable of describing inner relationships within the God-

[1] *Op. cit.*, 278.

head. Secondly, it is highly doubtful if New Testament teaching can find an appropriate vehicle of expression in the new nomenclature. Professor Hodgson says that Barth's trinitarian theology seems to him to be 'in flat contradiction to the biblical evidence'.[1] Even if we allow that the feat of expressing what St. Paul and St. John say of the Father, the Son, and the Holy Spirit in terms of a plurality of 'modes of being' is not entirely impossible, the results to say the least are odd. Is it through the second mode of being that we have our access in the third to the first? Did God so love the world that He gave a mode of His existence in order that by believing in it we may have eternal life? It may be replied that we are parodying the theory, by replacing the picturesque language of the biblical writers by theological jargon, and that strange results follow if we transpose their statements by the use of the word 'person'. But are we nearer or farther from New Testament teaching in the one terminology rather than the other? That is the decisive question. And the issue becomes sharper when it is seen in the words of Jesus. When He says that no one knows the Son save the Father, and that no one knows the Father save the Son, we seem nearer to His thought when we think of 'persons' rather than of 'modes of being'. The truth of the matter is that the suggested terminology breathes the air of philosophy rather than religion. It rebuts tritheism at the cost of confusion.

3. The third view we have to consider is the submission made by a group of Anglican scholars, including C. C. J. Webb, L. S. Thornton, and L. Hodgson, that the three Persons of the Trinity are 'Persons' in the modern sense of the term in a unity which is organic and not arithmetical. It is becoming common to speak of this view as 'the

[1] *Op. cit.*, 229.

social theory of the Trinity' and as 'the ultra-Cappadocian movement in modern Trinitarian thought', because of the prominence given to the analogy of the family and the use made by the Cappadocian Fathers, Basil of Caesarea, Gregory of Nyssa, and Gregory Nazianzus, of the analogy of three individual men. These characterizations are not altogether happy because the use of the psychological analogy is prominent in these writers, and because, as in all illustrations of the doctrine, the figure of the family is analogical. Professor Hodgson holds that the Trinity is the doctrine of God implied by the earthly life of Christ, when that life became the object of reflection by Christians in the light of their experience of being adopted to share His Sonship, and he maintains that the full personality of the Holy Spirit is taught in the New Testament. The evidence, he says, 'requires us to believe in a God whose unity unifies three activities each of which is known to us as a distinct Person in the full sense of that word'.[1]

Manifestly, such a theory has to meet the charge of being tritheistic. Although the three Persons are described as persons 'in the modern sense of the word', it is probable, in view of what is said of 'interpermeation' (περιχώρησις, circuminsessio),[2] that a form of personality is meant richer than its human counterpart; but this is not expressly said, possibly because of the objections to which such a term as 'extra-personality' is exposed. The charge of tritheism is anticipated by the considerable

---

[1] *The Doctrine of the Trinity*, 140. With Professor Hodgson's view may be compared that of Dr. G. L. Prestige who suggests that Patristic teaching, expressed in modern language, is that 'in God there are three divine organs of God-consciousness, but one centre of divine self-consciousness', *op. cit.*, 301. This view safeguards the divine unity, but is less easily capable of describing inter-trinitarian relationships, especially those of love.   [2] Cf. G. L. Prestige, *op. cit.*, 284.

attention which Professor Hodgson gives to the question of the divine unity. He makes use of ideas suggested in the first place by Professor J. Laird in *Problems of the Self* (1917), especially the view that the human self or soul, which expresses itself in the activities of thinking, feeling, and willing, is neither one of these several activities nor yet a fourth entity, but a mysterious unity in trinity postulated in faith by our reason. From this view Professor Hodgson develops a parallel conception relative to the constitution of the Godhead. The divine unity, it is maintained, is not arithmetical, but organic. It does not consist in the absence of multiplicity, but in the unifying of the elements of which it is composed, a process which is reflected in increasing complexity and upon different levels in the life of living creatures. It is a unity which casts light upon lesser unities. The act of faith required for the acceptance of the doctrine of the Trinity is faith in 'a dynamic unity actively unifying in one Divine life the lives of the three Divine Persons'.[1] It is not an irrational mystery, but it ends in mystery because on earth we know of no unity which so perfectly unifies so wide and rich a diversity of content.

It may, I think, be claimed that this conception of the Trinity illuminates the New Testament data, especially since the three Persons are not self-contained individuals, as in popular ideas of personality, but Persons who interpermeate one another in the life of divine love. It is open to argument whether Professor Hodgson's rejection of the *principium*, or primacy, of the Father is really necessary, if, as we have maintained, the subordination present in the New Testament is not a master and servant relationship, but a life of reciprocity exercised and fulfilled in the fellowship of mutual love. A marked feature of

[1] *Op. cit.*, 95.

this theory of the Trinity is its religious value. It provides a basis for a trinitarian religion in which there is ample room for meditation, contemplation, and adoration. The great hymns to the Trinity all confess a Trinity in Three Persons, as Bishop Heber's 'Holy, holy, holy, Lord God almighty!' and Charles Wesley's 'Hail, holy, holy, holy Lord!' testify. So far as we know, Personal Centres and Modes of Being have not as yet lent themselves to a comparable use; and in the foreseeable future it does not seem likely that they will prove liturgically attractive. This is no mere *argumentum ad hominem*, for it is a truism to say that a theology which does not express itself in hymns is found wanting.

II

A worthy theory of the Person of Christ can be formulated in terms of any one of the forms of the doctrine of the Trinity I have described, but for the reasons given the most serviceable, since it stands nearer to New Testament teaching, is the hypothesis that the three Persons are Persons in the full sense of the term.

Father, Son, and Holy Spirit, as we find them in the Gospels and the Epistles, are personal beings. The announcement, 'Thou art my beloved Son; in thee I am well pleased', is a converse between persons. The declaration that of the day or hour of the Parousia no one knows, 'not even the angels in heaven, neither the Son, but the Father', is a statement about persons. And so too in the Fourth Gospel and in the Epistles. When it is said that in the fulness of the time God sent forth His Son; when it is declared that the Father loves the Son, and has given all things into His hand; when God is said to have spoken first in the prophets and finally in His Son; in all these cases persons are named, and there is no reason to suppose that the language is only an accommodation to human thought. It is true that in some of these passages and in others of the kind the reference is to the Son as Incarnate, but this possibility leaves untouched the fact that the same language is used of the Father and the Holy Spirit and also of the Son as exalted and pre-existent. The language is human and pictorial, but it would be hazardous to suggest that it is consciously adopted to express relationships which are less than personal. Nor can it be convincingly shown that the counterpart to what the New Testament says of the Father, the Son, and the Holy Spirit is found in 'modes of being' or 'existence'. When it is argued that the three Persons are different manifestations of 'the Godness of God', although not merely aspects of His Being, we are still far removed from the immediacy and the clarity of New Testament revelation. With the richest meaning that can be poured into the word 'person' the Father, the Son, and the Holy Spirit are Persons in the full sense of that term.

Trinitarian relationships are the presupposition and background of the revelation of God in history and in Scripture. Since the New Testament has trinitarian implications, it is as a divine Person within the love of a unity of Persons that the Son of God must be conceived. Only on this theological basis will justice be done to His Person.

The consequences of this view must be indicated before further discussion is attempted. By general consent it is agreed that, if the Incarnation is in truth the invasion of the Triune God into human life, some form of divine self-limitation is involved in this historic process. The nature of this limitation, the form which it takes, and its connexion with trinitarian presuppositions must be the themes of the next chapter. Of necessity this inquiry, however speculative it may appear, involves a consideration of the psychological aspects of the Incarnation which fully recognizes the real humanity of the Son of God and the unity of the Trinity.

XIX

CHRISTOLOGY AND THE KENOSIS

FOR something like a generation the doctrine of the Kenosis, or the Self-emptying of the Son of His divine glory, has rested under much disfavour in contemporary discussions. This reserve is due to the overboldness of its earlier advocates and, in particular, to the wide rejection of the views of Thomasius of Erlangen. Indeed, it will be found that most of the objections to kenotic theories are really aimed at Thomasius or Gess. Discussion was broken off prematurely and has not been effectively renewed. Fashions in theological thinking are not altogether without profit. They provide an opportunity for new suggestions which often by contrast reveal the value of older methods. In the present case no good alternative has been advanced, and it is significant that when the opponents of kenoticism state their own theories, they are driven to put forward hypotheses which, because they must account for the human limitations involved in the Incarnation, prove to be to a considerable extent kenotic. In these circumstances it is necessary to review briefly the various forms this kind of Christology has taken and the objections to which it is exposed. The biblical basis for the doctrine is Phil. ii. 6–11 and 2 Cor. viii. 9. The former passage was examined in detail in Part I, where the claim was made that, while its teaching is primarily religious and ethical, it is at the same time of great Christological importance. It was because of the doctrine implicit in these passages that St. Paul was able to emphasize their bearings upon conduct.

To say this is not to claim that the kenotic hypothesis can be deduced from them. All that can be said is that they suggest and point to hypotheses of this kind.

I

I shall not attempt to give a full account of those writers who have developed kenotic hypotheses, but only to indicate outstanding contributions important for the study of modern Christology. The classic account is that of A. B. Bruce in his well known work, *The Humiliation of Christ* (1876).

Thomasius of Erlangen was not the first of these theologians, but in many ways he is the most important. In *Christi Person und Werk* (1853–61) he submits that in assuming human nature the divine Logos, without ceasing to be God, divested or 'emptied' Himself of the 'relative attributes' of omniscience, omnipotence, and omnipresence, while retaining the 'essential attributes' of holiness, love, and justice. In his *Die Lehre von der Person Christi* (1856) Gess goes further and advocates the hypothesis of a suspension of the influx of the life of the Father in the Son, so that the Logos parted with all the attributes of Deity and suffered the extinction of His eternal self-consciousness, only regaining it after the course of time as a human and variable consciousness. Ebrard, in his *Dogmatik* (1851), rejected the idea of the depotientiation of the incarnate Logos, maintaining that in becoming man the Son did not lose His divinity, but retained the divine attributes in a time-form appropriate to His humanity. In these views we have the three principal forms in which the kenotic hypothesis was presented.

In different ways these ideas were debated in Germany and France during the remaining decades of the nineteenth century, and subsequently, in the first quarter of the present century, kenotic hypotheses were received with much favour in Great Britain. As early as 1893 A. M. Fairbairn developed a kenotic form of Christology in his *Place of Christ in Modern Theology* and in 1898 Bishop Gore did the same in his *Dissertations on Subjects connected with the Incarnation*. In *Belief in Christ* (1922) he wrote: 'The Incarnation is the supreme act of self-sacrificing sympathy, by which one whose nature is divine was enabled to enter into human experience. He emptied Himself of divine prerogatives so far as was involved in really becoming man, and growing, feeling, thinking and suffering as man'.[1] He deprecated attempts to answer such questions as whether the self-emptying was a continual refusal to exercise His divine consciousness or was an original act by which He entered into the limiting conditions of manhood. 'We do well to be agnostics', he wrote, 'if we put our agnosticism in the right place'.[2]

The flowering period of British kenotic Christology which included the works of D. W. Forrest[3] and P. T. Forsyth,[4] culminated in H. R. Mackintosh's *The Doctrine of the Person of Jesus Christ* (1912). In this great work as well as in that of Forsyth we see this type of Christology in its best form.

---

[1] *Op. cit.*, republished in *The Reconstruction of Belief* (1926), 522.
[2] Ibid.
[3] *The Authority of Christ* (1906).
[4] *The Person and Place of Jesus Christ* (1909). Perhaps F. Weston (*The One Christ*, 1907), in spite of his rejection of all kenotic theories which carry over the self-emptying of the Logos into the eternal sphere (p. 115), ought to be included among these writers. He says: 'He has as incarnate no existence and no activity outside the conditions that manhood imposes upon Him' (p. 140); and again, 'He knew Himself as the Logos only in the measure that His human soul could be made to mediate that self-knowledge' (p. 153). 'The popular teaching that assumes in the Incarnate a full consciousness of divine glory side by side with a consciousness of certain occasional limitations', he writes, 'cannot be too strongly deprecated' (p. 157).

Forsyth does not hesitate to use human analogies in his Christology, knowing that examples of self-sacrificing love can be relevant only in part. Instead of speaking of the renunciation of divine attributes he prefers to think of their operation in a new mode of existence, of their retraction from the actual to the potential. They are not destroyed, but concentrated. The history of Christ's growth, as he sees it, is 'a history of moral redintegration, the history of his recovery, by gradual moral conquest, of the mode of being from which, by a tremendous moral act, he came'.[1] 'The diminuendo of the Kenosis went on parallel with the crescendo of a vaster Plerosis. He died to live'.[2] We cannot follow the steps, or make a psychological sketch. 'There is something presumptuous', he says, 'in certain kenotic efforts to body forth just what the Son must have gone through in such an experience.'[3]

The views of Mackintosh are more closely reasoned. Kenoticism in some form, he contends, cannot be avoided by any one who asserts (1) that Christ is now divine, the object of faith and worship, (2) that His divinity is eternal, (3) that His life on earth was unequivocally human, and (4) that we cannot predicate of Him two consciousnesses or two wills. 'It is impossible', he says, 'to think these four positions together save as we proceed to infer a real surrender of the glory and prerogatives of deity, "a moral act in the heavenly sphere", must have preceded the advent of God in Christ'.[4] He will not allow that the idea of the divine immutability rules out such an act of sacrifice. 'What is immutable in God', he affirms, 'is the holy love which makes His essence'.[5] Like Forsyth, Mackintosh mentions human analogies, but with the recognition that no analogy is commensurate with the divine

[1] *Op. cit.*, 308.   [2] *Op. cit.*, 311.   [3] *Op. cit.*, 320.
[4] *Op. cit.*, 470.   [5] *Op. cit.*, 473

s

fact. He rejects Thomasius' distinction between the relative and the essential attributes of God, and the idea of the abandonment of this or that attribute on the part of the Eternal Son. Attributes, he contends, may be transposed and may come to function in new ways. It is possible, he submits, to conceive the Son as subject to growth and progress, 'as now possessing *all* the qualities of Godhead in the form of concentrated potency rather than of full actuality, δυνάμει rather than ἐνεργείᾳ'.[1] He raises the question whether the Son Incarnate can have known Himself to be divine, and says, 'It can only have been in mature manhood and perhaps intermittently that Christ became aware of His divinity—which must have remained for Him an object of *faith* to the very end'.[2] Only by degrees can the full meaning of His relationship to the Father, with its eternal implicates, have broken upon the mind of Jesus.[3] He attempts no psychological theory regarding the relations of the divine and the human in Christ, and is silent about the 'Word' or 'Son' apart from His incarnation. This silence he defends by the insufficiency of the New Testament data and by the claim that certain traditional arguments appear to tend in the direction of ditheism.[4] In saying this he has in mind the objection that the cessation of the incarnate Word from His universal activities must produce cosmic chaos, and he counters this plea by recalling the *inseparabilis trinitatis operatio* emphasized by Augustine. Finally, in commenting upon 'the strongest blow aimed at the Kenotic principle', the objection of Ritschl, that for the Kenoticist 'Christ, at least in His earthly existence, has no Godhead at all',[5] he argues that the absence of certain divine qualities is simply essential to the personal advent of God in time;

[1] *Op. cit.*, 477. [2] *Op. cit.*, 481. [3] Ibid.
[4] *Op. cit.*, 484. [5] *Justification and Reconciliation*, 410.

and he commends the claim of Brierley,[1] that, wherever God reveals Himself, the veiling is as real as the revelation.

I have described the views of Mackintosh with some fulness because they have been widely accepted, and because it is in reply to him that some of the most powerful objections against kenotic doctrine have been directed. It will have been noted that his suggestions have more in common with those of Gess and Ebrard than Thomasius. This also is true of Forsyth's Christology.[2]

In his Hulsean Lectures for 1936 J. M. Creed observes that, although kenotic doctrine is no longer as much in favour as it was, he thinks it probable that most of those among us who have a Christology which they are prepared to state and defend are still kenoticists.[3] How far this is true at the present time it is not easy to say. Probably the opinion is still true, although a certain uneasiness is felt even by theologians who are not convinced by the powerful objections of Archbishop Temple and Professor D. M. Baillie. Since a decision, if it can be reached, is important in any modern evaluation of New Testament teaching concerning the Person of Christ, it is necessary to consider these objections carefully.

[1] *Aspects of the Spiritual*, 35.

[2] R. L. Ottley, in *The Doctrine of the Incarnation* (1896) had expressed similar views. He argued that God limited Himself in creation, and that 'the Incarnation is a further self-limitation' (ii. 285). Christ became 'poor' in such sense that He voluntarily laid aside the exercise of those attributes of Deity that would have hindered a real human experience. The voluntary act of love was maintained by a continuous act of unwearied will. 'The kenosis consisted in a deliberate abstention on the part of the Logos from the exercise of Divine powers that might at any moment have been resumed' (ii. 291f.).

[3] *The Divinity of Jesus Christ* (1938), 75. In his earlier essay on 'Recent Tendencies in English Christology' in *Mysterium Christi* (ed. by G. K. A. Bell and A. Deissmann, 1930), while supporting Mackintosh, Creed says that he does not wish to be understood as arguing for a kenotic Christology, for he is moved by the considerations which Dr. Temple and others have urged against it.

II

Dr. Temple's criticisms are made in his *Christus Veritas* (1924). He quotes the four points made by Mackintosh already mentioned and the kenotic inference drawn from them, and in a well known passage then says:

'But the difficulties are intolerable. What was happening to the rest of the universe during the period of our Lord's earthly life? To say that the Infant Jesus was from His cradle exercising providential care over it all is certainly monstrous, but to deny this, and yet to say that the Creative Word was so self-emptied as to have no being except in the Infant Jesus, is to assert that for a certain period the history of the world was let loose from the control of the Creative Word, and "apart from Him" very nearly everything happened that happened at all during the thirty odd years, both on this planet and throughout the immensities of space' (*op. cit.*, 143).

The suggestion is that a kenotic Christology would involve cosmic chaos.

Professor Baillie[1] asks if there is any answer to Dr. Temple's question, and says that he is not aware that a good reply has been made. He thinks it is vain to reply that the argument presupposes a crude and false separation between the Persons of the Trinity, or to invoke Augustine's principle, that the works of the Trinity without are indivisible, *opera Trinitatis ad extra sunt indivisa*. The kenotic Christology, he submits, proposes such a separation, and Dr. Temple's objection stands. He explains its apparent naïveté by saying that it is an example of *reductio ad absurdum*.

In fact, as we have seen, Mackintosh had anticipated the criticism by quoting Augustine and by insisting that, in trinitarian doctrine, 'person' is more than 'aspect' and less than 'individual'. What is perhaps surprising is that Dr. Baillie does not mention penetrating discussions of Dr. Temple's argument, including J. M. Creed's article

[1] *God Was in Christ*, 95f.

in *Mysterium Christi*[1] and his *Divinity of Christ* and O. C. Quick's *Doctrines of the Creed* published in 1938.

And in truth the objections to Dr. Temple's criticism are formidable. As we have seen, it is not New Testament teaching that the universe was created *by* the Son. The New Testament holds fast to the belief that God is the Creator and speaks of the Logos or the Son as the agent or medium of creation. It was *through* Him that God made the worlds. It does not seem reasonable therefore to argue that a kenotic Christology implies cosmic chaos, and certainly not the form in which it is presented by Forsyth and Mackintosh. Without presuming to define the manner of the divine operations, one might suppose that the resources of the Trinity would be equal to the situation. A claim that a kenotic Christology proposes a separation of the Persons of the Trinity does not seem well founded. It might be argued that it is the fear of cosmic chaos which is tritheistic. The objection is not without relevance when it is directed against the extremer forms of kenoticism but it is pointless against the Christology of Mackintosh. Indeed, it would appear that, while the criticism is directed against Mackintosh, it is the older exponents of kenoticism who are actually in mind. The arrow strikes the wrong target. Thomasius is attacked under the alias of Mackintosh. Further, the distinctive features in Mackintosh's views are not mentioned, especially his submission, which is also that of Forsyth, that the divine attributes were possessed in the form of 'concentrated potency'. Forsyth is not referred to by either critic, and in consequence his view that kenosis was followed by a vaster plerosis is not considered.

A second objection raised by Dr. Temple is that the kenotic theory has 'a mythological appearance'.[2] Pro-

[1] See footnote 3 on p. 265.   [2] *Op. cit.*, 143.

fessor Baillie puts the objection more strongly when he
says that it appears to him 'to give us the story of a
temporary theophany, in which He who was formerly
God changed Himself temporarily into man, or exchanged His divinity for humanity'.[1]   Again, the charge
could only be sustained against a particularly crude form
of kenoticism.   Neither Forsyth nor Mackintosh suggests that, while human, the historic Christ was not
divine.   They would have held rather that the divinity of
Christ is seen in His self-limitation.   And, in any case, the
objection is two-edged and dangerous, for precisely the
same might be said of any theory of the Incarnation.
The charge has a sceptical ancestry.   No matter how the
doctrine is presented, it must have a mythological appearance.   Even the names 'Father' and 'Son' are
pictorial.   The imagery of the 'sending' of the Son is that
of a journey, and no less the idea of His 'ascent' to heaven.
These are merely modes of speech, necessary if lucidity
of statement is to be gained.   In no way do they tell
against the doctrine of the Incarnation when presented in
any worthy manner and certainly not against the views of
Mackintosh.

A third objection is brought forward by Professor
Baillie alone.   He not only claims that in the kenotic
Christology Christ is God and man successively, a view to
which we have already referred, but submits that no room
is left for the Catholic doctrine of the permanence of
Christ's manhood.[2]   In reply we may say that kenotic
Christologies which do not renounce the hypostatic
union of the divine and the human in Christ have no need
to abandon the belief that

> 'He has raised our human nature
>   In the clouds to God's right hand'.

[1] Op. cit., 96.   [2] Op. cit., 97f.

It cannot be said that the modern attack on kenoticism is impressive. J. M. Creed says, 'I do not think that Dr. Temple shakes Professor Mackintosh's argument', and he observes that, if we take seriously the human conditions of the life of Jesus and His personal identity and continuity with the Eternal Word, 'then a Kenotic Christology appears to be indispensable'.[1] He maintains that, when Dr. Temple comes to develop his doctrine of the Incarnate Person, he puts forward statements which 'appear to presuppose that Kenotic principle which on theological grounds has been repudiated'.[2] Dr. Temple's view is that God the Son, who is the Word of God, 'without ceasing His creative and sustaining work, added this to it that He became flesh and dwelt as in a tabernacle among us'.[3] O. C. Quick's comment on this statement is that, 'What He added is precisely that experience in which His Divine consciousness was limited and His Divine state surrendered'.[4] This comment is well justified. In claiming that the life recorded in the Gospels is the very reality of God the Son, Dr. Temple speaks of it as 'set forth in terms of human experience', and accepts the view that on all matters of mere information the Eternal Son shared the views of His time.[5] Professor Quick claims that 'the difference between Dr. Temple and the kenotists concerns only events in the supra-mundane sphere, about which no direct revelation has been given, and man's knowledge is necessarily but guess-work'.[6]

There are, of course, difficulties. J. M. Creed points out the lack of Patristic support. While recognizing that in the writings of Bishop Gore and Dr. Mackintosh

---

[1] *Mysterium Christi*, 136.   [2] *The Divinity of Jesus Christ*, 75.
[3] *Christus Veritas*, 140.   [4] *Doctrines of the Creed*, 138.
[5] *Op. cit.*, 145.   [6] *Op. cit.*, 138.

kenotic teaching lends itself to a powerful interpretation
of the doctrine of the Incarnation, he recalls that F. Loofs
has shown that no real precedent for it can be adduced
from Patristic writers, and that the nearest approach to it
is to be found in the heresiarch Apollinarius.[1] Professor
Quick admits the truth of this contention, but maintains
that the Patristic theologians were committed to a Hel-
lenic conception of the changelessness of God. 'But if',
he says, 'we conceive of God's changelessness to consist
simply in the absolute steadfastness of his perfect will of
love, we can at once deny that the self-limitation of the
eternal Son in the historical manhood of Jesus involves
any real variableness in the deity; since it is the consistency of God's love for man which is the very cause and
ground of the self-limitation'.[2] 'Anglicans', he drily
remarks, 'can hardly be accused of heresy for appealing
to the Bible against a doctrine of the divine nature which,
whatever its value, is certainly derived from extra-
biblical sources'.[3]

In sum, I think we may claim that the modern reaction
against kenoticism is of value mainly as a protest against
the views of its first exponents, and further that the swing
of the pendulum must not prevent us from esteeming its
worth in the hands of its better advocates. The critics
were startled by the prelude and the first movement and
did not examine the second and the third. Theology,
however, is a science in which second thoughts are often
best. Some form of *kenosis* is essential to any worthy
doctrine of the Incarnation, and it should be the endeavour
of modern theology to ascertain, from the New Testament
and in the light of recent discussions, what the best form
is. The theologian of to-day is tempted to avoid the word
as hopelessly compromised by its history, and to speak

[1] *Mysterium Christi*, 133.   [2] *Op. cit.*, 135.   [3] *Op. cit.*, ibid.

rather of the self-limitation of the Son of God, but this is a form of capitulation which will hardly do him credit in the long run.

III

In much that has been said in the last section attention has been given to the conflicting opinions of modern theologians. No apology for this is needed, since the history of doctrine is a necessary discipline in the study of theology. It is desirable, however, to base conclusions on broader considerations, and this task will now be attempted.

There are two ways in which the problems of Christology may be studied. Either we may begin with the life of Christ as it is described in the Gospels and the Epistles, or we may find a starting-point in the doctrine of God as triune. Karl Barth, for example, begins his *Dogmatik* with the doctrine of God and the Trinity. Either method has its advantages. The former, as being more objective, is to be preferred, but the latter cannot be neglected. It will be submitted that in both ways we are led to much the same conclusion.

We have seen that the New Testament makes it clear that the life of Christ on earth was unambiguously human. Jesus Christ appeared as a man subject to the limitations of human finitude. He advanced in wisdom and in stature, grew in knowledge and experience, was exposed to disappointment, frustration, suffering, and death. His humanity was real. In all respects He lived as a man, with a humanity perfect and inclusive. Equally clearly He is divine, Lord and Christ, Son of Man and Son of God, with a unique knowledge of the Father as 'My Father' which is conveyed to Him by revelation from on high and burns during His earthly life with degrees of intensity in accordance with the conditions of His human existence. His Sonship is His secret, and His life is a ministry of redemptive suffering, death, and resurrection which establishes a new covenant between God and men.

The problem of the Person of Christ is the co-existence of these two manifestations of His divine-human personality. In His human life the Son of God is not omniscient and not omnipotent. There are things that He does not know, there are things that He cannot do, and yet He is the Lord and Son of God, venerated and worshipped, the object of faith, the inspiration of an obedience which has no parallel.

If we have regard to these circumstances the opinion is surely justified that some form of kenosis-hypothesis is unavoidable. Still more evident is this if, as will be argued in the final chapter, the Ego of His personality is divine. It can only have been by the deliberate acceptance of self-limitation that the Son of God appeared upon earth. Christology, in short, is incurably kenotic.

We reach the same conclusion if we approach the problem from the standpoint of the formulary adopted at Chalcedon with its doctrine of two natures, the human and divine, combined in the One Person of Christ. In the minds of many New Testament scholars this doctrine raises the greatest difficulties owing to the tendency in Patristic discussions to treat the two natures as separate metaphysical entities. Some of the greatest theologians of the last generation, of whom Forsyth and Mackintosh may be cited as examples, betray the greatest uneasiness when they discuss the doctrine. 'The formula of the union of two natures in one person', wrote Forsyth, 'is essentially a metaphysical formula, and the formula of a Hellenistic metaphysic', 'and', he adds, 'it is more or less

archaic for the modern mind'.[1] Mackintosh declared
that the doctrine, in the rigid shape given to it by tradition,
is 'detachable from the believing estimate of our Lord'.[2]

In considering the doctrine it is essential to distinguish between the form in which it appears in the
formula of Chalcedon and the detailed discussion of the
two natures in the *Tome* of Leo and later writings. The
Chalcedonian symbol confesses 'one and the same Son,
our Lord Jesus Christ, the same perfect in deity and the
same perfect in humanity, very God and very man'. It
describes the Son as 'consisting of reasonable soul and
flesh, of the same substance with the Father as touching
His Godhead, of the same substance with us as touching
His humanity'. It further confesses Him as

'one and the same Christ, Son, Lord, Only-begotten, in two
natures acknowledged, unmixed, unchanged, undivided; so that
the distinction of nature was never abolished by the union, but
rather the peculiarity of each preserved and combined into one
person and one hypostasis; not one, severed and divided into two
persons, but one and the same Son and Only-begotten, Him who is
God, Logos, and the Lord Jesus Christ'.[3]

The formulary is content to confess the reality of the
two natures, and by implication to rebut any attempt to
divide them into two persons as in Nestorianism, or to
affirm the existence of a single nature as in Eutychianism.
It is true that it offers no solution of the problem of the
co-existence of the two natures. But that is its merit. It
is the purpose of a credal statement to embody common
beliefs, not to develop theories. It was inevitable, however, that speculation should arise. It is present already
in the *Tome* of Leo, and there can be no doubt that in
framing the symbol Leo's views were in the minds of the

[1] *The Person and Place of Jesus Christ*, 229.
[2] *The Doctrine of the Person of Jesus Christ*, 298f.
[3] Cf. W. P. Du Bose, *The Ecumenical Councils*, 255.

members of the council. But his exposition is not introduced into the symbol. That is the significant fact, and,
while his views will always be of interest, they must be
distinguished from the doctrine itself.

In his exposition Leo introduces a duality into our
Lord's consciousness which the modern mind finds it
impossible to accept. The human Jesus, it is suggested,
does some things as man and other things as God. As
man He is hungry, as God He feeds the multitude. As
man He says, 'My Father is greater than I', but as God, 'I
and the Father are one'. As man He asks concerning
Lazarus, 'Where have you laid him?' as God He cries,
'Lazarus, come forth'. The tendency of these artificial
distinctions is to invest each of the natures with some kind
of real being, and so it becomes necessary to assign to the
Son two wills and two consciousnesses; or, where this
development is avoided, to emphasize the idea of the pre-
existent Logos as the Ego of the Son's Person to such a
degree that His humanity becomes impersonal. It is the
presence of these 'fatal difficulties', as Mackintosh calls
them, which leads him to reject the doctrine. It will be
recalled, however, that Mackintosh uses the phrase 'the
rigid shape given to it by tradition', and that Forsyth
speaks of it as 'a metaphysical formula'. Mackintosh,
however, is ready to recognize that the God-Man is a
living unity of two natures, if 'human nature' means 'everything pertaining to man's proper constitution', and if
'Divine nature' is 'equivalent to all that forms part of the
true being of God'. This is an opinion to which perhaps
too little attention has been given.

If this view is held to be an inadequate understanding
of the Creeds, the criticisms of Forsyth and Mackintosh
are amply justified. If, however, the two natures describe what is proper to the human and the divine in the

Person of Christ, it can be held that the doctrine is implicit in, or is a legitimate development of New Testament teaching.   In any case it would seem that only in this form can modern theology speak with conviction of the human and divine natures of Christ.   The situation is well described in the words of Leo himself when he says, 'Each nature keeps its own characteristics without diminution, and as the form of God does not annul the form of a servant, so the form of a servant does not impair the form of God'.[1]

If this view of the two natures of the Son is accepted, we come to the same conclusion as that suggested by the New Testament portraiture of Christ's humanity.   Some form of self-emptying is required if we are to apprehend how the two natures inhere in the One Christ.   The divine nature must be conceived as limited in its expression by the human conditions of the Incarnation.   This conclusion is not obviated by the subtle and attractive hypothesis of Leontius of Byzantium[2], that prior to the Incarnation the Logos already possessed all that was needful to live a perfectly human life; that, in theological terminology, the human nature of Christ is *enhypostatic*, having its hypostasis, or underlying reality, within the hypostasis of the Logos.[3]   We may welcome the suggestion that humanity at its best is already implicit in the Godhead; but we still need a Christology which finds the humanity of Christ, not only as a constituent element in

---

[1] Cf. J. Bethune-Baker, *An Introduction to the Early History of Christian Doctrine*, 289.

[2] Cf. H. M. Relton, *A Study in Christology* (1922); see A. R. Vine, *The Expository Times*, lxiv, 132–6.

[3] 'The Divine Logos was capable of becoming the Ego, not only of His Divine but also of His human Nature; because His Personality in virtue of its Divinity already embraced all that is most distinctive of a truly human personality'; 'His Ego was Divine—it was also human; therefore it could be the subject of both natures', H. H. Relton, *op. cit.*, 226f.

His being, but in a life lived out upon the human plane at a particular time and place subjected to self-limitation. To say this is to ask for some kind of kenotic Christology.

The truth is that we cannot get rid of kenoticism. If we dismiss it at the door, it comes back through the window. If we deny it in word, we affirm it in principle, however much theologically we may be upon our guard. The reason must be that self-limitation is an essential form of the divine manifestation. God is God when He stoops no less than when He reigns. He is a God who in revelation hides Himself.

It will be necessary to return to some of these questions in the final chapter. Meantime we must consider the bearings of modern psychology upon Christology, even though as yet little progress has been made in this field.

XX

CHRISTOLOGY AND PSYCHOLOGY

To what extent is it possible to approach the doctrine of the Person of Christ from the standpoint of
modern psychology? Has it any light to throw on
the theological problem?

The difficulties are great and in the opinion of many
insuperable. In its study of human life and behaviour
psychology is confronted with many difficulties. Dr.
D. J. West, the Research Officer of the Society of Psychical Research, has recently said that the whole subject
of psychical phenomena is under a big question mark, and
that so far the investigators raise more problems than they
solve.[1] The subconscious and the unconscious challenge
and defy complete analysis, and the problems of conscious
personality are exceedingly complicated because of an un-
predictable element in human reactions. Mental concepts such as the subconscious can never be verified by
direct observation in the same way as the existence of
germs, for example, can be confirmed.[2] With what hope,
then, can we attempt to describe the inner life of the
Divine Person presented to us in the Gospels? In this
matter there is much ground for reserve. One can fully
understand the point of view of those who think that
psychology has very little to contribute to the discussion of
Christological problems.

Nevertheless, it does not seem right to refuse to make a
psychological approach to Christology. In the early
Christian centuries psychological elements entered into

[1] *Psychical Research Today* (1954), 140f.   [2] *Op. cit.*, 133.

the philosophical aspects of Christological discussions and helped to shape the doctrine of the Trinity. We ought not, therefore, to neglect the better understanding of human personality made possible by the psychology of to-day.

I

A well known attempt to apply the findings of Psychology to Christology was made by Dr. William Sanday in 1910.[1] Its reception by learned opinion was not encouraging. In fact, it was rejected on all sides. Dr. A. E. Garvie included it in a series of articles entitled 'The Danger of Mares' Nests in Theology',[2] and the tendency has been to regard it as an aberration which might decently be interred. This tendency, I think, is to be regretted, for there is much to be learned from theories which prove to be wanting. Historically considered, Christology has developed by progress through error. How much the Catholic doctrine of Christ's Person owes to the discussion of the errors of Sabellius, Arius, Apollinarius, the authors of Nestorianism, and Eutyches! Dr. Sanday's intentions were fully orthodox and constructive, and nothing but good can result from a close study of his views.

Applying the hypotheses of William James and F. W. H. Myers, Dr. Sanday maintained that 'the proper seat or *locus* of all divine indwelling, or divine action upon the human soul, is the subliminal consciousness';[3] and he supported this contention by appealing to the history of mysticism. He went on to affirm that 'the same, or the corresponding, subliminal consciousness is the proper

[1] *Christologies Ancient and Modern* (1910), *Personality in Christ and in Ourselves* (1911).
[2] *The Expository Times*, xxiv, 305-7.
[3] *Christologies Ancient and Modern*, 159.

seat or *locus* of the Deity of the incarnate Christ'.[1]   We may draw a horizontal line, he suggested, between the upper human medium and those lower deeps which are the proper home of whatever is divine. 'Whatever there was of divine in Him, on its way to expression whether in speech or in act, passed through, and could not but pass through, the restricting and restraining medium of human consciousness'. 'This consciousness', he wrote, 'was, as it were, the narrow neck through which alone the divine could come to expression'.[2]   He had no doubt, it must be added, that this human life 'was, in its deepest roots, directly continuous with the life of God Himself'.

I need not describe in detail the discussions which followed.[3]   Dr. H. R. Mackintosh[4] asked if so vague and dubious a magnitude as the subconscious was calculated to help us to interpret the Person of Jesus. 'How shall we speak of a Holy Love', he asked, 'whose fit home is in the subliminal?'.   He questioned whether the new hypothesis really evaded 'the haunting dualism of tradition'.   Many criticisms were brought against the spatial and material metaphors Dr. Sanday employed and his apparent exaltation of the subliminal at the expense of the supraliminal.   To these and other objections he replied

---

[1] Ibid.

[2] *Op. cit.*, 167.   'That which was divine in Christ', he wrote, 'was not nakedly exposed to the public gaze; neither was it so entirely withdrawn from the outward view as to be wholly sunk and submerged in the darkness of the unconscious; but there was a sort of Jacob's ladder by which the divine forces stored up below found an outlet, as it were, to the upper air and the common theatre in which the life of mankind is enacted', *op. cit.*, 166.   He speaks of our human consciousness as a kind of 'narrow neck', 'a sort of porous material stretched entirely across this neck and closing the orifice', 'but not absolutely or imperviously'.   The process, he says, is like that of filtering: 'certain particles, very many particles pass through the pores and come to the surface', *op. cit.*, 176.

[3] Cf. A. E. Garvie's article mentioned above, and J. Baillie, *The Expository Times*, xxiv, 353–8.   [4] *The Person of Jesus Christ*, 487–90.

T

in *Personality in Christ and in Ourselves*, and in articles in *The Expository Times*[1] which are models of controversial courtesy. He disclaimed any intention of attributing superiority to the unconscious[2] and admitted his over-use of spatial metaphors.[3] He thought it possible to state the main hypothesis without bringing in the idea of locality and re-affirmed his belief that the psychology of the subliminal consciousness has matter of value to contribute to Christology.[4]

The importance of Dr. Sanday's hypothesis is that it is an attempt, although unsuccessful, to align the full recognition of the humanity of Christ and its necessary limitations with the conviction that He is in very truth the Eternal Son of God. It was a courageous and suggestive attempt, and one must regret that its failure discouraged others from making constructive contributions to Christology. Its defect was that it sought to localize the divine element in Christ's Person in 'the dreary depths of the subconscious'. Its failure suggests that one must find this element, not only in the hinterlands of human personality, but in His conscious experience of divine revelation and in its continuity with the triune life of God.

It may seem surprising that Dr. Sanday rejected the kenotic hypothesis on the ground that it rested upon an insufficient biblical and historical basis;[5] but it is to be recalled that he wrote at a time (1910) when the bolder and more vulnerable forms of kenoticism were current. Had he developed his views further, it is probable that, in spite of his disclaimer, he would have been compelled to accept some form of kenotic Christology. Indeed, it may be said that in principle he did so; for a view of

---

[1] Vol. xxiv, 438–44, xxv, 46.
[2] *Personality in Christ and in Ourselves*, 59.   [3] *Op. cit.*, 75.
[4] *Op. cit.*, 73.   [5] *Christologies Ancient and Modern*, 71–8.

Christ's Person which speaks of His divine consciousness passing through the restricting medium of His human consciousness is essentially kenotic in character. The opposition to his views prevented such a development for more than a generation. No successor came forward to grasp the robe of his master. The Alexandrian type of Christology, which spoke of Christ's humanity as added to His divinity, ruled Christological thought, with the result that Bishop Gore's restatement in 1920 of his earlier kenotic views made little impression, and even J. M. Creed, who spoke of kenoticism with much favour, was restrained by Dr. Temple's insistence upon its cosmic perils. It seemed better to think of Christ's humanity in terms of the Fourth Gospel, still held to be of Apostolic authorship, even at the risk of losing the virility of the Synoptic presentation in speculations which tended in the direction of an impersonal humanity, or sought to find the humanity as a constituent element in the personality of the Logos. The ghosts of docetism gained a new lease of life.

II

Whether, in the modern situation, psychology can help us to apprehend better the nature of Christ's Person remains at present uncertain. Dean W. R. Matthews, in *The Problem of Christ in the Twentieth Century*, has commended this possibility. He reminds us that much more is now known of the unconscious element in human selfhood. The speculations of Myers and of Sanday, he says, are out of date, but we shall find, he suggests, that these great men were pioneers of thought which cannot be ignored by those who seek insight into the nature of man and the nature of the Son of Man.[1] It was on the

[1] *Op. cit.,* 2.

basis of the God-consciousness that Schleiermacher built up his doctrine of the Person of Christ.[1]　Moreover, thanks to the researches of Freud and of Jung into the nature of the unconscious, and to investigations concerning telepathy and extra-sensory perception, we see that consciousness is perhaps only that minute portion of a larger whole which is illuminated.　'I cannot help thinking', Dean Matthews writes, 'that it is a reproach to modern theology that so little reflection appears to have been given to the bearing of this discovery on the doctrine of the Incarnation'.[2]　Very tentatively he suggests that we shall have to hold that 'the Libido was a reality for Jesus'.[3]　One cannot deny the interest of these suggestions, although it may be questioned whether the samples offered equal the attractiveness of the prospectus.

Progress in some measure has certainly been made in psychical research regarding basic questions.　It is widely thought that extra-sensory perception has been shown to exist, and precognition is said to be suggested by experimental evidence.[4]　The existence of the subconscious is a constant scientific assumption, although questions relating to the unconscious in its individual and racial aspects are matters of much controversy and speculation.　It may be agreed that, if C. G. Jung's theory of a racial unconscious gained fuller recognition, it would be bound to have profound consequences in shaping the doctrines of original sin, incarnation, and redemption. Already in Col. i. 20 the work of reconciliation is thought of as extending to 'all things', 'whether things upon the earth, or things in the heavens'.　Must its scope be extended further to include not only the conscious levels

---

[1] *Op. cit.*, 32.　　　　[2] *Op. cit.*, 44.　　　　[3] *Op. cit.*, 46.
[4] Cf. D. J. West, *op. cit.*, 131; J. B. Rhine, *Extra-sensory Perception* (1934), *The Reach of the Mind* (1947).

where by faith men enter into fellowship with Christ, but also the hidden depths of racial solidarity? And did the Incarnation involve participation in the unconscious? We shall probably feel that Jung's hypothesis, which depends on evidence supplied by dreams, is not sufficiently well grounded to encourage such speculations; but it is not unreasonable to entertain such thoughts on any theory of the unconscious. One thing at least is certain. It is too late in the day to disregard the doctrine of the Trinity because it is mysterious, or to deny that in Christ the human and the divine can co-exist.

Extra-sensory perception and precognition have a bearing upon the life story of Christ, but the evidence in the Gospels is not detailed enough to form a basis for scientific judgements. Thus, the saying of Jesus addressed to Nathanael, 'When you were under the fig tree, I saw you' (Jn. i. 48), is probably only an illustration of the Evangelist's theology. His statement regarding the cure of the Syro-Phoenician woman's daughter, 'The daemon has gone out of your daughter' (Mk. vii. 29), may be a case of precognition; but His knowledge concerning the colt (Mk. xi. 2) and the water-carrier at Jerusalem (Mk. xiv. 13–15) is adequately explained by arrangements previously made. In itself, the suggestion that Jesus experienced extra-sensory perception and precognition is probable enough, but these powers may be no more than the mark of a prophetic personality, and in most cases the psychological data are uncertain. In any case these psychical phenomena bear only indirectly upon the mystery of His Person. More important for Christology would be His marginal consciousness[1] and His subconscious life, if we possessed fuller information. It

[1] For the marginal consciousness in human life cf. H. R. Mackintosh, *Some Aspects of Christian Belief*, 215.

cannot be doubted that these realms of experience belonged to His human life, since they belong to the life of all men. Jesus must have been aware of things which were not the immediate object of attention, and convictions already formed in His conscious life may well have fructified in that little-known medium we call the subconscious. We can say these things because they are true of human life as we know it. Whatever may be the nature of the subconscious, too many instances are known to leave room for doubt that it plays a real part in human experience. Especially relevant are the many attested cases in which solutions of intellectual and personal problems have, as we say, 'leapt into the mind' after periods of apparent quiescence and inactivity, and have made definite contributions to human knowledge and understanding.[1] It is distasteful to many theologians to suggest that room should be found for the subconscious in the life of Jesus; and in truth the greatest care must be taken in shunning purely imaginative attempts to describe His inner life: but if we feel this distaste, we need to ask ourselves whether after all we have taken His humanity sufficiently seriously, and if we have fully grasped the vital truth that 'the Word became flesh' and that the Son of God was 'found in fashion as a man'.

These considerations enable us to make a better appraisal of Dr. Sanday's bold suggestions than was possible at the time when he wrote. He was fully justified in making use of the concept of the subconscious. His error, or misfortune, lay in supposing that it was the *locus*

[1] One illustration among many is recorded by the Rev. Nehemiah Curnock, the editor of *John Wesley's Journal*, who after many months and indeed years of reasoned inference and testing succeeded in deciphering the strange and unknown cipher in which Wesley's Diaries were written. 'It may be of interest', he writes, 'to note that the first effective clue was given to the writer in a dream', *op. cit.*, vol. I, 72.

or seat of the divine from which the knowledge of His
divinity emerged into the upper levels of His consciousness.   This is much too one-sided an account of His
Person, and one which does justice neither to the Gospel
records nor to the experience of prophets who came to
know God through divine revelation and fellowship
with Him.   But it is no more satisfactory to limit Christ's
life of Sonship to conscious levels, and to suppose that
subconscious experiences were either non-existent or were
sealed off from divine activity.[1]   There is not a little to be
said for reversing Dr. Sanday's hypothesis.   The *locus*
or seat of the divine, if we may use such expressions, was
His conscious life in decisive experiences of revelation,
meditation, and prayer; but, just because of this fact,
His subconscious life was also invaded by divine grace
and power, and although unperceived, was a matrix
through which His divine consciousness re-emerged
fructified and renewed in the abiding conviction that He
was in truth the Son of God.

[1] In *The Meaning of Sin* (1956), 74f., F. Greeves draws attention to the
danger of ignoring or minimizing the psychologically valuable characteristics of the unconscious itself, and quotes the significant remark of Freud:
'Not only what is lowest, but what is highest in the Ego can be unconscious'.

XXI

TOWARDS A MODERN CHRISTOLOGY

I N this final chapter I propose with considerable hesitation to suggest a presentation of the doctrine of the
Person of Christ which, I think, is implied in New
Testament teaching as a whole. This is a strictly limited
undertaking. For a full treatment of the doctrine it
would be necessary to discuss in detail the history of
Christological thought from ancient times down to the
present day, and to examine its philosophical aspects.
This task cannot be undertaken in these pages. Even as
it is, the more limited inquiry is difficult, since New
Testament teaching can be interpreted in different ways.
The easy way would be to close the investigation at the
point reached in the last chapter, but I think that anyone
who attempts to describe what the New Testament
teaches is bound to indicate what kind of a Christology, in
his judgement, it implies. There is no discharge from
this task because of its difficulty, or because conclusions
cannot be carried to the point of demonstration. Progress in theology cannot be made unless theologians are
ready to be found wanting in the endeavour to make
constructive statements.

The New Testament teacher, in particular, is tempted
to restrict himself to the problems of text, sources, and
exegesis on the ground that the history of the doctrine
and its religious and philosophical implications are the
proper concern of specialists in these fields. Without
doubt he must not claim to be a specialist in these subjects, but he cannot be said to have pursued his own dis-

ciplines completely unless he considers how New Testament teaching influenced later discussions and how it is
related to the thought of to-day.

If any defence of this opinion were needed, it would be
supplied by the history of the earliest Christological controversies, in which the protagonists on both sides appealed to the teaching of Scripture, and in which better
exegesis contributed largely to the victory of the orthodox
side. Hesitation about the use of the adjective *homoousios*
was due to the fact that it is not a biblical word, and it
was ultimately accepted only because it secured the idea of
that essential oneness of the Son with the Father which
the New Testament attests. In later controversies, when
doctrinal precision was obtained without its support,
problems were created and left unsolved for future discussions.

In the present inquiry results reached in earlier
chapters must be assumed. In particular, the Person of
Christ is presented in trinitarian terms and with full regard to that self-emptying which is the outstanding mark
of the incarnation of Christ. In what follows a general
Christological statement will first be submitted for
purposes of reference, and then a more detailed discussion
of the main points which are involved. It need hardly
be said that the two cannot be separated.

I

The Christology which seems most in accord with the
teaching of the New Testament is the doctrine that, in
becoming man, the Son of God willed to renounce the
exercise of divine prerogatives and powers, so that in the
course of His earthly existence, He might live within
the necessary limitations which belong to human finitude.
Divine attributes of omniscience, omnipotence, and omni-

presence were laid aside, not in the sense that they were abandoned or destroyed, but in such a manner that they became potential or latent because no longer in exercise. The knowledge of His heavenly origin and divine nature was given to Him by revelation and intuition, at His Baptism, Temptation, and Transfiguration, and during seasons of prayer and communion with His Heavenly Father. These experiences were remembered and formed the undertone of His life and ministry, but they were not always so central in His consciousness as to preclude the frustrations, disappointments, and trials of a truly human life. It is within this human life that one must find His divinity. In the words of Emil Brunner[1] His humanity was 'the incognito of His Deity'. While we must hesitate to say, with Calvin, that Christ *concealed* His divinity, we may agree with his submission that the splendour of His glory penetrated through the weakness and concealment of the flesh.[2] It is better, however, to speak of His divine powers as 'latent' rather than as 'concealed', since the idea of concealment introduces a duality into His earthly life which is not reflected in the Gospels. 'Concealment' is a term better applied to the pre-existent act of surrender on the part of the Son of God rather than to the conditions of His existence upon earth, true though it is that in His association with His disciples His glory breaks through His words and deeds.

Upon the normal levels of His human life His consciousness of divine Sonship does not always burn with the intensity of the season when He cries, 'All things have been delivered unto me of my Father, and no one knows the Son save the Father, neither does any one know the Father save the Son, and he to whom the Son

[1] *The Mediator*, 266, 337.
[2] Cf. G. C. Berkouwer, *The Person of Christ* (1954), 354.

wills to reveal Him'.   On less ecstatic levels it remains, in
the words of Mackintosh, 'an object of faith'.   And there
are times when for a season it is in eclipse.   Nevertheless,
at all times, in His humiliation as well as in His exaltation,
He receives through communion with His Father an
impress upon His human consciousness which is the secret
of His moral elevation and of His power to do 'mighty
works'.   The subject of His consciousness is divine, but
it is expressed within the compass of His human life.[1]

Such a statement as this is necessarily brief and may
justly be held to raise more problems than it solves.   It is
necessary, therefore, by way of commentary to take up the
main questions in greater detail.

II

1. In the first place, the question of the Ego of the
divine-human Son of God must be considered.   Is it
human or divine?   In the light of many elements in the
Gospel Story it is natural to wish to describe it as a completely human Ego, endowed with its own will and consciousness.   But this answer raises the greatest difficulties.   If His Ego were only human, He would be a
man, a prophet and a teacher, but not the Son of God.
Undoubtedly, His personality manifests itself as human,
and must indeed do so, but this fact does not necessarily
imply that it is human and nothing more.   All the relevant facts compel us to affirm that the subject of the
human life of Christ is the Logos, the Eternal Son, but
in the form and under the conditions of human existence.
It is not enough, I think, to say that the Logos added
humanity to His divine nature, for a Christology of this

[1] 'His self-consciousness as divine Son is at every moment to be measured
by the capacity of His human soul to mediate it', Bishop F. Weston, *The
One Christ*, 190.

kind suggests, or tends to suggest, that the human form is a guise or semblance; or, if this view is avoided, it leads to the conclusion that the humanity of Christ was impersonal. And neither of these views can be entertained without grievous loss. The unity of Christ's Person is complete. It is as a man, and within the limitations of manhood, that the Son of God is incarnate. Only by the exercise of a self-limitation, imaged and illustrated in the self-limitation of God in the creation of the world, can the Ego of the Son be operative in the conditions of time and space.

2. Secondly, in order to make this self-limitation possible, it is necessary to infer on the part of the Son, and in obedience to the Father, a pre-temporal act of will, whereby all that is alien to His ministry of humiliation and of redemptive work is set aside. We rightly hesitate to read too much into the words of St. Paul in Phil. ii. 6f., when he says that, being in the form of God, Christ did not regard equality with God as booty to be clutched, but emptied Himself, taking the form of a servant, being made in the likeness of men. We cannot say that in this passage the Apostle affirms a pre-temporal act of renunciation, but we are entitled to claim that here, and in 2 Cor. viii. 9, his teaching presupposes such an act and cannot be understood without it. His words imply that Christ 'emptied himself' of that divine glory which is the 'image' or 'godlikeness' of God,[1] and the further inference is justified that He divested Himself of the exercise of divine powers. This idea is not Pauline alone. The same idea is implicit in the Johannine Christology. St. John says of the incarnate Word, 'We beheld his glory', implying that that glory was visible in the earthly life of Jesus, but he also speaks of the resumption of the glory

---

[1] Cf. L. H. Brockington, *Studies in the Gospels* (ed. D. E. Nineham), 7f.

which the Son possessed with the Father before the world was. 'And now, O Father', prays the Johannine Christ, 'glorify thou me with thine own self with the glory which I had with thee before the world was' (Jn. xvii. 5, cf. xvii. 24).[1] Manifestly, the glory to be resumed is the glory that had been set aside. A pre-mundane act of surrender is implied. In its redemptive purpose this act is not only that of the Son, but is also one in which the Father shares: 'God so loved the world that he gave his only begotten Son'. The renunciation of divine glory, by which the Son of God enters into the world, is the supreme act of love which engages the activity of all the Persons of the Trinity, Father, Son, and Holy Spirit.

3. Thirdly, the Christology here presented presupposes that in the Son's earthly existence the divine attributes of omniscience, omnipotence, and omnipresence are potential and latent rather than continuously operative. They are not visibly present during His life and ministry. This claim is supported by the Gospels in the record of His words and deeds. That, in the Gospel Story, He is not omnipresent goes without saying. In the Fourth Gospel, and in the saying in Mt. xxviii, 18, 'All authority has been given to me in heaven and on earth', there are statements which might be held to suggest omniscience and omnipotence, as well as in the narratives which record nature-miracles. This evidence, however, is heavily discounted, and indeed refuted, by the consideration that the controlling interest in the Fourth Gospel is doctrinal; by the fact that Mt. xxviii. 18f. is a saying of the Risen Christ, and by the presence in the Synoptic Gospels of sayings to which repeated attention has been given, which reveal that Jesus was conscious of things which He did not know and things which He could not

[1] Cf. C. K. Barrett, *The Gospel according to St. John*, 421, 429.

do. If the nature-miracles are historical, they are occasional manifestations of divine power which match the divine revelations of Sonship made at the Baptism and Transfiguration. But in the normal course of His life the Jesus of history was not omniscient and was not omnipotent.[1] These facts are so manifest in the Gospel records that it is not surprising that they have been deemed sufficient in themselves to settle the question. This conclusion, however, may be premature. In addition to critical judgements doctrinal arguments must be considered if satisfactory conclusions are to be reached.

We have seen that Thomasius held that, in becoming man, the Son of God abandoned the attributes of omniscience, omnipotence, and omnipresence. Few doctrinal submissions have given greater offence; so much so that, as we have observed, many theologians identify kenoticism with the view of Thomasius. His claims are held to be crude and uninformed by wider Christological considerations.[2] This criticism is just, if we must limit our survey to the views of the Erlangen Professor and his adherents, for, as many critics have shown, the theological difficulties of his position are insuperable. The attributes of God are not accidental qualities which can be laid aside like a garment. They belong to His essence, so that without them He is not God. Equally, without these attributes, as well as those of justice, holiness, and love, the Son is no longer the Son. Divested of them He is only a man. So far, it must be conceded, the opponents of kenoticism have right on their side.

[1] Cf. Brunner, *The Mediator*, 363f.
[2] Cf. L. S. Thornton, *The Incarnate Lord*, 262. In this massive volume six lines are deemed sufficient to dispose of kenotic theories. Father Thornton claims that their exponents sought to solve the problem 'on too narrow a basis' and 'were sometimes crudely external in their treatment of the divine attributes'.

But the victory is Pyrrhic. It is so costly that it equals a defeat. No just reason has been given why, within the limitations necessary to the Incarnation, the attributes of omniscience, omnipotence, and omnipresence should not have remained latent or potential, existent, but no longer at the centre of the Son's consciousness and in conscious exercise, but undestroyed and capable of manifestation in appropriate circumstances. This is the contention of Forsyth[1] and Mackintosh;[2] and I do not think that it has been effectively challenged. An attribute is a form of the divine activity, but it is not essential to its existence that it should be constantly operative; nor, when potential, is it necessarily destroyed.

It may be argued that, if an attribute is potential, it is for all practical purposes abandoned. To say this is to claim too much, for to describe it as 'potential' means that its power exists, even though it is not visible. What is renounced is its conscious exercise. Outwardly it may appear to be wanting, but this does not mean that it is destroyed. As in all Christological questions our difficulty is that there is no really adequate illustration available; but with this necessary limitation, there are many cases in human life in which powers are latent, either by an act of will or because their presence is not known. Conscious life is the progressive discovery of powers which in earlier stages are not suspected. It is possible that in this matter psychology can give greater assistance to theology than has otherwise been afforded in the study of the subconscious.

Whether in His incarnate life the Son was aware of powers latent but not operative we do not know. It has been suggested that He held in check attributes of which He was conscious, but while this is a possible view to take,

[1] *Op. cit.*, 308f.   [2] *Op. cit.*, 477–9.

it comes near to the idea of *occultatio* or concealment, and it is hard to reconcile it with the reality of Christ's humanity. It has this in its favour, that the experiences of revelation, in which Jesus was assured of His Sonship, must have carried with them a knowledge of divine power which transcended the level of His normal life. If the saying in Mt. xxvi. 53f., 'Do you think I cannot beseech my Father, and he shall even now send me more than twelve legions of angels?', were more strongly attested, support might be claimed for this view from the Gospel tradition. But, with M'Neile,[1] the genuineness of the saying, which is found in Matthew alone, must be considered doubtful. On the whole, the hypothesis of a pretemporal act of surrender is more probable.

Only on the assumption that the divine attributes are potential rather than active does a true incarnation seem possible. If the Son comes into the world omniscient and omnipotent, His coming is a theophany; if He completely strips Himself of these attributes, He is downgraded to the level of a man. In the one case the humanity is a semblance; in the other the divinity is lost; in neither case is there a veritable incarnation of the Son of God. This dilemma is resolved in a Christology in which these attributes are latent, conditioned in operation by the circumstances of a truly human existence.

4. Fourthly, it is a merit of the Christology in question that it does full justice to the unity of Christ's Person, as both human and divine. It hangs no iron curtain between the earthly life of Jesus and His heavenly mode of existence. A curtain there is, but through it shines a celestial glow, and there are breaks in the fabric through which the light shines. This type of Christology presupposes one Christ, who is not cut off from the life of

---

[1] *The Gospel according to St. Matthew*, 395.

God, and yet consents to live on earth within the bounds of human finitude. His human nature is the life He leads as a man, subject to the conditions of time and space; His divine nature is the existence which He shares with the Father and the Holy Spirit. The uniting bond between these two modes of existence is His divine will, which in His human life is limited and confined by the conditions appropriate to that life, but is unlimited and unconfined within the triune life of God. This hypothesis does not mean that the Son has no operative human will. The human will is the divine will restrained by conditions which are accepted fully and completely. His will is the subject of His divine life, and by self-limitation is also the subject of His human existence.

The hypothesis of a single will transcends the unreal distinctions faced in the Monothelite controversy, which ended in the decision of the Sixth General Council of Constantinople in A.D. 680 to affirm two wills and two consciousnesses, one human and one divine. This decision was the logical consequence of the tendency to hypostasize the two natures of Christ. As Dr. Temple has said, there could be no escape from this conclusion in the terms in which the problem was stated.[1] If Christ has no human will, it was argued, His human nature is imperfect; if no divine will, He is not divine. The existence of two wills has usually been defended by emphasizing the perfect unity which exists between them, so that, in fact, they act as one. This subtle explanation is artificial, since the unity renders the separation unnecessary. Dr. Temple's comment is, 'Yet we are thus brought very near Nestorianism; for if there is a divine Will side by side with a human will, how is this to be distinguished from a divine Person side by side with a human Person?'[2]

---

[1] *Christus Veritas*, 135.   [2] *Op. cit.*, 135f.

u

The danger is overcome if we affirm not a divine will in contrast with a human will, nor a human will which is in no sense divine, but a divine will which can function in both realms, unconfined in its trinitarian relationships, limited in its expression by human conditions. This hypothesis is not refuted by the argument that a divine will cannot be limited, for by such a contention we are well on the way to a denial that an incarnation is possible; and further, we rule out the possibility of creation, which entails divine self-limitation. The restraint is not imposed from without, but is self-imposed by divine love and by the redemptive purpose flowing from it. This claim is possible only if there be a fundamental affinity between the human and the divine, such as is involved in the biblical statement that man is made in the image of God; and the hypothesis is tenable, it would seem, only on kenotic presuppositions. It is the mark of a kenotic Christology that, along with other advantages, it can give whole-hearted assent to the unity of Christ's Person by taking seriously that self-limitation which is the sign of the grace of God.

Bishop Gore, it is true, presented a form of kenoticism in which two wills, two consciousnesses, and two natures are affirmed by the submission that the greater will and consciousness and nature 'are acting under the conditions of the lesser, within the sphere of the incarnate and mortal life'.[1] These distinctions do not appear to be

---

[1] *The Reconstruction of Belief*, 862. Bishop Weston, who rejects kenotic theories which carry over the self-emptying of the Logos into the eternal sphere, affirms the existence of one consciousness, but two wills. 'The importance of arriving at a conception of a single consciousness', he writes, 'cannot be over-estimated', *The One Christ*, 157. Two wills, he says must always be confessed 'for they are two essential functions of God in Manhood' (p. 170).

more than verbal.[1] If 'the greater will' can act under the conditions of 'the lesser', there does not appear to be any advantage in distinguishing or separating the two. It seems better to predicate one will, the will of the Eternal Son, manifesting itself under different conditions. In this way we are true to the spirit and intention of the Sixth General Council, while avoiding the manifest embarrassments of its statements. A Christology which affirms self-limitation would seem to make this solution possible.

5. Lastly, it must be said that while a kenotic Christology can make its contribution to speculative questions, no just demand can be made upon it, or indeed upon any Christology, that it should be able to solve ultimate problems. It ought not to be expected that its exponents should be able to describe the life of the Incarnate Son within the fellowship of the triunity of God. Of these matters we know nothing at all. Scripture throws no light upon them, and it is presumptuous to pretend otherwise. I have mentioned earlier Bishop Gore's remark about 'agnosticism in the right place'. He instances the very point under discussion. 'Or again', he says, 'we are asked how to relate this "limited" condition of the Son as incarnate with His exercise of all the cosmic functions of the eternal Word—what the New Testament calls "the sustaining" or "bearing along of all things" or holding all the universe together—and again I think we had better give no answer'.[2] When reflection has reached its bounds

---

[1] The modern student is apt to feel a sense of impatience at these subtle distinctions, but he should remember the theological situation as it was in the seventh century, and the desire to repudiate Nestorianism on the one hand and Eutychianism on the other. To-day, in a different theological climate, it is possible for those who affirm two wills and those who prefer to think of one to mean much the same thing. Much depends on whether the decision of the Sixth Council is felt to be binding.

[2] Op. cit., 522.

it is not escapism to quote the dictum of the Schoolmen, 'Omnia exeunt in mysterium', or to say, with D. M. Baillie, that 'the paradox of the Incarnation' has its parallel in 'the paradox of grace'.[1] The only obligation upon us is that we should not say these things too soon, before theological reflection has reached its limits.

We are entitled to claim that no doctrine of the Incarnation which recognizes the limitations accepted by the Son during the conditions of His earthly existence threatens the cosmic functions of the triune God. It is not a tenable objection to the Christology under discussion, which affirms the potentiality but not the continuous exercise of the powers by which the universe is sustained, to say that its consequences would be cosmic chaos. How God acts, while the Son lives on earth as man, we do not know. Neither can we describe the part of the Incarnate Son in the sustaining of the universe. It has been conjectured that, in consequence of the Incarnation, the cosmic functions of the Son are taken over by the Father and the Holy Spirit;[2] but this suggestion is crude and mischievous. The Son is not separated from the Father by the fact that He is sent. As the Incarnate, He is still, as the Fourth Evangelist declares, 'in the bosom of the Father', because triune relationships are not temporary and local, but eternal and spiritual. To say that the cosmic activities of the Son are not suspended although not present to His consciousness, is an alternative speculation which may be entertained, but cannot be established by human reason. In what way the divine consciousness of the Son functions while He is incarnate, is not revealed to us, but it would be idle to suppose that the Godhead is impoverished by the supreme act of love by which the Son of God is sent into the world.

[1] God Was in Christ, 106–24.   [2] By Godet and others.

III

It is incumbent upon those who defend a kenotic Christology to consider the objections to which it is exposed. This task must now be attempted.

1. First, it may be objected that the Christology in question is not new, and that, in fact, it has been rejected by a considerable body of opinion. The truth in this objection may be admitted. We have seen, however, that the kenotic hypothesis commonly opposed is that which presupposes an abandonment of the divine attributes. The better forms, including the views of Ebrard, Forsyth, and Mackintosh, which prefer to describe the divine attributes as potential, or as expressed in new ways, have not received the same attention, and have certainly not been refuted. Judgement has gone by default. Shocked by earlier and vulnerable forms of the kenotic hypothesis, many theologians have not taken second thoughts concerning its validity. For this reason it is open to anyone who ponders the teaching of the New Testament to claim that some form of *kenosis* is an essential element in a modern theology and to consider what the best form may be.

2. The objection that a kenotic Christology is mythological is felt by many to be strong. It suggests, it is said, the idea of 'a temporary theophany' reminiscent of stories told of the pagan gods. It has 'a mythological appearance', and is 'more like a pagan story of metamorphosis than like the Christian doctrine of the Incarnation'.[1] It is even claimed that it is a story of a Divine Being who changed Himself temporarily into man, or exchanged His divinity for humanity. This surely is the language of exaggeration. No reputable kenoticist, not even Thomasius or Gess, has suggested any such thing. It would be impossible to

[1] See earlier, p. 267f.

show that Bishop Gore or Dr. Forsyth or Dr. Mackintosh entertained for a moment the idea of divinity exchanged for humanity, or suggested that the Son temporarily changed Himself into man. On the contrary, these writers maintain that He was divine in His humiliation as well as in His pre-incarnate glory, in His self-abasement no less than in His exaltation. In these forms of the kenotic theory the objection is robbed of much of its force.

The question, to what extent we are at liberty to use symbolic and anthropomorphic concepts, is important.[1] A certain vocabulary based on these ideas has established itself, and a better terminology is still to seek. A Christology which speaks of the Son as 'sent', as One who 're-nounced' divine powers, and who 'came' into the world in humiliation, implies a picture of the universe as 'a three-storied structure', and to this extent has 'a mythological form'.[2] To a greater or less degree this is true of any Christological hypothesis. But, provided we know what we are doing, we are no more barred from using such ideas any more than we are from speaking of the sun as 'rising' and 'setting' because science has taught us better. Not to use such concepts is either to be reduced to silence or to be seriously hampered in the presentation of a Christology.[3] It is a surprising and unforeseen turn of the theological wheel that the objection under review anticipates the plea that we should demythologize the theology of the New Testament. As regards the kenotic hypothesis such a plea would have point only if it compromised the substance of Christology; and this

[1] Cf. A. Farrer, *The Glass of Vision.*
[2] Cf. R. Bultmann, *Kerygma and Myth*, 1, 12.
[3] 'It needs to be recognized that it is impossible for mortal men to comprehend or to discuss God except by using symbols derived from mortal experience', G. L. Prestige, *God in Patristic Thought*, 299.

we have denied. The objection to the hypothesis would be just if, in Miltonic fashion, we attempted to portray what happened in the courts of heaven before the Son of God came to earth. But the best exponents of kenoticism are aware of this peril. Their reason for presupposing an act of self-limitation on the part of the Son is not a pretended knowledge of the secrets of heaven, but the implications of the doctrine of the Incarnation as it is unfolded in the New Testament. It is a human inference suggested by observable facts.

3. The strongest objection to a kenotic Christology is the charge that, on its presuppositions, the divine consciousness of the Son is not always at the same pitch of intensity, and at times may even be in eclipse. The sense of Sonship is intermittent, it is said, so that successively Christ is God and man.

Dr. Mackintosh himself uses the word 'intermittently',[1] and our first reaction is one of surprise. This phrase, however, is not applied to the actuality of Christ's Sonship, but to its expression in His human consciousness. Christ is in truth the Son of God at all times, in His humiliation as well as in His exaltation, both when He affirms it and when He is silent. Even so the word 'intermittently' is not well chosen, since it suggests an oscillation in the consciousness of Sonship comparable to the revolving light in a lighthouse when bright illumination is followed by deeper darkness. There is variation, but it is not so sharply defined. If we have regard to the evidence contained in the Gospels, there are different levels of consciousness, and it is the merit of a kenotic

---

[1] In the passage already quoted (p. 264): 'It can only have been in mature manhood and perhaps intermittently that Christ became aware of His divinity—which must have remained for Him an object of *faith* to the very end'.

Christology that it takes account of this evidence. As a babe, Christ was unconscious of His divine Sonship, and this condition may have extended into youth and early manhood, although, according to Lk. ii. 41–52, already at the age of twelve He spoke in an intimate sense of 'My Father'. Moreover, the times when His knowledge of divine Sonship was at its full intensity imply, as their correlative, seasons when it was less intense. The analogy of the lighthouse has at least this suggestiveness that even when the beam is not visible, its potentiality is not destroyed, since after darkness light flashes yet again across the waters.

But all analogies are partial, and if pressed too far, misleading. I have suggested that Christ's consciousness of Sonship was at its zenith in high moments of revelation and intuition, and in hours of prayer and communion with His Father. But this claim does not mean that at other times there was no remembrance of these experiences. It is true that what is remembered cannot have the intensity of an immediate experience. Nevertheless, these seasons of illumination could not be forgotten. They must have left behind them a continuous consciousness of Sonship, less intense, but real.

In Browning's *Ring and the Book*, the Pope describes a lightning flash which reveals the city of Naples

'thick and plain with spires.'

There are parallels in the life of Jesus, but with the difference that the flash is followed by a permanent glow. The revelation is remembered, the intuition recalled. To this extent the Fourth Gospel is historical in presupposing an abiding knowledge of Sonship, but it is less historical in representing that consciousness as steady, continuous, and unbroken. The revelation is remembered, but it does not always glow. The intuition is felt, but it is not always regnant. There must have been times when knowledge was less clear, and even clouded, so that the Son of God cries, 'My God, my God, why hast thou forsaken me?'. One can never forget that there was a Friday when, for a season, the heavens were as brass. In psychological terms, the consciousness of Sonship is both central and marginal, and at times subconscious. But even when subconscious, it is not destroyed. Partial focus, and even darkness, are subsumed in creative experiences when the Son of God cries, 'All things have been delivered to me of my Father'.

There is nothing in such a Christology for which apology is needed. It 'shines in its own light'. It can affirm *vere Deus, vere Homo*, finding divinity in humanity. On the other hand, it can claim that, in often allowing its thought to be determined by an uncritical evaluation of the Fourth Gospel, the Church has sometimes lost much of the wonder of the Incarnation. It has been wounded by the docetism it rejected, so anxious to affirm divinity that it has failed to estimate fully the humanity in which the divinity was manifested. The Synoptic Gospels restore the balance and thereby, with the Fourth Gospel, make known the full glory of the Word made flesh. They imply rather than describe, a moral and spiritual development which marks the experience of Jesus from the time that He first draws breath as a babe to the moment when He breathes forth His spirit in death. It is through growth that the consciousness of Sonship emerges, not as a dark suspicion from below, but as a revelation from on high. It is no disparagement of this development to say that it has its heights and its lower levels also. So it must have been in a life which St. Luke describes in one of the greatest of Christological truths, in the words, 'And Jesus advanced in wisdom and in stature, and in favour with God and man'.

IV

In conclusion, the merits of the hypothesis supported in these pages may with advantage be summarized for purposes of reference.

1. It unequivocally accepts the divinity of Christ, its trinitarian foundations, and the possession of two natures, or modes of existence, each appropriate to the conditions of His existence. It affirms the divine Ego of His Person which manifests itself by a supreme act of self-limitation within the confines of a humanity which is complete in every respect.

2. It preserves the unity of His divine-human Person by presupposing a pre-temporal act of surrender of the exercise of divine powers necessary to a true participation in humanity. It maintains that this self-emptying is implied in both Pauline and Johannine teaching, and is suggested by the primitive records of the earthly life of Jesus.

3. Above all, it sets the Incarnation within the context of eternal love and sacrifice. It is not to be questioned that in any worthy form of the doctrine love is presupposed; but it is claimed that by setting self-limitation and surrender at the centre of the Godhead, it gives expression to the exercise of the love and sacrifice of the Triune God as no other Christological presentation does, or can. It finds the final proof of divine love in the Son's journey into a strange country at supreme cost for the redemption of mankind. 'Greater love', declares the Fourth Gospel, 'hath no man than this, that a man lay down his life for his friends'. The Son's sacrifice sets this truth within the life of God. It can have no greater setting.

EPILOGUE

OUR study of the Person of Christ in New Testament teaching is ended. Inevitably the investigation has proved to be a matter of exegesis and inference. I therefore think it important to say in conclusion that results are not reached by these methods alone. It is certainly necessary to pay attention to what Scripture and the Church teach, since otherwise the revelation of God in Christ is not brought home to us. It is in this persuasion that this investigation has been undertaken. But the problem of the Person of Christ is not solved by any process of reasoned argument; otherwise, different conclusions would not be reached, as they are, by different scholars who survey the same evidence thoroughly and with a strong desire for impartiality.

The investigation has shown repeatedly how worship, as well as reflection, has prompted the greatest Christian affirmations. Throughout the centuries worship has opened the eyes of men to truth concerning Christ. From this fact, it is apparent that if the conclusions suggested by New Testament teaching and embodied in the Creeds are to be accepted with conviction, a personal response to the challenge with which God confronts us in Christ is necessary. We do not first discover who Christ is and then believe in Him; we believe in Him and then discover who He is.

This claim is an affront to human pride. The natural man assumes that the secret of Christ's personality must be solved intellectually without self-committal to Him. To think otherwise, he believes, is to beg the question.

History and experience show that this attitude, while natural, is mistaken. The penalty of treating the Person of Christ as a purely intellectual problem is that He remains an enigma. In the words of John the Baptist, 'There stands in the midst of you one whom you know not'. The veil is not lifted. The incognito is not interpreted. In addition to the study of New Testament teaching a personal response to the revelation is necessary. The encounter is a challenge to faith. Faith alone knows who Jesus is.

This demand for faith is wrongly conceived if we imagine that we can short-circuit the issue by neglecting the study of Scripture and the fellowship of the Church, for while God speaks to us directly by His Spirit, He speaks also through His Word and through the life of the Christian community. Faith is the response to this threefold witness. Only when this response is made do we learn the truth of the words addressed to Thomas, 'Because thou has seen me, thou hast believed; blessed are they that have not seen, and have believed'. Then only do we cry, 'My Lord and my God'.

BIBLIOGRAPHY

J. Moffatt, *The Theology of the Gospels.*

H. A. A. Kennedy, *The Theology of the Epistles.*

G. B. Stevens, *The Theology of the New Testament.*

R. Bultmann, *Theology of the New Testament.*

A. E. J. Rawlinson, *The New Testament Doctrine of the Christ.*

C. A. Anderson Scott, *Christianity according to St. Paul.*

W. F. Howard, *Christianity according to St. John.*

H. R. Mackintosh, *The Doctrine of the Person of Jesus Christ.*

P. T. Forsyth, *The Person and Place of Jesus Christ.*

W. Sanday, *Christologies Ancient and Modern,* and *Personality in Christ and in Ourselves.*

G. C. Berkouwer, *The Person of Christ.*

V. Taylor, *The Names of Jesus, The Life and Ministry of Jesus.*

W. P. Du Bose, *The Gospel in the Gospels.*

W. F. Lofthouse, *The Father and the Son.*

T. W. Manson, *The Teaching of Jesus, The Sayings of Jesus, The Servant-Messiah.*

C. H. Dodd, *The Apostolic Preaching and its Development, The Interpretation of the Fourth Gospel.*

W. Temple, *Christus Veritas.*

L. Hodgson, *The Doctrine of the Trinity.*

C. Welch, *The Trinity in Contemporary Theology.*

J. Weiss, *The History of Primitive Christianity.*

R. S. Franks, *The Doctrine of the Trinity.*

J. N. D. Kelly, *Early Christian Creeds.*

D. M. Baillie, *God Was in Christ.*

K. Barth, *The Doctrine of the Word of God.*

A. B. Bruce, *The Humiliation of Christ.*

C. Gore, *The Reconstruction of Belief.*

R. L. Ottley, *The Doctrine of the Incarnation.*

F. Weston, *The One Christ.*

O. C. Quick, *Doctrines of the Creed.*

J. M. Creed, *The Divinity of Christ.*

J. Bethune-Baker, *The Way of Modernism, An Introduction to the Early History of Christian Doctrine.*

W. R. Matthews, *The Problem of Christ in the Twentieth Century.*

E. Percy, *Die Botschaft Jesu.*

W. Bousset, *Kyrios Christos.*

E. Brunner, *The Mediator.*

W. D. Davies, *Paul and Rabbinic Judaism.*

O. Cullmann, *Early Christian Confessions, Baptism in the New Testament, Die Christologie des Neuen Testaments.*

W. L. Knox, *Some Hellenistic Elements in Primitive Christianity.*

J. S. Whale, *Christian Doctrine.*

R. Otto, *The Kingdom of God and the Son of Man.*

J. Jeremias, *The Parables of Jesus, The Eucharistic Words of Jesus.*

W. F. Flemington, *The New Testament Doctrine of Baptism.*

G. W. H. Lampe, *The Seal of the Spirit.*

L. S. Thornton, *The Incarnate Lord.*

R. C. Moberly, *Atonement and Personality.*

J. Scott Lidgett, *Sonship and Salvation.*

E. F. Scott, *The Fourth Gospel ; its Purpose and Theology.*

R. H. Fuller, *The Foundations of New Testament Christology.*

INDEX OF SCRIPTURE PASSAGES

INDEX OF PROPER NAMES

PRINTED IN GREAT BRITAIN
BY ROBERT MACLEHOSE AND CO. LTD
THE UNIVERSITY PRESS, GLASGOW